W9-CDE-040

WAR ON THE FRONTIER

The Trans-Mississippi West

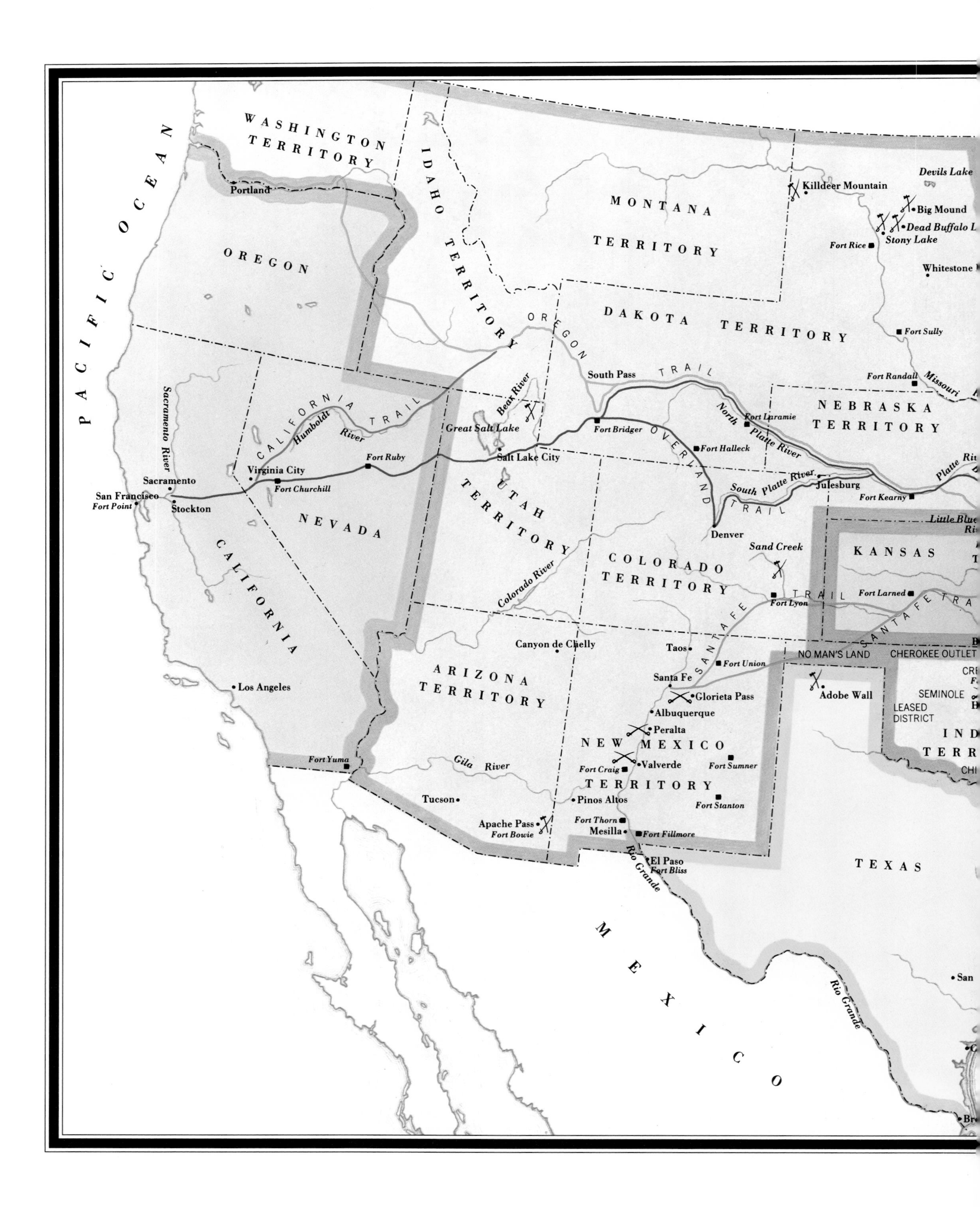

PACIFIC OCEAN
WASHINGTON TERRITORY
IDAHO TERRITORY
MONTANA TERRITORY
DAKOTA TERRITORY
NEBRASKA TERRITORY
OREGON
NEVADA
CALIFORNIA
UTAH TERRITORY
COLORADO TERRITORY
KANSAS
ARIZONA TERRITORY
NEW MEXICO TERRITORY
TEXAS
MEXICO
NO MAN'S LAND
CHEROKEE OUTLET
SEMINOLE
LEASED DISTRICT
OREGON TRAIL
CALIFORNIA TRAIL
OVERLAND TRAIL
SANTA FE TRAIL
Portland
Sacramento River
Sacramento
San Francisco
Fort Point
Stockton
Virginia City
Fort Churchill
Fort Ruby
Humboldt River
Great Salt Lake
Bear River
Salt Lake City
Fort Bridger
South Pass
Fort Laramie
North Platte River
Fort Halleck
South Platte River
Julesburg
Fort Kearny
Platte River
Denver
Sand Creek
Fort Lyon
Fort Larned
Little Blue
Colorado River
Canyon de Chelly
Taos
Fort Union
Santa Fe
Glorieta Pass
Albuquerque
Peralta
Valverde
Fort Craig
Fort Sumner
Fort Stanton
Pinos Altos
Tucson
Gila River
Fort Yuma
Los Angeles
Apache Pass
Fort Bowie
Fort Thorn
Mesilla
Fort Fillmore
El Paso
Fort Bliss
Rio Grande
Adobe Wall
Killdeer Mountain
Devils Lake
Big Mound
Stony Lake
Fort Rice
Whitestone
Fort Sully
Fort Randall
Missouri

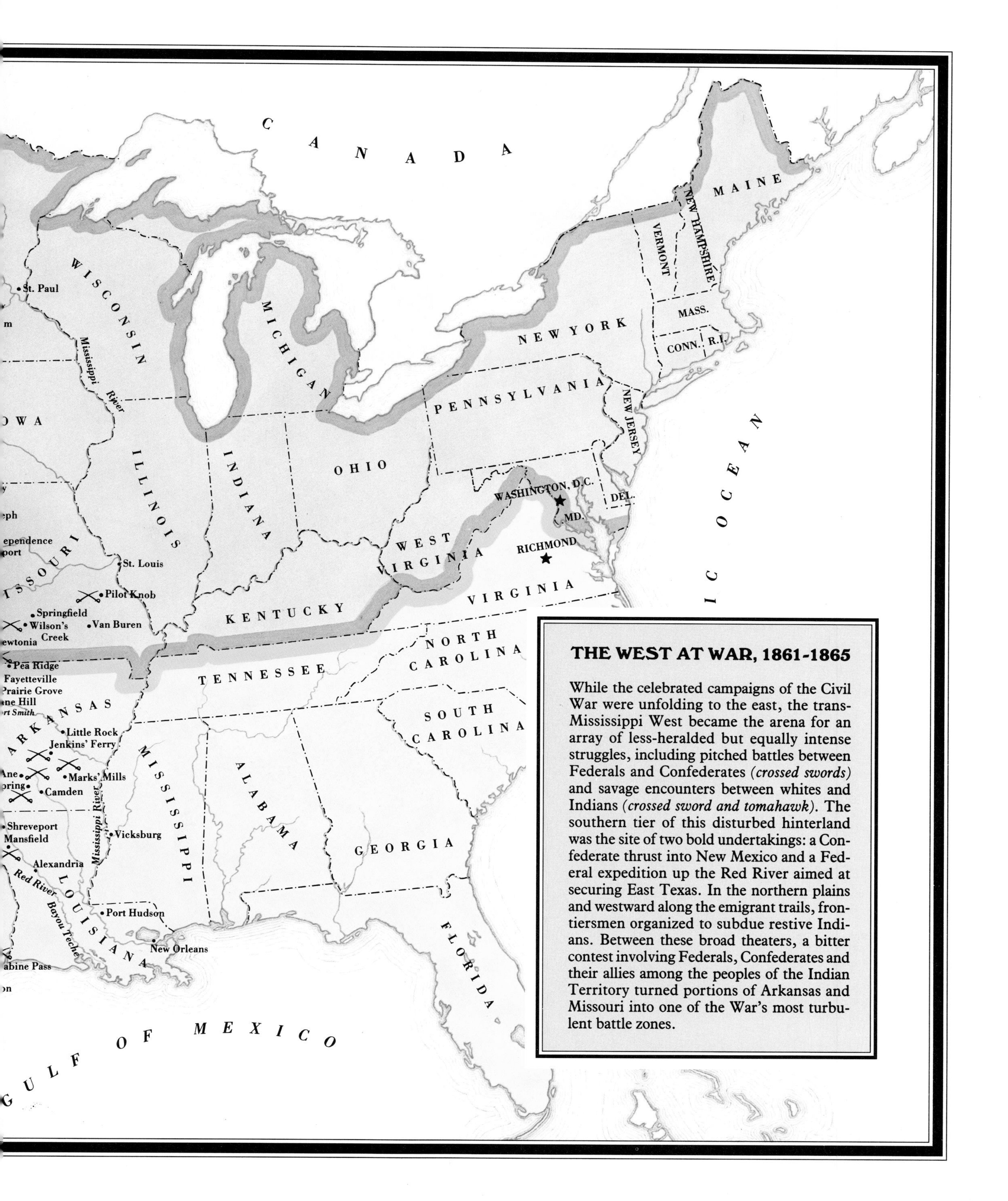

THE WEST AT WAR, 1861-1865

While the celebrated campaigns of the Civil War were unfolding to the east, the trans-Mississippi West became the arena for an array of less-heralded but equally intense struggles, including pitched battles between Federals and Confederates *(crossed swords)* and savage encounters between whites and Indians *(crossed sword and tomahawk)*. The southern tier of this disturbed hinterland was the site of two bold undertakings: a Confederate thrust into New Mexico and a Federal expedition up the Red River aimed at securing East Texas. In the northern plains and westward along the emigrant trails, frontiersmen organized to subdue restive Indians. Between these broad theaters, a bitter contest involving Federals, Confederates and their allies among the peoples of the Indian Territory turned portions of Arkansas and Missouri into one of the War's most turbulent battle zones.

Other Publications:

TIME-LIFE LIBRARY OF CURIOUS AND UNUSUAL FACTS
AMERICAN COUNTRY
VOYAGE THROUGH THE UNIVERSE
THE THIRD REICH
THE TIME-LIFE GARDENER'S GUIDE
MYSTERIES OF THE UNKNOWN
TIME FRAME
FIX IT YOURSELF
FITNESS, HEALTH & NUTRITION
SUCCESSFUL PARENTING
HEALTHY HOME COOKING
UNDERSTANDING COMPUTERS
LIBRARY OF NATIONS
THE ENCHANTED WORLD
THE KODAK LIBRARY OF CREATIVE PHOTOGRAPHY
GREAT MEALS IN MINUTES
PLANET EARTH
COLLECTOR'S LIBRARY OF THE CIVIL WAR
THE EPIC OF FLIGHT
THE GOOD COOK
WORLD WAR II
HOME REPAIR AND IMPROVEMENT
THE OLD WEST

For information on and a full description of any of the Time-Life Books series listed above, please call 1-800-621-7026 or write:
Reader Information
Time-Life Customer Service
P.O. Box C-32068
Richmond, Virginia 23261-2068

This volume is one of a series that chronicles in full the events of the American Civil War, 1861-1865.
Other books in the series include:
Brother against Brother: The War Begins
First Blood: Fort Sumter to Bull Run
The Blockade: Runners and Raiders
The Road to Shiloh: Early Battles in the West
Forward to Richmond: McClellan's Peninsular Campaign
Decoying the Yanks: Jackson's Valley Campaign
Confederate Ordeal: The Southern Home Front
Lee Takes Command: From Seven Days to Second Bull Run
The Coastal War: Chesapeake Bay to Rio Grande
Tenting Tonight: The Soldier's Life
The Bloodiest Day: The Battle of Antietam
War on the Mississippi: Grant's Vicksburg Campaign
Rebels Resurgent: Fredericksburg to Chancellorsville
Twenty Million Yankees: The Northern Home Front
Gettysburg: The Confederate High Tide
The Struggle for Tennessee: Tupelo to Stones River
The Fight for Chattanooga: Chickamauga to Missionary Ridge
Spies, Scouts and Raiders: Irregular Operations
The Battles for Atlanta: Sherman Moves East
The Killing Ground: Wilderness to Cold Harbor
Sherman's March: Atlanta to the Sea
Death in the Trenches: Grant at Petersburg
The Shenandoah in Flames: The Valley Campaign of 1864
Pursuit to Appomattox: The Last Battles
The Assassination: The Death of the President
The Nation Reunited: War's Aftermath
Master Index: An Illustrated Guide

The Cover: Confederate troops and their Indian allies storm a Federal battery during the battle waged at Pea Ridge in Arkansas on March 7, 1862. Many of the Indians involved in this assault later switched their allegiance to the Union, further complicating the chaotic struggle for control of the frontier west of the Mississippi.

THE CIVIL WAR

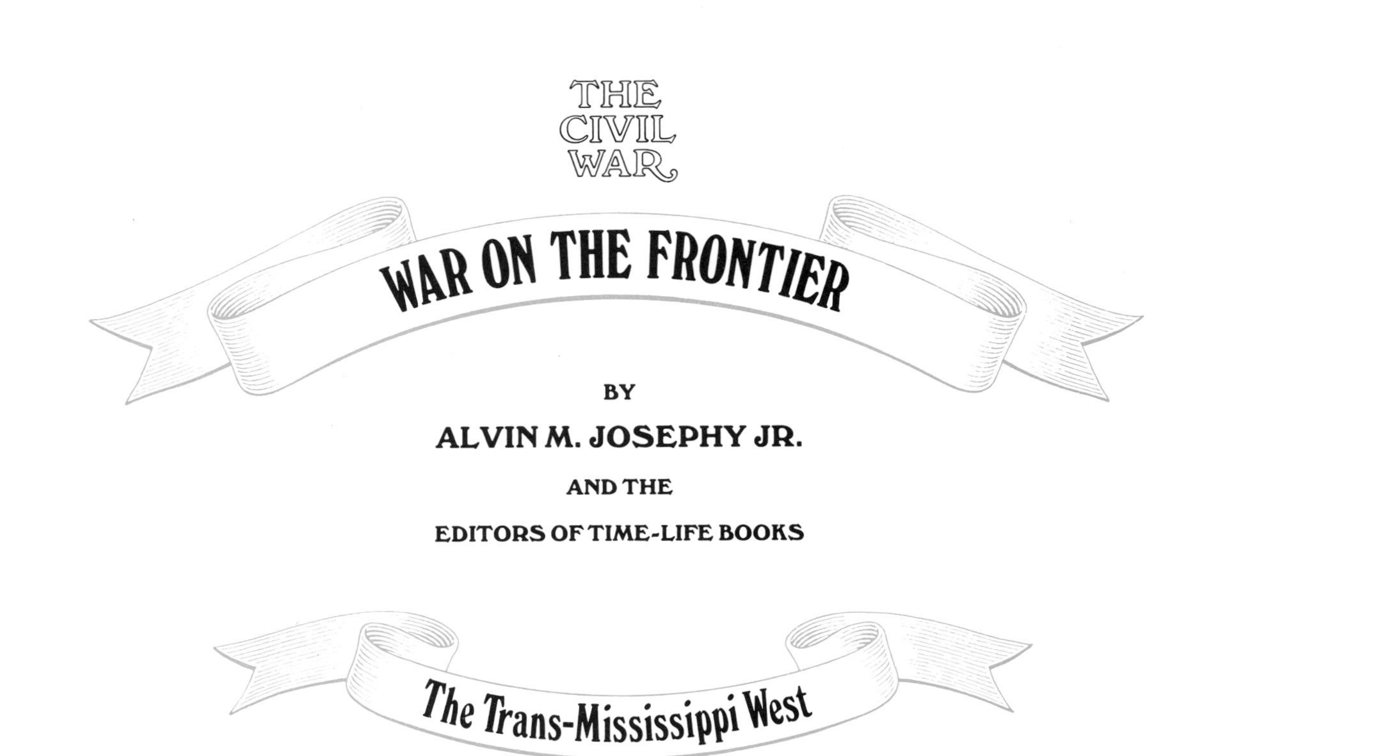

WAR ON THE FRONTIER

BY

ALVIN M. JOSEPHY JR.

AND THE

EDITORS OF TIME-LIFE BOOKS

The Trans-Mississippi West

TIME-LIFE BOOKS, ALEXANDRIA, VIRGINIA

The Civil War
Series Director: Thomas H. Flaherty
Designer: Edward Frank
Series Administrator: Jane Edwin

Editorial Staff for *War on the Frontier*
Associate Editors: John Newton, David S. Thomson (text); Marion F. Briggs (pictures)
Staff Writers: Stephen G. Hyslop, Daniel Stashower
Researchers: Kristin Baker, Karen F. Monks (principals); Harris J. Andrews, Brian C. Pohanka
Copy Coordinator: Jayne E. Rohrich
Picture Coordinator: Betty H. Weatherley
Editorial Assistant: Donna Fountain
Special Contributor: Elissa E. Baldwin

Editorial Operations
Copy Chief: Diane Ullius
Editorial Operations: Caroline A. Boubin (manager)
Production: Celia Beattie
Quality Control: James J. Cox (director)
Library: Louise D. Forstall

Correspondents: Elisabeth Kraemer-Singh (Bonn); Maria Vincenza Aloisi, Josephine du Brusle (Paris); Ann Natanson (Rome). Valuable assistance was also provided by: Letitia Baldwin (Mexico City); Christina Lieberman (New York); Janet Zich (San Francisco).

The Author:
Alvin M. Josephy Jr., a former Associate Editor of *Time,* was also Editor-in-Chief of *American Heritage* magazine for several years. He has a long-standing interest in the history of American Indians and the West and has written numerous books on the subject, among them *The Patriot Chiefs, Black Hills, White Sky* and *Now that the Buffalo's Gone.*

The Consultants:
Colonel John R. Elting, USA (Ret.), a former Associate Professor at West Point, is the author of *Battles for Scandinavia* in the Time-Life Books World War II series and of *The Battle of Bunker's Hill, The Battles of Saratoga, Military History and Atlas of the Napoleonic Wars, American Army Life* and *The Superstrategists.* Co-author of *A Dictionary of Soldier Talk,* he is also editor of the three volumes of *Military Uniforms in America, 1755-1867,* and associate editor of *The West Point Atlas of American Wars.*

William A. Frassanito, a Civil War historian and lecturer specializing in photograph analysis, is the author of two award-winning studies, *Gettysburg: A Journey in Time* and *Antietam: The Photographic Legacy of America's Bloodiest Day,* and a companion volume, *Grant and Lee, The Virginia Campaigns.* He has also served as chief consultant to the photographic history series *The Image of War.*

Les Jensen, Director of the Second Armored Division Museum, Fort Hood, Texas, specializes in Civil War artifacts and is a conservator of historic flags. He is a contributor to *The Image of War* series, consultant for numerous Civil War publications and museums, and a member of the Company of Military Historians. He was formerly Curator of the U.S. Army Transportation Museum at Fort Eustis, Virginia, and before that Curator of the Museum of the Confederacy in Richmond, Virginia.

John Phillip Langellier, a former museum director of the U.S. Army, is Wyoming's Director of State Museums. A specialist in North American frontier-military subjects, he is the author of more than 40 publications, including *The Drums Will Roll* and *Continually Wear the Blue,* concerning the military's participation in the development of the West.

Michael McAfee specializes in military uniforms and has been Curator of Uniforms and History at the West Point Museum since 1970. A fellow of the Company of Military Historians, he coedited with Colonel Elting *Long Endure: The Civil War Years,* and he collaborated with Frederick Todd on *American Military Equipage.* He is the author of *Artillery of the American Revolution, 1775-1783,* and has written numerous articles for *Military Images Magazine.*

James P. Shenton, Professor of History at Columbia University, is a specialist in 19th-century American political and social history, with particular emphasis on the Civil War period. He is the author of *Robert John Walker* and *Reconstruction South.*

Third printing 1991. Printed in U.S.A.
Published simultaneously in Canada.
School and library distribution by Silver Burdett Company, Morristown, New Jersey 07960.

Library of Congress Cataloguing in Publication Data
Josephy, Alvin M., 1915-
War on the Frontier.
(The Civil War)
Bibliography: p.
Includes index.
1. West (U.S.) — History — Civil War, 1861-1865 — Campaigns. I. Time-Life Books. II. Title. III. Series.
E470.9.J67 1986 978'.02 86-14413
ISBN 0-8094-4780-0
ISBN 0-8094-4781-9 (lib. bdg.)

CONTENTS

A Prize Worth Fighting for

"Every sunset which I witness inspires me with the desire to go to a West as distant and as fair as that into which the sun goes down." So wrote Henry David Thoreau in 1862, voicing a sentiment that remained poignant for many Americans in the midst of war. "Though we may be estranged from the South," Thoreau said of his fellow Yankees, "we sympathize with the West. There is the home of the younger sons."

Yet the South had seen many of its own sons head West in recent years to mingle with avid young Northerners in far-flung river ports, mining towns and trading posts. Such was the lure of the frontier that for most of those who yielded to it, the political issues dividing the nation seemed remote. Life in the raw West, as depicted here and on the following pages, offered practical challenges aplenty to preoccupy its new inhabitants.

In the end, however, the frontier proved too tempting a prize to be spared the intrusions of war. As the conflict spread, some men heeded old sectional loyalties and became eager volunteers. Others were simply caught up in the tide. William Cody, a scout in Kansas who later earned renown as Buffalo Bill, awoke after a night of carousing in February 1864 to find himself enrolled as a Federal cavalryman. "I did not remember how or when I had enlisted," he said later, "but I saw I was in for it."

A Western scouting party peers into the sunset in this painting by William Ranney, a Connecticut-born artist whose passion for frontier subjects grew out of his stint as a paymaster for the Texas troops who won independence from Mexico in 1836.

Linking a Restless Realm

When historian Francis Parkman boarded a steamboat at St. Louis in 1846 to begin his journey up the Missouri River to the head of the Oregon Trail, he found the vessel a microcosm of the restless frontier: "In her cabin were Santa Fé traders, gamblers, speculators, and adventurers of various descriptions, and her steerage was crowded with Oregon emigrants, 'mountain men,' negroes, and a party of Kansas Indians, who had been on a visit to St. Louis."

For many of the passengers — as for most Americans venturing West before the War — the voyage was just one episode in an arduous passage. Beyond the navigable waters lay rough wagon trails that time and traffic had hardly improved. Plans for a railroad to the Pacific that would shorten the cross-country trek from months to days remained mired in Congress through the 1850s by wrangling over a northerly or southerly route. Amid the turmoil, though, the nation was afforded a glimpse of a more cohesive future: Late in 1861 the first transcontinental telegraph line was linked up in Utah.

Driving their livestock, a party of German farmers heads west on the Oregon Trail in a painting by Albert Bierstadt, who observed this scene near Fort Kearney in Nebraska in 1863. Undeterred by war, an estimated 65,000 westward-bound emigrants followed this path from 1861 to 1865.

Work on the transcontinental telegraph line culminated here at the Western Union office in Salt Lake City on October 24, 1861, as wires strung from the opposite coasts were joined. The first cross-country telegram sent over the span was a message to President Abraham Lincoln in Washington from Stephen Field, Chief Justice of California, pledging his state's loyalty to the Union.

Steamboats crowd the levee at St. Paul, Minnesota, in 1858. In just eight years, traffic on this stretch of the Mississippi River had increased tenfold. Many of the vessels carried settlers bound for rich farmland in southwestern Minnesota that had been ceded to the Federal government by the Sioux in 1852; a decade later, that territory would be the site of a bloody Indian uprising.

The Lure of Untapped Bounty

The first whites to exploit the bounty of the West were trappers, roaming the wild in small bands. By the 1840s the fur trade they had fostered was declining, but other veins of wealth were being tapped. Lodes of gold and silver enticed miners in droves, while dense forests drew thousands of lumbermen. When war broke out, some of these hardy adventurers proved ready recruits: One Union regiment culled from the mining camps of Colorado would play a pivotal role in the struggle for New Mexico.

In this painting by William Ranney, two trappers take advantage of a stream to conceal their trail — a ruse learned from the Indians with whom such backwoodsmen alternately traded and fought. Some trappers became army scouts.

Logs clog the Mississippi at a sawmill near Minneapolis in 1857. The first loggers in this area were U.S. soldiers, who built the outpost of Fort Snelling in the early 1820s; later, experienced timbermen flocked to the area from New England and Scandinavia.

Colorado miners, photographed around 1860, shovel earth into a sluice box to separate the gold at a claim owned by Scottish immigrant David Henderson *(foreground)*, who left an estate of nearly $150,000 in gold at his death. Word of such strikes lured prospectors from both ends of the continent: "greenhorns" from the East and seasoned "yondersiders" from California.

Ships lie at anchor at the Navy yard established in 1854 on Mare Island, near San Francisco. The Navy's Pacific Squadron had wrested control of the California coastline from Mexico in 1846 during a war of conquest that added more than 500,000 square miles to U.S. territory.

Security Spread Thin

America's irrepressible westward surge tested the limits of the country's military resources in the 1850s. The Pacific fringe of the new Federal domain could be patrolled by the Navy, but the burden of policing the vast interior, where friction between Indians and whites was increasing, fell to a Regular Army of scarcely 15,000 men.

Many of the Army's frontier garrisons were located at trading posts, where the troops had to deal with Indians embittered by the shady practices some traders engaged in. When tribal resentments boiled over, the soldiers had a fierce and agile foe to contend with. "In a campaign against Indians," one officer noted, "the front is all around, and the rear is nowhere."

Assiniboin Indians assemble outside Fort Union in the Dakota Territory. The Army held the fort during the War, but it was a trading station of the American Fur Company, whose representatives were known to lure Indians into the stockade with gifts, ply them with alcohol and divest them of their pelts for a pittance.

Frustration in New Mexico

"We charged up a hill towards an enemy who were hidden and invisible and who waited patiently for us to approach to shoot us down. Up we went, taking advantage of every bush and tree to shelter us. We saw no foe till in twenty yards of them, and then they rose from behind their breast works of rocks and poured into us a deadly volley."

SERGEANT ALFRED B. PETICOLAS, 4TH TEXAS MOUNTED VOLUNTEERS, AT GLORIETA PASS

1

In Taos, New Mexico Territory, a mostly Spanish-speaking town of low, mud-walled buildings, the usually even-tempered Christopher (Kit) Carson seethed with anger. It was the summer of 1861, and a crowd of Confederate sympathizers had torn down the United States flag and was about to raise the Confederate stars and bars above the town's dusty plaza. Newly commissioned a lieutenant colonel of the United States 1st New Mexico Volunteer Infantry Regiment, the famous explorer and guide would have none of it. Aided by several townspeople, Carson nailed an American flag to a long cottonwood pole. Then, facing the crowd, he ordered the Federal colors raised. Taos, he declared, had been Union since the Territory was won from Mexico in 1848, "and will stay Union!"

Carson was not yet aware of it, but the future of Taos, the rest of New Mexico and other regions of the American West was much in doubt as the Civil War began. The Confederate government avidly wanted the huge area and was planning to seize it. Gold from Western mines would give the South financial credit with which to buy arms abroad. Possession of California's ports, too distant to be blockaded by a Federal Navy concentrated along the Atlantic and Gulf Coasts, would ensure that the arms and other supplies could be delivered. The West might still be largely empty and unexplored — only about five million Americans, or 14 percent of the population, lived beyond the Mississippi in 1861 — but it was nevertheless an enormous prize, offering "plenty of room," as one Southern officer noted, "for the extension of slavery which would greatly strengthen the Confederate states."

Controlling even a portion of the trans-Mississippi West — the southern tier running through Arkansas and Texas to the Pacific Coast — would give the Confederacy great advantages in the conflict that was beginning. As the first shots were fired at Fort Sumter in April 1861, Confederate sympathizers in Texas were raising troops to secure the southern tier. Possession of that area might lead to conquest of the whole region.

The Federal government in Washington also was alert to the value of the 2,000-mile expanse from the Mississippi to the Pacific. The Union's treasury, like the Confederacy's, needed the gold and silver being mined in Nevada, California and other states and territories to finance the war effort. But that was a small matter compared with the threat of having large sections of the West — especially the Pacific Coast — fall to the Confederates and become slaveholding areas. So the government launched its own effort to secure the West, mobilizing volunteers — like Kit Carson and his New Mexicans — wherever they were to be found and sending them on campaigns designed to bind the vast region firmly to the Union cause.

This flag of the Federal 1st Colorado was torn by Confederate grapeshot during the decisive battle for control of New Mexico fought at Glorieta Pass on March 28, 1862. The banner was carried through the fight by Color Sergeant William Moore, whose battered Company D had 36 of its 100 men killed or wounded that day.

Preoccupied as it was with fighting the main Confederate armies east of the Mississippi, the Federal government often made a terrible botch of the war on the frontier. The violence of early confrontations between Union and Confederate volunteers in the southwest spread like a contagion to Indian tribes already angry at white encroachment on their lands, and the often brutal efforts of the inexperienced volunteers to contain the Indians only made the outbreaks worse. Federal attempts to flush the Confederates from the southeasterly parts of the trans-Mississippi region — Arkansas, Louisiana and Texas — were often so badly mismanaged that they became odysseys of frustration and hardship.

Despite misdirection and tragic bungling, the struggle on the frontier formed an important and dramatic part of the Civil War. In contrast to the fighting in Virginia, most of which took place in a cramped corridor only 100 miles long between Washington and Richmond, the conflict in the West spread from Minnesota to Oregon, from southern California to the Louisiana bayous. Armies trudged hundreds of miles to engage the enemy — and if defeated they fell back in harrowing retreats half the breadth of Texas. Ill-trained troops found themselves crossing trackless deserts and unexplored reaches of the Sierra Nevada and the Rocky Mountains. They fought furious engagements in an untamed land still inhabited by people the troops thought of as savages. It was warfare in its rawest state and often so implacable that it would have appalled even veterans of Gettysburg or Spotsylvania.

When the War began, more than 100,000 Southerners with strong ties to their home states were living in California alone, and Southern sympathizers were prevalent in every mining district from Washington Territory to western New Mexico. Although New Mexico had only 85 blacks in its population, the legislature had passed a slave code in 1859 and secessionists controlled southern and western portions of the Territory. Moreover, many officers in the prewar Army's Western departments were Southerners and the outposts they commanded were stocked with valuable military equipment. The Confederates were confident they could rely on secession-minded officers to secure strategic Federal forts and supplies for the South.

The principal seizure of Federal arms and other property occurred in Texas. Secessionists in the Texas legislature had taken the state out of the Union even before Lincoln's inauguration, by a vote of 166 to 8. Shortly thereafter, 71-year-old Major General David E. Twiggs, commander of the U.S. Army's Department of Texas, was threatened by a Confederate force of 1,000 men under Colonel Ben McCulloch, a flamboyant Texas Ranger and hero of the Mexican War. Twiggs, a Georgia-born officer, surrendered all of the Federal posts, government property and military stores in the state.

The attack on Fort Sumter set off a run of defections elsewhere in the West. More than 300 Southern-born officers resigned their commissions and hastened East to offer their services to the Confederacy. Two heads of departments — Brigadier General Albert Sidney Johnston in California and Colonel William Wing Loring in New Mexico — packed and left. So did many promising junior officers such as Major James Longstreet and Lieutenant Joseph Wheeler. A number of them would become generals of the Confederacy. "We were practically an army without officers," complained one Western soldier who remained staunchly Unionist.

The Federal government further depleted its forces in the West by ordering most of the loyal officers and their troops to hurry East. They were needed to add some professionalism to the volunteer armies being raised to fight the main Confederate forces. Frontier posts were abandoned or were held only by small detachments of Regulars. To fill the vacuum, the government urged the Western states and territories to raise volunteer units of their own. By 1862 an almost wholly new force of about 15,000 men policed the West for the Union, standing guard against both Confederates and hostile Indians.

While the Federals were recruiting this new volunteer army in the West, Texas was raising its own force, combining the state militia with newly enlisted volunteer units. Sent to head the Confederacy's Department of Texas was Colonel Earl Van Dorn, a hard-living Mississippian who arrived in San Antonio on March 16, 1861. Van Dorn had

This rare ambrotype of troops in San Antonio, Texas, was taken on Soledad Street, near the city plaza where the U.S. forces under Major General David Twiggs laid down their arms in February 1861. The mounted men bearing guns at right are probably Confederates; the soldiers in the road beyond may be Federals bound for the surrender ceremony.

Ben McCulloch *(above)*, the Mexican War hero who raised 1,000 volunteers to force General Twiggs *(below)* to surrender the Federal posts in Texas, had little trouble with his obliging adversary. Said Twiggs, "If an old woman with a broomstick should come with full authority from the state of Texas to demand the public property, I would give it up to her."

served earlier on the Texas frontier, leading units of the 2nd Cavalry in savagely fought campaigns against the Comanche. Now he formally mustered the Texas troops into the Confederate service and looked west toward a foe more important than the Indians — the Union forces in New Mexico.

Late that spring, Van Dorn ordered Lieutenant Colonel John R. Baylor's battalion of the 2nd Texas Mounted Rifles to ride westward, occupy the abandoned Fort Bliss at El Paso and guard against a Federal invasion from Union-held forts on the upper Rio Grande in New Mexico. Significantly, Van Dorn gave Baylor, who had been a ruthless Indian fighter himself, authority to take the offensive. If Baylor thought it advisable, he could invade New Mexico from Fort Bliss and attack Fort Fillmore, 40 miles north of El Paso and the probable staging point for any Federal countermove into Texas.

There was in fact little danger of a Union invasion from New Mexico. After the rash of Southern defections, Lieutenant Colonel Edward R. S. Canby, a tall, unassuming but efficient officer who had taken charge of the department at Santa Fe, was too busy reorganizing and strengthening his forces to contemplate any offensive move.

Canby found his domain rife with the spirit of secession. The people of Mesilla, a town on the Rio Grande only six miles from Fort Fillmore, were flying the Confederate flag. To the west 300 miles, secessionist miners around Tucson were planning to send a delegate to the Confederate Congress.

Worried by Southern sympathizers at home, Canby soon received the unsettling news that Colonel Baylor's Texans had arrived at El Paso and appeared ready to ride up the Rio Grande into New Mexico. Canby strengthened Fort Fillmore, placing its 700-man garrison — seven companies of the U.S. 7th Infantry and three companies of Captain Alfred Gibbs's Mounted Rifles — under the command of one of the few experienced officers left in the Territory, a gray-bearded, 55-year-old major from Vermont named Isaac Lynde. At the same time, Canby called on New Mexico's Territorial Governor, Abraham Rencher, for volunteers. Among those who responded were Kit Carson and the 1st New Mexico.

Canby's fears were well founded. The combative Baylor took immediate steps to attack Fort Fillmore. After reconnoitering the post — a collection of adobe buildings vulnerable on three sides to attack from high ground — Baylor ordered his small force of 258 men to cross into New Mexico on July 23, 1861, and ride northward along the Rio Grande. By the following night his horsemen were camped undetected within 600 yards of the Union fort, intending to take it by surprise at daybreak. Major Lynde was warned of the Texans' presence, however, by one of Baylor's pickets, who deserted during the night. Drums sounded, and Lynde's troops manned their positions. Realizing that the Federals were ready, Baylor called off the assault and, crossing the Rio Grande, entered Mesilla, whose Southern-leaning population gave him a rousing welcome.

Although a veteran of 34 years in the infantry, Lynde was unsure what to do next. Should he defend Fort Fillmore or attack the intruders? After pondering his situation most of July 25, he sallied forth with several companies in the late afternoon and made a halfhearted attempt to drive the Texans from Mesilla. After a brief exchange of fire — three Federals were killed and six wounded — darkness fell, and Lynde withdrew to the protection of his fort.

But the following night the nervous major had another change of heart. Either because he overestimated Baylor's strength or because he was overcome by panic, Lynde decided to abandon Fort Fillmore and retreat toward Fort Stanton, 140 miles across the desert to the northeast.

In the excitement of packing and departing, some of Lynde's soldiers broke into the post's stock of medicinal whiskey and filled their canteens. It was the worst thing they could have done. Lynde ordered Fort Fillmore evacuated at 1 a.m. on July 27, and during the night his men made good progress along the desert road. But after daylight, the July heat and a lack of water — combined with the whiskey, which merely increased the men's thirst — took a terrible toll. Under a blazing sun, scores of agonized men fell by the way. Lynde and some of his hardier troops finally reached San Agustín Springs, but much of his command was strung out in total disorder on the road behind him.

Baylor learned that Fort Fillmore had been evacuated, and he started off after the Federal column. Riding up the road — which, he reported, "was lined with fainting, famished soldiers who threw down their arms as we passed and begged for water" — Baylor easily overtook Lynde at the spring. The distraught Union leader drew up the remnants of his force for defense and then meekly surrendered his entire command. "I could not bring more than 100 men of the infantry battalion on parade," he later wrote in justification.

Baylor's stunning victory, achieved without firing a shot, had effectively cleared the Federal presence from southern New Mexico. Union troops who had been marching toward Fort Fillmore from Forts Buchanan and Breckenridge to the west abruptly changed direction and headed for Fort Craig, 100 miles farther north on the Rio Grande. At the same time, the Federal commander at Fort Stanton, 80 miles to the east, hurried his men northwestward to Albuquerque and Santa Fe. With the exception of the isolated garrison at Fort Craig, no Union troops stood guard below the 34th parallel, which bisected the Territory. The way to California stood open.

Baylor's force was too small to continue the offensive unaided. While he waited for reinforcements, he settled in at Mesilla and on August 1 issued a proclamation establishing the Confederate Territory of Arizona, including all of New Mexico south of the 34th parallel. He named Mesilla the capital and himself as Governor.

The effort to reinforce Baylor was already under way, propelled by a veteran officer and fire-breathing secessionist named Henry Hopkins Sibley. Inventor of the prewar Army's cone-shaped Sibley tent as well as the portable Sibley stove, he had become familiar with New Mexico before the War while campaigning against the Navajo under Canby, who had been a fellow cadet at West Point. Now a Confederate brigadier general, Sibley had orders from President Jefferson Davis to organize an army in Texas and drive the Federals out of all of New Mexico. After that, Sibley's orders read, he was to be "guided by circumstances and your own good judgment" — implying that if New Mexico fell, he had permission to extend his offensive to California, Nevada, Colorado and other areas.

During the summer and fall of 1861, while

A Critical View of Rebel Texans

Not long after General David Twiggs surrendered his command in Texas to Ben McCulloch, a detachment of state troops departed San Antonio to take possession of the abandoned Federal forts to the west. Accompanying the men was an accomplished artist, Carl G. von Iwonski *(below, left)*, who seized the opportunity to make some of the first sketches of secessionist forces in the field. If the Texans had known Iwonski's political views, they might have sent him packing. For like many other German immigrants in the state, he remained a Unionist at heart.

Iwonski's low opinion of the troops he traveled with is betrayed in a study done in pencil and brown wash near Fort Clark in March 1861 *(below, right)*, showing the Texans making free with provisions from U.S. supply wagons they had commandeered. The artist submitted this drawing to *Harper's Weekly*, whose engraver then executed a fair likeness of the sketch *(bottom)* for publication. The scene appeared in *Harper's* on June 15 with a note from Iwonski, who wrote archly that the "Dons" — as he dubbed the Anglo Texans — had left it to those of Mexican descent to "do all the hauling of wood and drawing of water, the Dons being engaged in smoking cigarritos, eating sardines, drinking Pat's 'favorite,' superintending the killing of a *stray* pig, etc."

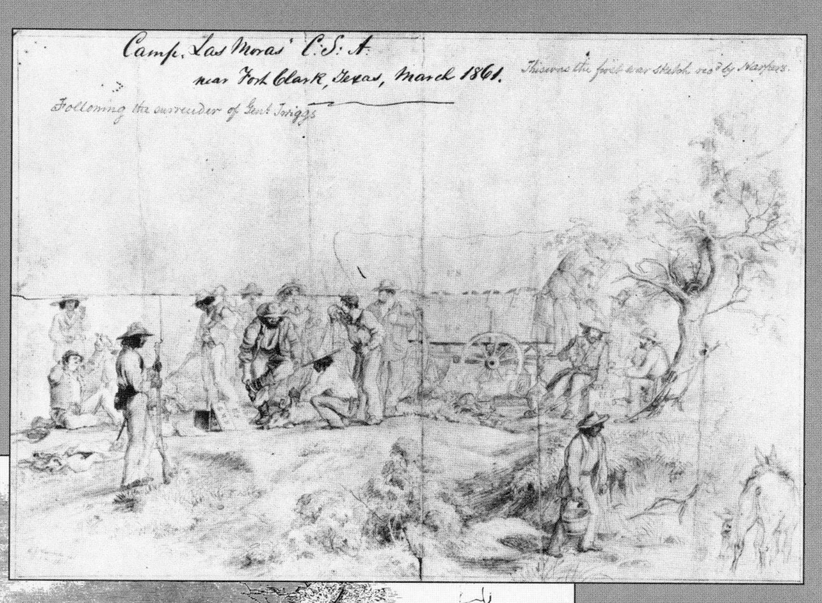

Diversely clad members of Terry's Texas Rangers — officially the 8th Texas Cavalry — ride jubilantly off to fight for the Confederacy in a painting attributed to Carl G. von Iwonski. One of the many mounted units formed in San Antonio early in the War, the Rangers distinguished themselves in the 1862 Battle of Shiloh, where their tenacity earned a Texas-size tribute from their colonel: "Not even when fighting at the odds of sixty to one did the men fall back until ordered."

Baylor maintained his forward position at Mesilla, Sibley raised three regiments totaling 3,500 mounted volunteers in San Antonio. Equipped with artillery and other weapons surrendered by Twiggs, the hard-riding Texans also carried, as one of them wrote proudly, "squirrel guns, bear guns, sportsman's guns, shotguns, both single and double barrels, in fact, guns of all sorts." Leaving San Antonio amid wild cheers from the populace on October 22, 1861, the Texans rode the 700 miles across the West Texas desert to Fort Bliss. They traveled in small detachments, to allow the precious waterholes along the way to replenish themselves.

In January 1862 Sibley's three regiments regrouped at Fort Thorn, an abandoned Federal post about 40 miles north of Mesilla and 90 miles south of Union-occupied Fort Craig. They were joined by six companies of Baylor's 2nd Texas Mounted Rifles and an independent unit organized locally and known as the Brigands.

At the same time, Sibley sent one of Baylor's companies, led by Captain Sherod Hunter, riding westward to occupy Tucson and keep watch for Union troops who might threaten him from California. Hunter's command of about 100 men crossed the desert through Apache country and on February 28 entered the old adobe pueblo of Tucson — "a city of mud-boxes, dingy and dilapidated, cracked and baked into a composite of dust and filth," according to a contemporary observer. They received an enthusiastic welcome from Tucson's secessionist inhabitants.

Three weeks before Hunter completed his long ride, Sibley had started up the Rio Grande with his main force to attack Fort Craig. His mounted column now totaled 2,515 effectives — many of those he had led west across Texas had already been lost to disease — and included 15 artillery pieces. Accompanying the troops were a long supply train and a herd of beef cattle.

Canby waited for the Confederates at Fort Craig with 3,810 men. Only 900 of them were Regulars — an assortment of companies from the 5th, 7th and 10th Infantries along with Gibbs's Mounted Rifles (now called the 3rd Cavalry) and men from the 1st Cavalry. The rest were New Mexico volunteers, including Kit Carson's regiment; a company of New Mexican scouts; some state militia; and a company of Colorado volunteers who had rushed to New Mexico in response to Canby's appeal for assistance.

It was a mixed bag of troops, some of doubtful reliability in a fight; but the fort — 22 adobe and stone buildings enclosed by an adobe-and-earthen wall — provided a strong position on the west bank of the Rio Grande. When members of the 5th Texas Mounted Volunteers appeared within a mile of the post on February 16, Canby refused to be drawn into battle, preferring to remain at the fort and await attack.

Bold and confident though he was, Sibley decided Fort Craig was too strong to assault head on. Instead, he chose to cross to the east bank of the fordable Rio Grande and bypass the fort, then recross the river six miles north at Valverde. From there he could follow an almost straight track paralleling the Rio Grande to Albuquerque and Santa Fe. The stratagem would leave Fort Craig's defenders isolated in their remote bastion and cut their supply line to the north.

Sibley waited two days for a sandstorm to subside before withdrawing several miles south of the fort and fording the river on February 19. The next morning he started north through rocky, sandy terrain one and a half miles east of the river. Although Canby had placed a protective force on the river's east bank, it failed to detect Sibley's movements until the afternoon, when the Texans appeared on higher ground. Canby realized what Sibley was planning and decided his only course was to fight. Moving most of his troops eastward from the fort, he tried to intercept the Texans. But the difficult terrain broken by sandy ridges and ravines slowed his advance and prevented his artillerists from placing their guns. For a time the two small armies watched each other as they moved along parallel ridges. Eventually, Confederate artillery shells panicked members of the 2nd New Mexico. The confusion spread to other units, and as darkness approached, Canby ordered most of his men back to the fort, leaving only an infantry picket line along the west riverbank.

That night Captain James (Paddy) Graydon, leader of the New Mexican company of scouts and spies, concocted one of the more bizarre schemes of this or any war. Intending to stampede Sibley's beef herd and deprive the Confederates of their steaks-on-the-hoof, Graydon and several companions tied boxes of howitzer shells to the backs of a pair of elderly mules and led the animals across the shallow river. Lighting the shell fuses, Graydon headed the mules toward the Texans' cattle. The mules turned around, however, and began following Graydon and his helpers, who were forced to race for safety back to their own lines. Far behind them, the shells exploded harmlessly — except for the unfortunate mules.

Early the following morning, Sibley again started the main body of his Texans up the east bank of the Rio Grande, aiming for the ford at Valverde. When Canby learned of the movement he sent Lieutenant Colonel Benjamin S. Roberts and a detachment of 220 cavalrymen, followed by infantry and artillery, hurrying up the west side of the river to block the Confederate crossing.

The Federals arrived opposite Valverde to find an advance unit of 180 Texans under a rancher and Mexican War veteran, Major Charles L. Pyron, occupying a cottonwood grove on the east bank. Roberts sent three companies of the 3rd Cavalry and one company of the 1st Cavalry splashing across the stream. After prolonged maneuvering, the troopers drove Pyron's Confederates away from the river to the protection of some nearby sand hills. Roberts then set up two artillery batteries, supported by skirmishers, on the west bank and commenced firing as more of Sibley's men began to appear.

Lieutenant Colonel John Baylor, who led the Confederate advance into the New Mexico Territory in July 1861, had been conditioned to combat in bloody encounters with Commanches along the Texas frontier. Such was Baylor's aversion to Indians that in 1860 he had stirred up sentiment against them in a newspaper he published, provocatively called *The White Man*.

Brigadier General Henry Hopkins Sibley, who took over command of the New Mexico operation from Baylor, was a seasoned West Pointer who had contended with the Seminoles in Florida, the Mexicans at Vera Cruz and jayhawkers in Kansas. Yet some feared that his combative instincts had been eroded by alcohol; detractors called him a "walking whiskey keg."

The Battle of Valverde, the first major encounter of the war in the southwest, increased in intensity about 11 a.m., when the 4th Texas Mounted Volunteers under Lieutenant Colonel William Scurry rushed up, followed by a Confederate light howitzer battery. During an exchange of artillery fire Scurry, who had become famous before the War as an adroit politician in East Texas, made an unsuccessful attempt to retake the cottonwood grove. Toward noon Union reinforcements led by Captain Henry R. Seldon, including a company of Colorado volunteers, joined Roberts on the west bank. Soon afterward Kit Carson arrived with eight companies of his New Mexicans.

Fearing a threat to his left flank, Roberts sent these fresh troops upstream. There Seldon's command waded the cold waters of the Rio Grande and in a fierce bayonet charge drove a force of dismounted Texans from some woods, only to face a counterattack by a 5th Texas company of lancers.

Coming at full gallop, the troopers, armed

Colonel Edward R. S. Canby, in charge of the Federal Department of New Mexico, was hard pressed to meet the Confederate threat there. Recruiting proved difficult among the Spanish-speaking populace, Canby reported, and few seeking commissions inspired confidence: His stated goal was to have among the officers of each company "at least one American who could be relied upon."

with nine-foot-long wooden lances tipped with three-inch-wide steel blades, nearly panicked the Coloradans. But their commanding officer, Captain Theodore H. Dodd, coolly closed up his ranks and shouted, "They are Texans. Give them hell!" A volley shattered the Texans' front line, knocking men and horses to the ground. Some of the horsemen, a Colorado private wrote, "came near enough to be transfixed and lifted from their saddles by bayonets, but the greater part bit the dust before the lances could come in use." Only three Texans escaped unharmed; the survivors fell back to their own lines in disorder. Encouraged by the Coloradans' success, Roberts now crossed his artillery to the east bank.

As the fighting raged on, Sibley became ill. Placing Colonel Thomas Green of the 5th Texas in command, he retired from the field. Some of Sibley's men claimed he was drunk: "The Commanding General," one of his men wrote, "was an old army officer whose love for liquor exceeded that for home, country or God." Baylor later contended that Sibley spent the rest of the battle cowering in an ambulance.

Whatever the truth of these charges, Sibley had chosen an excellent officer to take his place. Under Green, a transplanted Virginian who had battled both Mexicans and Indians during the Texas Republic's early days, the Texans fought furiously, beating off Federal attacks until, in the late afternoon, they made a climactic rush of their own that carried the day.

The stage had been set about 3 o'clock. Colonel Canby arrived from Fort Craig and took over field command. Recalling Kit Carson's regiment from its position upstream, he ordered Carson's troops and the 2nd New Mexico to cross the river and join in an assault on the Texas left. Carson's regiment quickly moved into position, but most of the men of the 2nd New Mexico refused to obey Canby's order. During the confusion caused by the aborted Federal assault, Green launched a two-pronged counterattack. Forming up out of sight behind some high sand ridges, about 200 Texans led by Major Henry W. Raguet suddenly emerged and charged down a slope against the battery on Canby's right wing. The attack was met by some dismounted Federal cavalrymen and other units, including Kit Carson's New Mexicans, and was hurled back with 40 men killed or wounded.

A different story, however, was unfolding on the other flank. There about 4 p.m. Green sent a yelling mass of 750 dismounted Texans, led by the gallant Major Samuel A. Lockridge, across a plain toward the Federal battery commanded by Captain Alexander

The Confederate hero of the 1862 Battle of Valverde, Colonel Thomas Green, who replaced the faltering General Sibley as field commander, had two invaluable assets that his superior lacked: a zest for battle and the wholehearted respect of the troops. "His men adored him," a fellow officer noted, "and would follow wherever he led."

McRae. A storm of canister met the Texans and they wavered momentarily, taking heavy losses; but then they dashed forward until they had reached the Federal guns.

Once within the Union lines, the Texans began firing their pistols at point-blank range, clubbing gunners with rifle butts and slashing left and right with their feared Bowie knives. Two companies of the 2nd New Mexico supporting the artillery abandoned their positions "in the wildest confusion," according to Canby. They demoralized in turn a company of 7th Infantry. As the fighting swirled around the guns, both Lockridge and McRae were killed — some claimed by simultaneously shooting each other across one of McRae's artillery pieces.

Lockridge's attack sent the Federals reeling, and when a counterattack failed to retake McRae's guns, Canby ordered a general withdrawal to the walls of Fort Craig. As the Federal troops splashed back across the Rio Grande, shells from McRae's captured guns fell among them, killing a number of men and horses whose bodies floated slowly downstream. The Texans pursued Canby's retreating men as far as the river, but they halted when the chivalrous Colonel Green agreed to Canby's request for a truce to recover the Federal dead and wounded.

Losses in the wild, sporadic fighting had been about even. Canby reported 68 men killed, 160 wounded and 35 taken prisoner. Green reported 36 dead and 150 wounded. The Confederates also lost half their cavalry mounts and were forced to convert one of their regiments to infantry. But Valverde clearly had been a Confederate triumph, opening the way for a continued march northward into the heart of New Mexico.

Two days after the victory, General Sibley, his health recovered, formed his columns and struck out for Albuquerque and Santa Fe. Within a week Sibley's advance units, encountering only feeble resistance from scattered Federal detachments, had covered the 100 miles to Albuquerque. The Texans seized all the Federal stores that had not been burned or removed to Santa Fe.

In a first-hand impression of the Battle of Valverde, sketched by a Confederate, the charging T

Lieutenant Colonel William Scurry, a formidable stump speaker in Texas before the War, used his oratorical skills to inspire his troops above the din of battle. At Valverde, Colonel Green recalled, "the cheering voice of Lieutenant Colonel Scurry was heard where the bullets fell thickest on the field."

d *center)* focus their attack on Alexander McRae's battery *(right)* near the Rio Grande.

Another cache of military supplies fell into their hands when four bold Southern sympathizers forced a garrison of 47 New Mexico volunteers to surrender a post at Cubero, 60 miles west of the city.

Their supply wagons replenished, Sibley's Confederates moved on to Santa Fe, entering the Territorial capital on March 10. The Federal Governor had already left, establishing a temporary seat of government in the hamlet of Las Vegas 30 miles to the east. An army train of 120 wagons, escorted by all the Federal troops in Santa Fe, had also headed eastward, seeking refuge in an old frontier post called Fort Union.

With the capture of Santa Fe, the Confederate conquest of New Mexico was virtually complete. Canby was isolated at Fort Craig. Only Fort Union now barred the way to a Confederate invasion of Colorado, and Sibley viewed that post as no obstacle. Spies told him that the 800-man garrison was demoralized by Canby's defeat at Valverde and the approach of the triumphant Confederate army. Foreseeing a quick victory, Sibley ordered his men to march on the fort.

Sibley's next moves were not to be as easy as he expected. The Federal government in Washington and the Union commands in both Colorado and California had belatedly awakened to the precarious situation in New Mexico. Help came first from Colorado, where Acting Governor Lewis Weld responded to an Army request: "Send all available forces you can possibly spare to reinforce Colonel Canby." In late February and early March, the scattered companies of the 1st Colorado Volunteer Infantry Regiment under Colonel John P. Slough, a prominent Denver attorney, set out for New Mexico.

The 1st Colorado was a rough, brawling outfit composed largely of miners, frontiersmen and the denizens of Denver's saloons. Bored by inaction in their Colorado camps, the troops were spoiling for any kind of a fight. Their swift march south across the high plains and over the Raton Mountains in freezing weather put the hardiest of them to the test. While still trudging through southern Colorado, they learned of the Federal defeat at Valverde and increased their pace, making 40 miles a day, sometimes through several inches of snow. They moved even faster after March 8 when, climbing the Raton Pass between Colorado and New Mexico, they got word that Sibley had occupied Albuquerque and was starting an advance on Fort Union. Carrying only their blankets and arms, the Coloradans marched 30 miles during the night, battling bitterly cold winds that whipped at them with hurricane force. The Pike's Peakers, as the Confederates came to call them after one of Colorado's tallest mountains, finally tramped into Fort Union on March 11 with drums beating and colors flying. Only a few had ridden; most of the 900 men had walked more than 400 miles in 13 days.

Over the objection of the fort's commander, Colonel Gabriel R. Paul, Slough claimed seniority and assumed charge of the post and all its men. Paul was angered and alarmed when Slough, ignoring Canby's orders to defend Fort Union, made plans to strip the garrison and march immediately against the Confederates. On March 22 Slough set the bulk of the troops — Coloradans, Regulars and New Mexicans, totaling 1,342 men — marching southwestward on the road to Santa Fe. Sibley's Confederates were already moving in the opposite direction. On March 25 they approached Glorieta Pass, a high, narrow corridor through the southern tip of the pine-covered Sangre de Cristo Mountains. It was in this rugged country that the two armies would collide.

Slough's advance guard of 400 men was led by Major John M. Chivington, a tall, powerfully built Methodist preacher from Denver with a booming voice he often exercised delivering fire-and-brimstone sermons. As Chivington and his troops approached Glorieta Pass after dark, they stopped near a ranch owned by Martin Kozlowski, a Polish immigrant. During the night some of Chivington's pickets captured four Confederate scouts and learned that the enemy was not far off. Chivington ordered an advance early the next morning, March 26. By 2 p.m. his troops had reached the summit of the pass and, while descending its western slope, surprised a scouting party of 31 Texans, taking them prisoner. One of the captors rushed back to Chivington's main camp shouting, "We've got them corraled this time. Give them hell, boys!"

Flinging aside knapsacks and other extra equipment, Chivington's men hurried forward on the double-quick, entering a narrow, rocky defile at the western end of Glorieta Pass called Apache Canyon. Turning a bend where the canyon widened into a long, open space, they came face to face with the vanguard of Sibley's Confederates — the 2nd Texas Mounted Rifles and four companies of the 5th Texas — carrying the Lone Star flag and commanded by one of the heroes of Valverde, Major Pyron. Momentarily startled, the Texas horsemen nevertheless managed to unlimber two small mountain howitzers and began firing.

The grapeshot and shells sent the Union troops running for cover, but Chivington soon restored order, dispatching his infantry and some dismounted cavalry up the wooded mountainsides where their flanking fire forced the Confederates to retreat. Withdrawing to a point where the canyon narrowed again, the Texans crossed a log bridge over a 15-foot-wide arroyo, destroyed the bridge and prepared a new defense. While

:olonel Christopher (Kit) Carson :op), in command of the Federal 1st ˈew Mexico at Valverde, had reason ɔ be proud of his troops, who stood p to Confederate pressure until or- ered to fall back. Carson was accus- ɔmed to seeing men through tight crapes: As a prewar scout, portrayed bove with his rifle cradled in his rms, he had guided dozens of parties cross hostile Indian country.

Pyron placed his howitzers beyond the arroyo to command the narrow road, his men emulated the Federal tactic, scrambling up the rocky slopes on both sides of the defile to support the gunners.

Chivington's troops soon advanced, halting about 200 yards short of the howitzers. Quickly sizing up the situation, Chivington ordered most of his infantry and dismounted cavalry to climb still higher up the rocky slopes to get above the Confederate riflemen. The rest, finding what protection they could, opened a frontal fire on the road. Chivington rode among this group fiercely, a Colorado private named Ovando J. Hollister reported, "with a pistol in each hand and one or two under his arms," urging his men toward the enemy battery. While the Federals in the center inched forward, their comrades on the mountainsides gradually forced the Confederates down to the road, where they were vulnerable.

At this point Chivington called on a company of Colorado cavalry he had in reserve. The mounted men charged down the road, yelling as they leaped the arroyo and crashed into the Texans' crowded ranks. The ferocity of the Coloradans' attack stunned the

Confederates. "On they came to what I supposed certain destruction," a Texan later wrote his wife, "but nothing like lead or iron seemed to stop them, for we were pouring it into them from every side like hail in a storm. In a moment these devils had run the gauntlet for a half mile, and were fighting hand to hand with our men in the road." With his troops in disorder, Pyron called another retreat. Chivington ended his pursuit as darkness approached, and the Confederates got away with their howitzers intact.

The engagement in Apache Canyon, although it had been small in scale, was the first Union victory in the New Mexico Territory. The Confederates suffered losses of 32 killed, 43 wounded and about 70 taken prisoner. The Federals' casualties were only five killed and 14 wounded.

The battle, however, had not involved the main forces on either side. At the start of the fighting, Pyron had sent a message asking for help to Colonel Scurry, who was with the 4th Texas and part of the 7th Texas Cavalry at

Two drummers stand beside troops of Company G, Federal 1st Colorado, as they turn out for guard duty in the mining town of Empire early in 1862. Sent to New Mexico in March, the rough-and-tumble volunteers showed surprising discipline; one rancher on whose property they camped recalled gratefully, "They never robbed me of anything, not even a chicken."

Colonel John P. Slough, commander of the 1st Colorado, was regarded suspiciously by Republicans in the regiment because of his former prominence in the Democratic Party of his native Ohio. Slough soon dispelled any doubts as to his loyalty, yet he remained remote. "His aristocratic style savors more of eastern society than of the free-and-easy border," one private complained.

the town of Galisteo, 16 miles away. Scurry marched immediately, arriving at Johnson's ranch, Pyron's camp in Apache Canyon, about 3 a.m. on March 27, the morning after the encounter. When the expected Federal attack failed to materialize, Scurry ordered his and Pyron's commands, between 600 and 700 effectives, to advance up the canyon. They were to beat back the Federals who had blocked Pyron's way and take Fort Union. So as not to impede his movements, Scurry left his large supply train at Johnson's ranch, watched only by a small guard.

Chivington also was reinforced late on the the 27th of March when Slough's main column reached Kozlowski's ranch. Eager to capitalize on Chivington's victory, Slough at once made plans to push ahead. By dawn the next day he had dispatched Chivington with seven companies — almost one third of his force — with orders to cross the mountains by a circuitous route. Coming out at Apache Canyon, they were to occupy the heights above the canyon and, if possible, harass the enemy's rear. With the remainder of his troops, fewer than 900 men, Slough then entered Glorieta Pass and marched cautiously as far as Pigeon's ranch — so named because its owner, a Frenchman, was said to resemble a pigeon when he danced the fandango.

Slough's men had scarcely paused when pickets rushed back with word that Texans were advancing in force through a stand of pine and cedar about 800 yards ahead. "Suddenly the bugles sounded assembly," recalled Ovando Hollister. "We seized our arms, fell in and hastened forward perhaps 500 yards, when their artillery commenced cutting the tree tops over our heads."

A partially wooded depression lay between the two forces, and Slough sent a cavalry unit into it to try to locate the Texas artillery. Riding toward thicker timber on their left, the Federal horsemen came under fire and dismounted, seeking shelter at the foot of a small hill. Meanwhile, Slough established a battle line below the brow of a ridge, placing two batteries of four guns each, supported by infantry companies, in the center. He then sent two other companies forward on the right and left with orders to climb the wooded hills bordering the battlefield and flank the Texans.

Scurry countered by disposing his dismounted cavalry in three columns, with Pyron's command on the right, the artillery supported by Henry Raguet's Texans on a slight elevation in the center, and the third unit, commanded by himself, on the left. Once begun, the fighting soon became furious; the air was filled with the roar of artillery, the rattle of small arms and the yelling of men as the two sides lunged and parried, the men half-blinded by clouds of rock dust. Slough's company on the right moved first, rushing forward to flank the Texans' left. Scurry's men replied by charging into the Federals, "pistol and knife in hand," driving them back with heavy losses. Confederate pressure on the opposite side of the line forced the Federals there to withdraw as well, relinquishing their ridgetop positions to the Texas artillery.

The Union howitzers were soon set up again, however, and this time the gunners managed to get the range with deadly precision. Direct hits put two of the Confederate guns out of action. Federal sharpshooters picked off a number of the gunners serving the remaining pieces. "The Texan battery soon slackened its fire until it almost ceased," Private Hollister reported.

Although Scurry's troops now had lost most of their artillery support, the combative Confederate commander was in no mood to give up. First he launched several head-on attacks. When these were thrown back, he sent Majors Pyron and Raguet with their commands up some rocky ledges on the Federal right with orders to flank the Union line. The move succeeded. The Texans gained the ledges, beat off attempts to dislodge them and drove the Federals back. Scurry then combined his columns and ordered a general charge against the Federal guns.

But now it was the Federals' turn to gain the upper hand. Fierce fire from Union artillerists and their supporting infantry halted Scurry's initial charge and four more that stubbornly followed. On the sixth and final try, the Confederates withered under point-blank volleys. Seeing their advantage, the Federals counterattacked with bayonets. A wild melee ensued, the troops fighting hand to hand. Raguet was killed, Pyron had his horse shot from under him and Scurry was twice bloodied by grazing shots.

But the Confederates were not through. Enfilading fire from one of Scurry's detachments holding higher ground on the Union right again forced the Federal artillery and infantry to withdraw. As the Federal line pulled back to a new position below Pigeon's ranch, the Texans charged once more.

Although the Federals managed to beat back the assault, Slough had had enough. Shortly after 5 that afternoon he broke off the engagement, ordering his battered units back to Kozlowski's ranch. Both armies were exhausted. They had fought without interruption for six hours.

As Slough's Federals trudged away from the Glorieta battlefield, they were sure that they had lost the day. But a Confederate ambulance flying a white flag soon caught up with them. Its occupant, the former Secretary of New Mexico Territory and a secessionist, asked for a truce until the following noon. Slough agreed.

At 10 p.m. the reason for the Confederate request became clear. Into the Union camp came Major Chivington and his 430 men, returned from their mission with a stunning report. Guided by a New Mexican who knew the area, they had circled 16 miles through the mountains to a wooded precipice directly overlooking Johnson's ranch, where Scurry had left his supply train. Lowering themselves over the cliff with ropes and leather straps, Chivington's troops had stormed the ranch, driven away the guard and destroyed the entire train of 73 wagons. They burned all of Scurry's ammunition, food, baggage, saddles, tents, clothing and medical supplies — everything the Texans would need to continue their campaign.

In addition, the Federal detachment had found 500 horses and mules — mostly mounts left behind by Scurry's cavalry — corraled in a ravine about half a mile from the ranch, and they had destroyed the animals with bayonets. As the Coloradans prepared to leave, a Confederate courier emerged from the canyon, saw what had happened and galloped away. It was his shocking news that had induced Scurry to ask for a truce.

Chivington's astonishing exploit made it clear that Glorieta Pass, far from being a Union defeat, had been a debacle for Sibley's Texans, ending at a stroke Confederate aspirations of conquering the southwest. The dismayed Texans, leaving their wounded at Pigeon's ranch, swiftly fell back on Santa Fe. There they were joined by six companies of the 5th Texas and by General Sibley, who had been at Albuquerque throughout the action at Glorieta. The Confederates ransacked Santa Fe, commandeering everything available including some wagons, ammunition and a store of blankets intended for distribution to Indians. Still Sibley saw that his force was in no condition to continue the offensive. Clinging to a thin hope, he wrote the Governor of Texas requesting reinforcements. "We have been crippled, and for this reason ask assistance," he pleaded.

Colonel Canby, still at Fort Craig, was unaware of what had happened at Glorieta Pass.

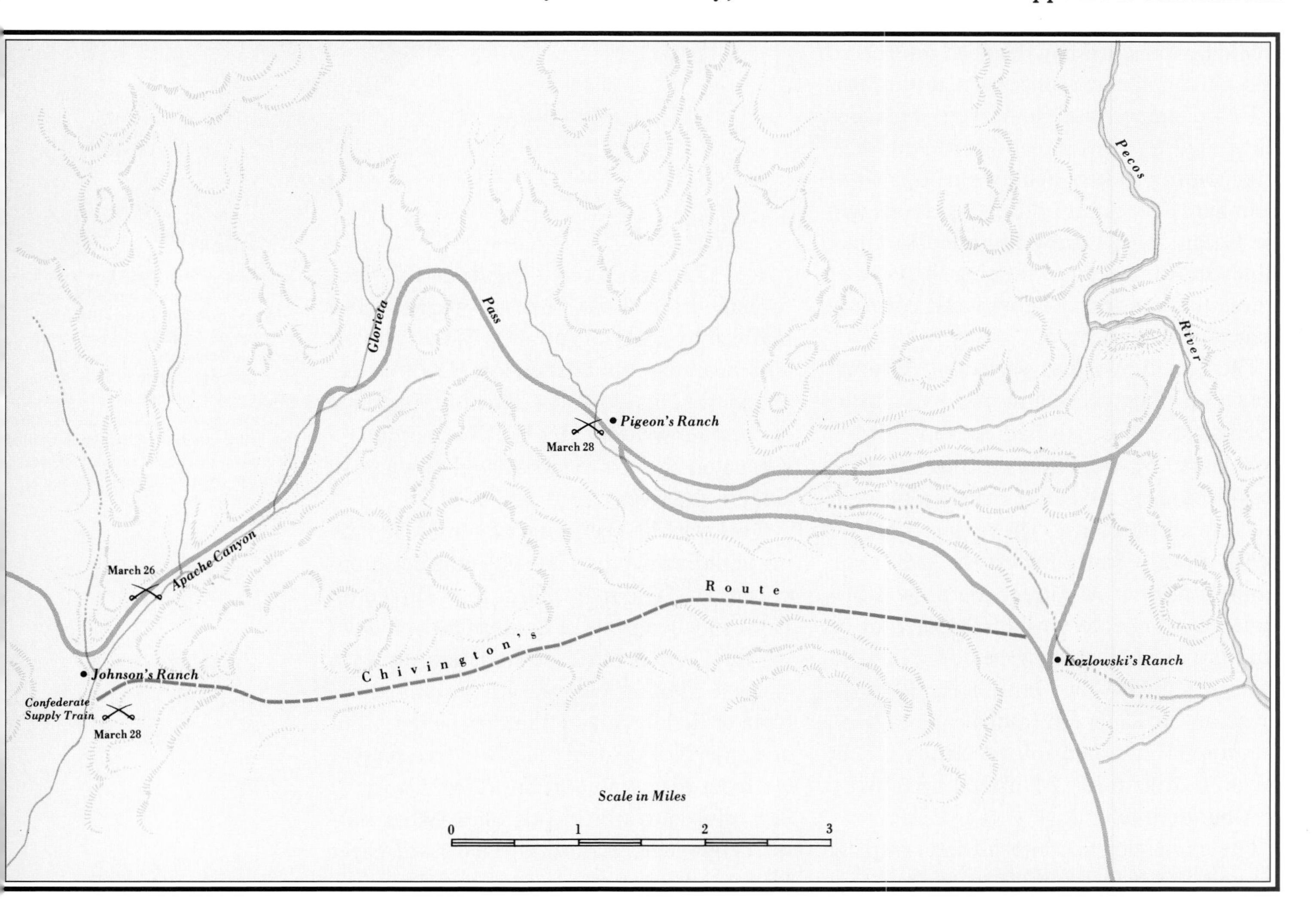

)n March 28, Colonel William ;curry marched his Confederates ast through Glorieta Pass, leaving a detachment to guard his supplies at Johnson's ranch. Colonel ohn Slough, meanwhile, sent part of is Federal force under Major ohn Chivington to threaten the enmy rear, then marched his remaining men to meet Scurry. Slough nd Scurry fought furiously near 'igeon's ranch until Scurry learned hat Chivington had destroyed his upplies, making retreat inevitable.

Running low on supplies himself and concerned that the impetuous Coloradans had left Fort Union exposed, he sent a messenger to Slough, ordering him to return at once to protect that post. Then on April 1 Canby set out from Fort Craig with 1,210 men to try to join the northern forces.

At Socorro, 30 miles north of Fort Craig, Canby learned of the Texans' disaster and their withdrawal from Glorieta. Abruptly altering his plans, Canby came up with a scheme designed to force the Confederates from Santa Fe, then from Albuquerque and finally from New Mexico. First he ordered the Coloradans, who by then had returned to Fort Union, to march once more toward Santa Fe and an eventual rendezvous with him. He started his own force toward Albuquerque, hoping to lure Sibley's troops south from Santa Fe. After uniting his troops with the Coloradans, Canby intended to attack Sibley in Albuquerque, forcing the Confederates to abandon the town and continue their retreat southward.

The scheme worked perfectly. Although the Coloradans were angered by Canby's original order, which had prevented them from pursuing the Texans through Glorieta Pass — Slough in fact had resigned his commission in disgust — they now marched swiftly toward Santa Fe. At the same time, Canby's feint at Albuquerque drew Sibley southward to protect what remained of his supplies, most of which were stored in Albuquerque's mud-walled buildings. With Sibley gone, the Colorado troops entered Santa Fe unopposed, then joined Canby's main force as planned, 15 miles northwest of Albuquerque.

The climactic encounter of the campaign seemed about to occur. But it never took place. Outnumbered — his plea for reinforcements had not been answered — and hobbled by a lack of supplies, Sibley was left with no choice but to abandon New Mexico. On April 12 his Texans — after burying some of their brass howitzers in Albuquerque — evacuated the town and started down both sides of the river.

This was the beginning of a long, agonizing withdrawal punctuated by only occasional combat. The main flare-up occurred on April 15 when some of Canby's men, following the Confederates south, caught up with Colonel Thomas Green's 5th Texans at the town of Peralta, about 15 miles below Albuquerque. Not wishing to have to feed prisoners from his own short supplies, Canby at first refused to attack. But when Green's artillery opened fire, the Coloradans, still eager for a scrap, pitched into the Confederates.

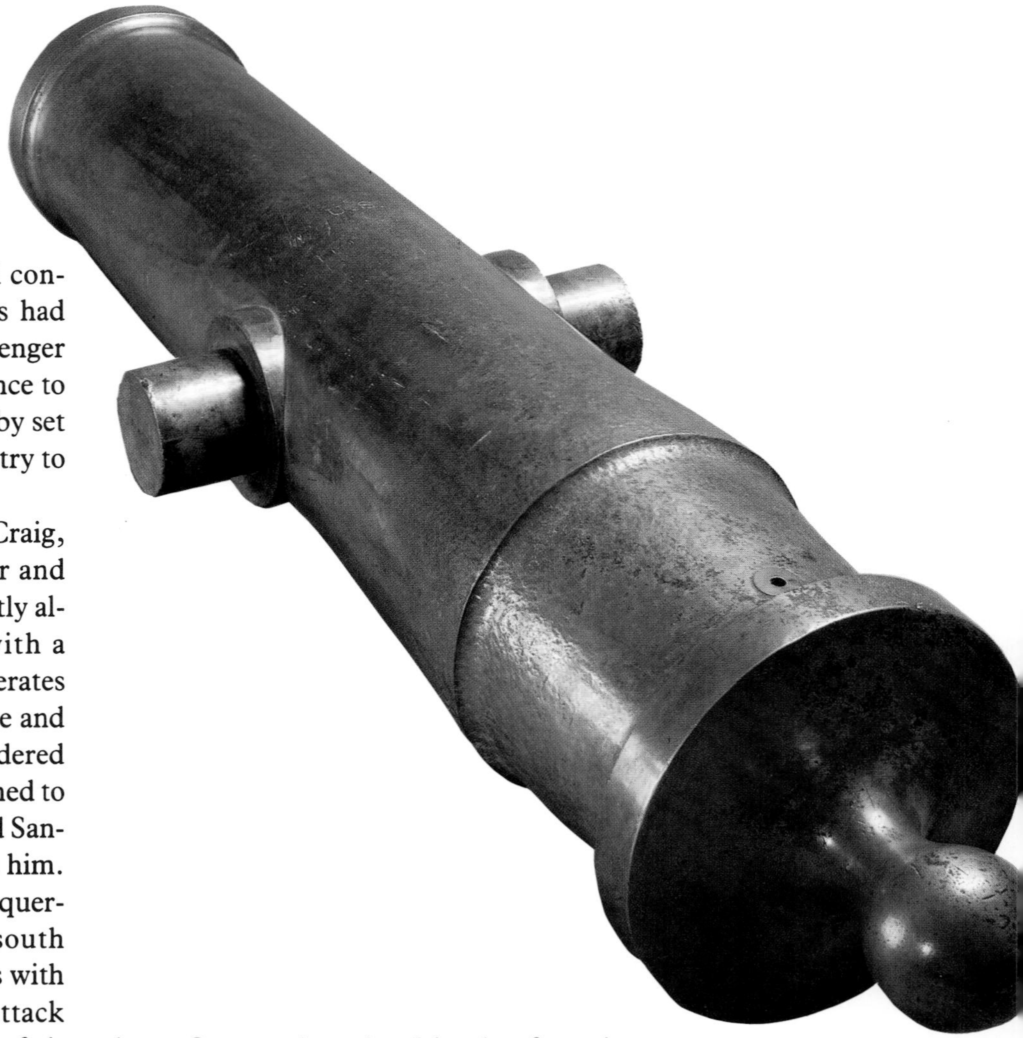

This 12-pounder brass howitzer was one of eight cannon buried at General Sibley's orders in a corral in Albuquerque on April 12 to keep them from the Federals. The guns had been in the stockpile of U.S. arms and supplies handed over to the Confederates at San Antonio the year before; since then they had been hauled through sand, snow and icy streams for more than a thousand miles.

The fighting soon spread, the large Union force driving the Confederates into Peralta, whose thick-walled adobe buildings ran for two miles along the river. Seeing no reason to risk heavy casualties in house-to-house fighting, Canby again ordered his men to halt and hold their lines. The Battle of Peralta thereafter consisted of little more than sporadic skirmishing and desultory artillery fire. "It was the most harmless battle on record," wrote Private Hollister. "We lay around on the ground in line of battle, asleep."

The pressure from the pursuing Federals nevertheless hurried Sibley southward. Abandoning his sick and wounded as well as all wagons, baggage and supplies not deemed essential, he set off on a hazardous detour across deserts and mountains 20 miles west of the Rio Grande. His plan was to circle Fort Craig, then return to the river south of the armed post.

The difficult march did little for the Texans' morale, which was already cracking. They blamed Sibley for mismanaging the campaign, and at Peralta 250 men had mutinied, threatening to shoot their officers if ordered into battle. Now, as the men struggled over ragged mountains and cut their way through dense thickets of desert brush with axes and Bowie knives, the Confederate Army of New Mexico virtually disintegrated. The 100-mile-long detour took them eight days to complete. Discipline dissolved, and according to one survivor, it was every man for himself. Famished and exhausted men collapsed and were left to die. Others too sick to be carried along were thrown out of the few wagons and abandoned.

On April 25, Sibley finally reached the Rio Grande and made his way past Mesilla to Fort Bliss by the first week in May. Behind him, his tattered, half-starved troops, cursing him for his "want of feeling, poor generalship and cowardice," were strung out for 50 miles. And the Texans' nightmare had not ended. At Fort Bliss, Sibley learned that a fresh Federal army had left California and was moving in his direction.

The oncoming Federals were California volunteers backed by an artillery company of Regulars that had been assembled at Fort Yuma on the California-New Mexico border. In command was James H. Carleton, a veteran cavalry colonel and rigid disciplinarian. Marching rapidly eastward, elements of Carleton's so-called California Column had reached the neighborhood of Tucson by March 15. Carleton had then started detachments across the desert toward the Rio Grande. Despite severe fighting with Indians at Apache Pass, the site of a spring in the arid southeastern part of present-day Arizona, the first detachment arrived at the Rio Grande above Mesilla on July 4 and raised the American flag.

By that time Sibley and many of his remaining men were in flight back to San Antonio. A rear guard of about 600 Texans had been left at Fort Fillmore under the command of Colonel William Steele, but on July 8 they, too, withdrew before the approaching Californians. With their departure, the last semblance of a Confederate presence in New Mexico vanished.

The 700-mile journey across the West Texas desert, from waterhole to waterhole, was the ultimate ordeal for the remnants of Sibley's army. In the burning heat of midsummer, men abandoned their last possessions, even their weapons, in order to keep moving. A stagecoach from El Paso passed

Diary of a Retreat through Hell

"No order was observed, no company staid together; the wearied sank down upon the grass, regardless of the cold, to rest and sleep; the strong, with words of execration upon their lips, pressed feverishly and frantically on for water."

Thus did Sergeant Alfred B. Peticolas describe in his diary the retreat of Sibley's Confederates through the arid high country of New Mexico in April 1862. For the 23-year-old Peticolas, who supplemented the entries in his journal with detailed sketches *(right)*, the withdrawal was made all the more unpalatable by memories of the triumph he had tasted two months earlier at the Battle of Valverde. "Never before have I felt such perfect happiness," he had written after that battle.

In the weeks following Valverde, Peticolas and his fellow Texans had been lashed by sandstorms and late-winter blizzards, weakened by hunger and outflanked by the enemy. Now as they headed home, swinging away from the Rio Grande to elude the Federals, they found themselves engaged in a daily battle for survival. "Water is still 10 miles ahead and the column is already reeking with sweat and parched with thirst," Peticolas noted on April 22. Hours later he and his mates finally caught sight of the stream they were seeking. "We dashed recklessly down the steep sides of the rocky canion," he wrote, "and there we threw ourselves upon the rocks, regardless of the crowding horses and mules, regardless of the swearing men, regardless of everything, and drank the cool clear soft water."

In Sergeant Peticolas' sketch of the Battle of Valverde, mounted Texans face Federals armed with cannon along the Rio Grande. In time, Peticolas noted, many troopers dismounted to fire more accurately on foot: "Not a man shot without taking sight, for Texas boys are accustomed to the use of arms and never shoot their ammunition away for nothing."

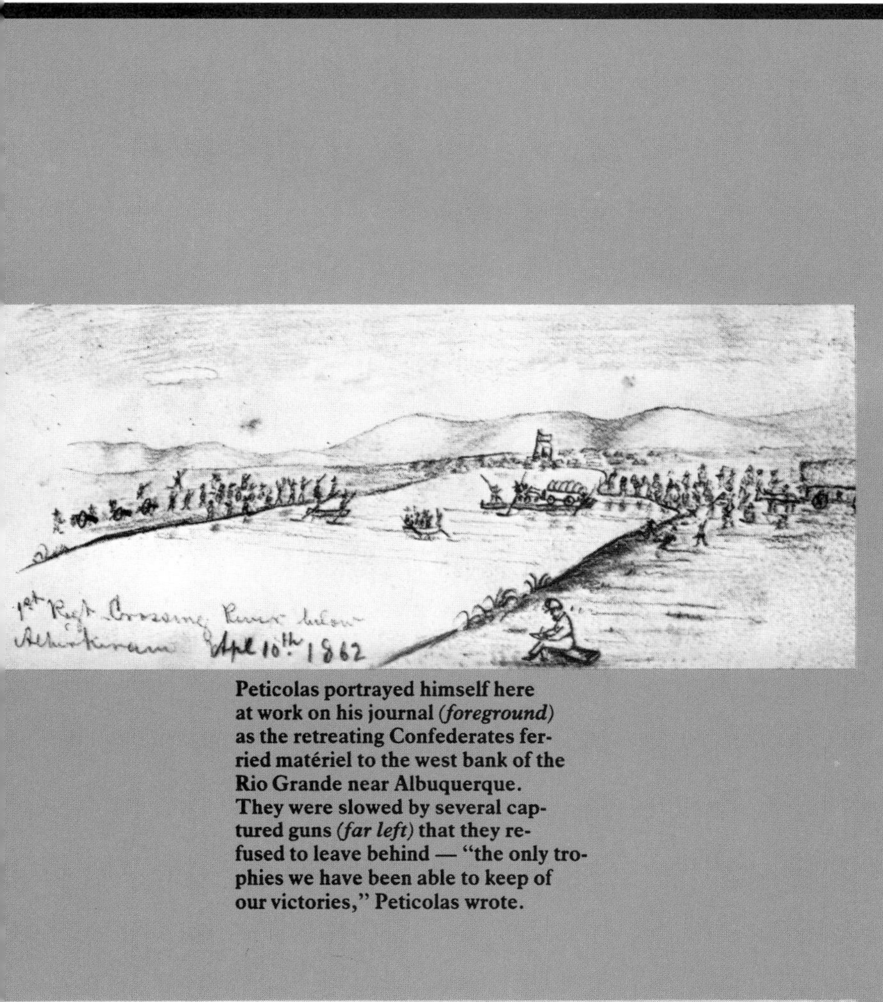

Peticolas portrayed himself here at work on his journal *(foreground)* as the retreating Confederates ferried matériel to the west bank of the Rio Grande near Albuquerque. They were slowed by several captured guns *(far left)* that they refused to leave behind — "the only trophies we have been able to keep of our victories," Peticolas wrote.

Mules pull Confederate supply wagons near Star Mountain in this drawing done by Peticolas in western Texas on June 14. The teamsters were lucky to be riding, for most of the troops had lost their mounts; many of those on foot would "give out on the road," Peticolas predicted, "and when we reach San Antonio the brigade will be dwindled to a regiment."

some of the troops, and a woman passenger wrote that the wretched men "were suffering terribly from the effects of heat; very many of them were a-foot, and scarcely able to travel from blistered feet. They were subsisting on bread and water, both officers and men; many of them were sick, many ragged, and all hungry."

News of the soldiers' plight traveled ahead of them, and as they neared San Antonio, friends and relatives rushed to meet them with wagon trains of provisions. Men straggled in all summer, but of the approximately 3,500 Texans who had ridden west with Sibley the previous year, 1,500 never returned.

The collapse of Sibley's campaign ended the Confederacy's grand dream of expansion to the Pacific. For the rest of the War, New Mexico remained firmly in Union hands. Edward Canby was promoted to brigadier general and called East to another assignment. He turned over his command in New Mexico to Carleton, who also received a commission as brigadier general. Chivington took his Pike's Peakers back to Colorado, and Kit Carson and his New Mexicans joined Carleton at Santa Fe. All four officers would be heard from again in later campaigns in the trans-Mississippi West.

In San Antonio, Sibley's veterans had one prize to show for their valor. At Colonel Scurry's insistence, they had managed to drag all the way home the six brass artillery pieces of McRae's Union battery that they had captured at Valverde. A special unit, formed by volunteers from Sibley's regiments, was equipped with the guns. Proudly named the Valverde Battery, it soon would see action with other Texas units against Federal troops in the bayous of Louisiana.

Emperor Napoleon III, who was able to seize control of France in 1852 largely because of French nostalgia for the reign of Napoleon I, shared his famous uncle's dreams of military expansion. Failing to extend his power in Europe, he engaged in several overseas adventures in addition to his brief conquest of Mexico.

A Menacing Presen South of the Borde

The war on the frontier was made even more troublesome for President Lincoln' government by French adventurism south of the Texas border. Taking advantage of a civil conflict in Mexico that threatened President Benito Juarez' government, Emperor Napoleon III of France landed a small army at Vera Cruz in October 1861. A surprising Mexican victory at Puebla, a fortress guarding Mexico City, stalled the invasion, but the French eventually crushed the Mexican resistance. Seizing his opportunity, Napoleon placed a puppet emperor Archduke Maximilian of Austria, on the Mexican throne.

The French conquest posed a direct affront to the Monroe Doctrine, infuriating Lincoln. The president was concerned that Napoleon's government might enter into a formal alliance with the Confederacy and use Mexico as a base for further incursions in Latin America. Out of fear of American reprisal, the French ultimately did neither. Throughout the Civil War, however, Mexico's turmoil influenced Washington's already discordant military policies in the Southwest.

The approach of French troops eventually forced President Juarez to flee Mexico City, but he refused to give up and leave his country. "Show me the highest and driest mountain," he declared, "and I will go to the top of it and die there, wrapped in the flag of the Republic, but without leaving the national territory. That never!"

Mexican lancers help drive back Zouaves in this painting of the defense of Puebla in 1862. Lacking supplies and heavy guns, the outnumbered French withdrew.

A Valiant Mexican Stand

Shocked by the initial French setback at Puebla, Napoleon dispatched reinforcements, including three battalions of the vaunted Foreign Legion, to Mexico along with a new commander, Major General Elie Frédéric Forey. On March 17, 1863, French infantry backed by siege guns renewed the assault on the city.

The Mexicans made a valiant stand. Using rifled cannon of the most modern design and old weapons so outdated that their counterparts rested in European museums, they made the French pay dearly. But after two months, the defenders' resources were exhausted, and Puebla's fall on May 17 opened the road to Mexico City.

Major General Elie Forey, engineer of the French victory, wears a full-dress uniform in a painting commemorating the capture of Puebla. A Crimean War veteran, Forey was known for a gruff joviality between battles that earned him the playful nickname "the Bear."

The Marquis de Gallifet *(near right)* stands with two other French officers hurt at Puebla. When news of his injury reached Paris, Empress Eugénie forbade her staff to use ice — then employed to slow bleeding — in sympathy for Gallifet, who might die from the lack of it.

French troops storm the huge San Xavier penitentiary at Puebla after two months of relentless shelling had blasted the walls to rubble. Inside the stronghold, the besieged Mexican troops had been reduced to eating rodents and pets to stay alive.

In one of the few defeats of Forey's campaign, the last survivors of a company of French Legionnaires — ambushed while scouting ahead of a payroll train — make a last stand at Camerone, 20 miles from Puebla, on April 30, 1863. The Legionnaires' captain, Jean Danjou *(above)*, who wore a wooden left hand as a result of injuries sustained in the Crimean War, was among the first killed.

Gentle Emperor for a Volatile Throne

With Mexican resistance crumbling after the fall of Puebla, Napoleon quickly set about establishing a monarchy on the ruins of Juarez' republic. His choice for Emperor was a self-effacing Austrian nobleman, Archduke Ferdinand Maximilian Joseph, an amateur botanist who was reigning quietly in Trieste, a port city on the Adriatic then controlled by Austria.

Amid the ceremonies celebrating the April 1864 departure of Maximilian and his wife, the Archduchess Carlota, on their 4,000-mile sea voyage to Mexico, a single cautionary voice was heard. Anyone aspiring to rule politically volatile Mexico, warned the United States consul in Trieste, "ought to be extraordinarily happy if he escapes with his life."

The vanguard of Napoleon's conquering army, led by General Forey *(right of center, on white horse)* enters Mexico City on June 8, 1863, a few hours after President Juarez' departure. To bolster the enthusiasm of the crowd, the French plied bystanders with centavos and quaffs of a beerlike drink called pulque.

Eager to please their new subjects, Maximilian and his wife, Carlota, were studying the Spanish language and Mexican history when this photograph was taken shortly before they left Europe. A less than gracious reception awaited them in Mexico. The welcoming committee arrived two hours late, and the only decorations — a pair of hastily constructed triumphal arches — had blown over.

In Trieste on October 3, 1863, Maximilian *(far left)* listens as Gutierrez de Estrada, spokesman for a delegation of Mexican monarchists, reads a document offering him the crown of Mexico. When the Archduke insisted he could accept only if the Mexican people willed it, Gutierrez produced a petition with thousands of signatures. Unknown to Maximilian, they had been procured by the French army, often at gunpoint.

Three *Juaristas* — soldiers who remained loyal to President Benito Juarez — sit in a photographer's studio, dressed in their Mexican army uniforms, which were cut in the French military fashion. Their determined fight for Mexican independence got a boost in 1865 when weapons from U.S. arsenals began to flow across the Texas-Mexico border.

The *Juaristas'* Revenge

Shortly after the end of the American Civil War in April of 1865, events in Mexico took another dramatic shift. Unbowed by their defeats, Mexican troops kept on fighting. More important, the U.S. government, no longer wary of offending France, dispatched a 50,000-man "Army of Observation" to patrol the border of Mexico.

Unwilling to risk war, Napoleon began withdrawing his forces, leaving the unfortunate Maximilian to be deposed and executed. Facing the firing squad, the former emperor behaved with quiet dignity. "Boys, aim well," he told the riflemen, pointing to his heart. "Aim right here."

Urging his red-coated Contra Guerrillas forward with sword upraised, Captain Michel Ney leads a clash with Mexican irregulars on June 8, 1865. Napoleon's decision gradually to withdraw French troops triggered increased Mexican guerrilla raiding. The fighting would continue until the last French soldier left in early 1867; Maximilian's reign ended a few months later.

Dressed in the uniform of the Contra Guerrillas and bedecked with medals, French Colonel Charles Dupin sports a fancy sombrero as well as high soft boots. Dupin organized the Contras, but he was soon dismissed as a useless incompetent.

Red River Odyssey

"Oh the mud and slosh. No one can form an idea of it unless he has once been in the swamps of Louisiana."

CAPTAIN ELIJAH P. PETTY, WALKER'S TEXAS DIVISION, C.S.A.

No state or territory in the trans-Mississippi West — and few places in all the divided nation — suffered more during the War than Louisiana. First came the fighting for New Orleans. Then the rich sugar- and cotton-growing parishes opposite Baton Rouge, Port Hudson and Vicksburg were laid prostrate during the long, bitter struggle for control of the Mississippi. "The houses are all deserted," wrote a Confederate officer. "You can behold mansion after mansion, including costly sugar houses, going to decay."

Nor did the devastation cease in July 1863 when the Federals under Ulysses S. Grant finally took Vicksburg and Port Hudson was surrendered, clearing the Mississippi. Soon other Union armies were marching and countermarching through Louisiana, inflicting damage both near the Mississippi and in the state's western uplands.

The main cause of this renewed fighting was an obsession in faraway Washington, D.C., with the Confederate-controlled flatlands of East Texas. Still a wild and mostly empty area, East Texas nevertheless possessed economic and strategic importance. And the most feasible overland route for a Federal invasion of Texas lay directly across Louisiana, or more precisely, up the Red River from the already ruined parishes north of Port Hudson to Shreveport, in Louisiana's northwest corner.

In 1864 the government in Washington ordered just such an invasion. The expedition that followed was the largest and most ambitious of all the military operations west of the Mississippi. About 30,000 Federal troops, supported by a large fleet of shallow-draft gunboats and transports, would force their way up the Red River — and meet about 20,000 brilliantly led Confederates in ferocious battles that left the opposing forces reeling and exhausted. All this would take place in country that the men on both sides agreed was as miserable a place to fight in as could be imagined. The landscape progressed from dank bayous and swamps filled with poisonous snakes to a frontier region of sandy uplands and scorpion-infested pine barrens. "I would not give two bits for the whole country," complained one disgusted Confederate. Yet much more than that was to be invested in the Red River Campaign.

East Texas loomed large in the eyes of President Abraham Lincoln and his advisers for several reasons, some of them barely pertinent to the war effort. One was intense political pressure from the mill owners of New England, whose looms had been idle for lack of Southern cotton almost since the conflict began. Their clamor for military action to wrest coastal Texas cotton fields from the Confederates reached a crescendo as the election year of 1864 approached.

A second irritant was the Confederate arms traffic across the Rio Grande from Mexico into East Texas. Foreign ships tying up at Bagdad, a Mexican port immune to the U.S. Navy's blockade, were busily trading

This regulation brass bugle, shown with its original braided-cotton strap, was carried during the Red River Campaign by Private Edgar Aldrich of the 3rd Rhode Island Cavalry. The so-called pig's tail attachment at the mouthpiece could be removed to change the key of the bugle call.

Enfield rifles and other war supplies for bales of Texas cotton, needed by the spinning mills of Europe. This traffic could be choked off only by gaining control of the Rio Grande crossing points.

But most important in Lincoln's view was what appeared to be a dangerous threat from a foreign power. The invasion of Mexico by Emperor Napoleon III of France was a growing concern throughout the War. Putting a Federal army in Texas would help discourage any French move to aid the Confederacy — or to annex Louisiana and portions of the southwest.

For these reasons and others, President Lincoln and his chief military adviser in Washington, Major General Henry Halleck, began bombarding the Federal commander in New Orleans with orders to concentrate the troops in his Department of the Gulf and move against Texas. The officer entrusted with this task was Nathaniel P. Banks, a 47-year-old political general who had received his rank solely because before the War he had been Speaker of the U.S. House of Representatives and a three-term Republican governor of Massachusetts.

Banks looked the model of a major general in tailored uniforms set off by gleaming boots. He was an honest, energetic officer, but he had not always fared well on the battlefield. During the Shenandoah Valley fighting of 1862 he had been soundly drubbed by Stonewall Jackson, losing so many supply wagons that Jackson's hungry troops, feasting on the captured Federal stores, had nicknamed their unwilling benefactor "Commissary Banks." Shifted to New Orleans, Banks in 1863 had commanded the Federal attack on Port Hudson, and although his campaign had been marred by mistakes, the eventual capture of the Confederate stronghold had restored some luster to his reputation.

Banks viewed General Halleck's orders to invade Texas with distaste. He agreed with General Grant, then the Federal commander of the Mississippi region, that a move in the other direction, toward Mobile, Alabama, would do more damage to the Confederacy. And he shuddered at Halleck's suggestion that the invasion proceed via the Red River. Plainly a difficult undertaking, it might prove a failure and ruin forever Banks's hopes of someday being elected President. So he cast about for other, less risky ways to move a Federal force into Texas.

His first solution was to attack Sabine Pass at the mouth of the Sabine River, which forms the Louisiana-Texas border. From there, he thought, his troops could move down the Texas coast and capture Galveston, then take Houston and Beaumont as well. Loading 5,000 men on 22 transports, he sent them off under the command of Major General William B. Franklin. A veteran of the Army of the Potomac, Franklin had been in disfavor since his poor performance at Fredericksburg and had only recently been assigned to Banks. Escorting the transports were four gunboats under a young Navy lieutenant named Frederick Crocker.

After his bold New Year's Day attack drove off a Union flotilla, Confederate General John B. Magruder *(left)* issued a proclamation *(below)* to announce the resumption of Confederate trade in Galveston. The proud general, called "Prince John" by his men, also had a message for the Federals: "We are preparing to give them a warm reception should they return with a larger fleet."

HEADQUARTERS,

District of Texas, New Mexico and Arizona,
***Galveston*, January 4th, 1863.**

Whereas the undersigned has succeeded in capturing and destrc ing a portion of the enemy's fleet and in driving the remainder o of Galveston Harbor and beyond the neighboring waters, and th blockade has been thus raised, he therefore hereby proclaims to a concerned, that the Harbor of Galveston is open for trade with a friendly nations, and their merchants are invited to resume their usu commercial intercourse with this Port.

Done at Galveston, this, the Fourth day of January, Eighteen Hu dred and Sixty-Three.

J. BANKHEAD MAGRUDER,
(Official,) Major General Commanding.
E. F. TURNER, Capt. & A. A. Gen'l.

Cottonclad Victory at Galveston

Early on January 1, 1863, Major General John Magruder's fleet of five Confederate cottonclads — so called for the protection afforded by bales of cotton on their decks — steamed into the harbor at Galveston, Texas, determined to end the Union blockade and occupation of the port. The steamer *Westfield,* with Fleet Commander William B. Renshaw aboard, was the first of six Federal warships to respond to the attack; but the *Westfield* ran aground. As other Federal ships moved to her aid, Confederate batteries fired from the opposite shore, driving them away. With capture imminent, Renshaw tried to blow up the *Westfield;* but the explosion was early, killing Renshaw and several of his crew.

Nearby, the Confederate gunboat *Bayou City* dueled the Federal sidewheeler *Harriet Lane.* The *Bayou City* blasted a hole in the *Harriet Lane's* wheelhouse before the Confederate ship's 32-pound gun blew apart. The *Bayou City* rammed the *Harriet Lane;* whooping Confederates swarmed onto the deck of the Federal cutter and captured her. The remaining Union vessels slipped away under a flag of truce, and the harbor returned to Southern control. "The victory was won," wrote a jubilant Confederate, "and a New Year's gift was made to the people of Texas."

Confederate soldiers clamber aboard the Federal steamer *Harriet Lane* after ramming the ship with their "cottonclad" steamer, the *Bayou City (background)*. After her capture, the *Harriet Lane* was used by the Confederates to run a cargo of Texas cotton to Havana.

An explosion meant to prevent the capture of the stranded Federal gunboat *Westfield* becomes a tragedy as the charge touches off prematurely. Most of the crew had transferred to the transport *Mary A. Boardman (right)* a few minutes earlier; but the last party preparing to leave, including Fleet Commander William Renshaw, died in the explosion.

Major General Nathaniel P. Banks led a Federal army up the Red River in March 1864, to invade Texas. Banks, who had risen from bobbin boy in a cotton mill to become Governor of Massachusetts, was thought by some to be the best of the Union's so-called political generals.

It seemed like a mismatch when the Federal flotilla arrived off the bar at Sabine Pass on September 7, 1863. Only a single company of 47 Texas artillerymen manning a small Confederate fort at the pass was ready to oppose the invasion force. But the Texans' accurate fire soon crippled two of Crocker's gunboats, and Franklin, afraid to land his troops in the face of artillery, called off the attack. The entire expeditionary force sailed ignominiously back to New Orleans.

Leery of any more coastal operations, Banks next directed Franklin to prepare an expedition that would ascend the Bayou Teche, a broad stream heading generally north into central Louisiana, then strike overland through western Louisiana and enter Texas near Beaumont. Franklin assembled his army, now swollen to almost 20,000 men, at Fort Bisland on the lower Teche and on October 3 began advancing slowly. Along the way the Federals skirmished with Confederates led by Major General Richard Taylor, the 37-year-old son of Zachary Taylor, hero of the Mexican War, and a hero himself earlier in the Civil War as one of Stonewall Jackson's ablest lieutenants.

By October 21 Franklin had advanced about 75 miles and occupied the town of Opelousas, but there he dawdled indecisively. He had learned that food would be exceedingly hard to find in sparsely inhabited western Louisiana, and he was loathe to move without a large, well-stocked wagon train. In late October he began to pull back — only to have his northernmost brigade surprised in its camp near Grand Coteau by two cavalry brigades of aggressive Texans under newly promoted Brigadier General Thomas Green, the Confederate leader at the Battle of Valverde in New Mexico the previous year. Green's Texans, supported by three infantry regiments from Major General John Walker's Texas division, routed the Federals and captured almost 600 men. With the Texans harassing his withdrawal, Franklin retreated to New Iberia, 100 miles west of New Orleans, and went into camp for the winter.

Frustrated again, Banks decided to try another water-borne expedition to the Texas coast. This time the Navy and elements of his army would seize the mouth of the Rio Grande, closing that part of the Mexican border to Confederate commerce, then occupy other points along the coast.

The expedition accomplished more than the fiasco at Sabine Pass, but the benefits to the Union cause were paltry nonetheless. On

November 2, Federal troops landed at Brazos Santiago, where the Rio Grande flows into the Gulf of Mexico. They soon took Brownsville and closed the area to further Confederate-Mexican trade. But trains of cotton-filled wagons merely followed more westerly routes, crossing the river upstream. In the same manner, European arms continued to flow into Texas. The Federals also established beachheads at Corpus Christi, Matagorda, Indianola and Port Lavaca, but they were largely symbolic because the coast was already blockaded by the U.S. Navy. Holding them merely tied up numbers of Banks's troops.

Henry Halleck, in Washington, was far from satisfied with Banks's modest successes on the coast. The only sensible way to approach Texas, he again insisted, was to send a large expedition up the Red River to Shreveport. Such a campaign would clear the Confederates from Louisiana and position Banks's army for a full-scale invasion of the more important parts of Texas.

Once again Banks demurred — and he was strongly backed by U. S. Grant, who still wanted Banks to move on Mobile. But Halleck was adamant. An invasion of Texas, he said, was "a matter of political or State policy" — which meant Lincoln was still concerned about the French presence in Mexico. There was little that even Grant could do in the face of the President's wishes, and in January 1864 Banks began planning the venture up the Red River that would test to the breaking point his army and his personal abilities as a commander.

As Banks issued orders from his headquarters in New Orleans, he began to look upon the expedition with more optimism than he would have dreamed possible a month or two earlier. One reason for his sanguine view: Grant had promised him reinforcements — 10,000 or more veteran troops to be drawn from William Tecumseh Sherman's armies in Tennessee. Grant also assured Banks that he could count on help from the 15,000-man Federal army in Arkansas commanded by Major General Frederick Steele, who had just chased the Confederates from Little Rock. And there was a political lure. The wharves and warehouses on the upper Red, Banks was told, were piled high with cotton bales that he could seize and ship to the starved mills of his native Massachusetts, where the voters would surely be grateful.

Suspending further operations in Texas, Banks recalled most of his troops to the lower Teche. Then on March 1 General Sherman arrived in New Orleans to confer on the upcoming campaign. Sherman would indeed furnish troops and Rear Admiral David Porter would send his fleet of ironclads, which had been instrumental in the Union victories on the Mississippi. Sherman had one proviso: His troops would have to be returned east of the Mississippi by April 15 for his planned spring operations in Georgia. But this hardly seemed a problem to Banks. He planned to be ensconced in Shreveport by then.

On March 7, 1864, an advance cavalry division started up the Teche. Heavy rains and muddy roads delayed the bulk of Banks's command, but by March 15 all of his troops were on their way — XIX Corps and two divisions of XIII Corps recalled from Texas, about 17,000 men in all. On March 10, the XVI and XVII Corps from Sherman's hard-bitten Army of the Tennessee, commanded by Brigadier General Andrew J. Smith, sailed from Vicksburg for the mouth of the Red in 20 transports. With them came Brigadier General Alfred W. Ellet's Marine Brigade and Porter's gunboat flotilla and supply ships. The armada totaled about 60 vessels mounting 210 guns, the largest naval force ever seen in Western waters.

In Arkansas, General Steele took his time departing from Little Rock. Many of his troops were on furlough, he explained. Besides, Arkansas roads were impassable from the spring rains and forage was difficult to obtain. Instead of moving against Shreveport, Steele proposed merely making a demonstration in Arkansas. This would divert Confederate troops who might otherwise rush to defend the Red. Grant, who early in March had superseded Halleck as general in chief, had never liked the idea of a Red River expedition, but he did not want it to fail either. "Move your force in full cooperation with General N. P. Banks's attack on Shreveport," he ordered Steele. "A mere demonstration will not be sufficient." Receiving this blunt command, Steele reluctantly committed his small army.

Yet there was a major flaw in the Federal scheme. Banks and Steele, far removed from each other, would find it impossible to coordinate their movements. In addition, the sometimes arrogant Porter, although under orders to cooperate with Banks, also exercised independent command. The result: No single commander had complete charge of the various forces — about 45,000 Federal soldiers and sailors — that were heading toward Shreveport. "The difficulty in regard to this expedition," Banks would write later, "was that nobody assumed to give orders."

The Confederates in Louisiana, Arkansas and Texas were aware of all this activity. General Edmund Kirby Smith, in charge of the Confederacy's Trans-Mississippi Department since his abortive invasion of Kentucky in 1862, quickly began deploying what defensive forces he possessed. The troops already in Louisiana under Richard Taylor — which included Walker's Texans and a separate brigade of Texas infantry led by a young French enthusiast for the Southern cause named Camille Polignac — were told to harass the Federal advance as best they could. At the same time, Kirby Smith summoned reinforcements from Texas, including Thomas Green's veterans, ordering them to join Taylor as fast as possible, and he instructed Major General Sterling (Pap) Price to march south from Arkansas toward Shreveport with his divisions of Missouri and Arkansas Confederates. As he moved, Price would try to thwart Steele's advance from Little Rock.

Rear Admiral David D. Porter, brother of Commodore William Porter and cousin of General Fitz-John Porter, commanded the Federal fleet that escorted Banks's army up the Red River. When Southerners branded him "the Thief of the Mississippi" for his policy of seizing Confederate cotton, the admiral was obliged to assure his mother that his cabin was not, as she had heard, full of stolen silver.

Only Walker's 3,800 Texans and three companies of Louisiana cavalry were anywhere near the mouth of the Red River, however, when Porter's fleet entered the river

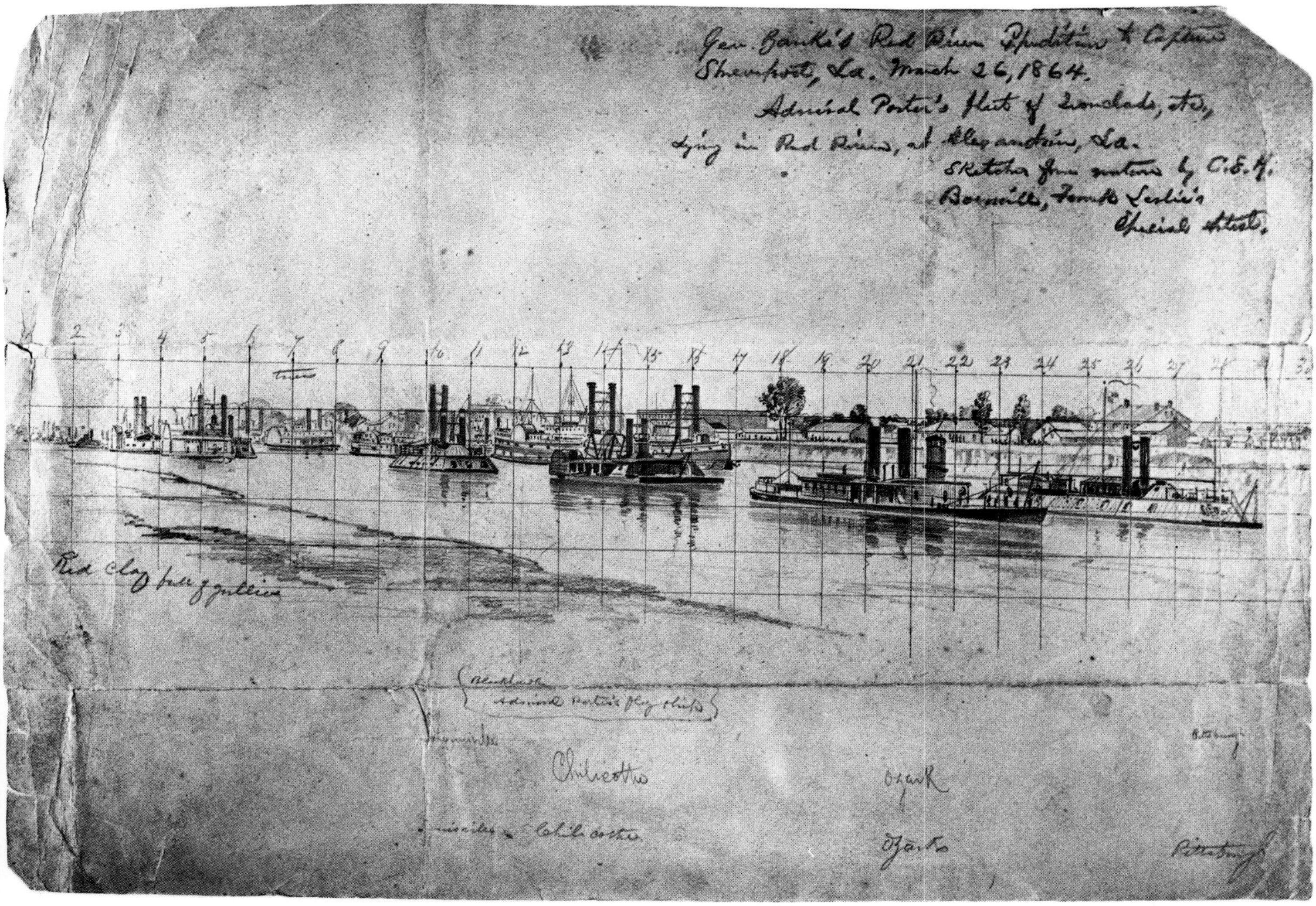

In a newspaper artist's annotated sketch, Admiral Porter's flotilla lies at anchor at Alexandria, Louisiana, on March 26, 1864, after its bombardment contributed to the capture of nearby Fort De Russy. Porter, who described the movement to Alexandria as most orderly, evidently was unaware that one of his gunboat crews had threatened to destroy a town along the way unless its citizens paid a bribe.

and landed A. J. Smith's two corps at Simsport on March 12. Heavily outnumbered, the Confederates evacuated a half-completed entrenchment on nearby Yellow Bayou and fell back past their principal bastion in the region, Fort De Russy, leaving only a small garrison there.

The Federals soon showed the sort of combined naval and military muscle that Banks was counting on to win the campaign. While Porter's gunboats moved up the river, one of A. J. Smith's divisions under Brigadier General Joseph A. Mower prepared to attack by land. A onetime carpenter from Vermont who had begun his military career as a private in the Mexican War, Mower was a hard-fighting, hard-marching soldier. He wasted no time leading his men across the lush Avoyelles Prairie south of the Red to come at Fort De Russy from the rear. Then, as Porter's heavy guns blazed away at the fort from the river, Mower's men stormed the earthworks. At a cost of only 38 killed or wounded, the Federals captured 300 of the shell-dazed defenders along with 10 cannon.

The way was now open for A. J. Smith and Porter to move another 30 miles up the Red to the town of Alexandria; there they were scheduled to meet Banks's troops, who were still marching overland up the Teche. Accordingly Smith reembarked most of his two corps on the naval transports, leaving behind only enough men to thoroughly dismantle Fort De Russy. After a one-day trip up the winding, mud-banked river, the fleet reached Alexandria on March 15. Four days later, lead elements of Banks's cavalry rode into town; within a week the rest of the main Federal force of 17,000 men had arrived. Muddy and disheveled from their march through the swampy country of the Teche — and almost a week behind schedule — the men, like their leader, seemed nonetheless eager to get on with the expedition.

In the meantime, Mower had struck another blow at the Confederates. On the stormy afternoon of March 21, in rain, hail and sleet, he had led six regiments of infantry, a battery of artillery and a brigade of Banks's newly arrived cavalry into a swampy area 23 miles northwest of Alexandria. That night at Henderson's Hill, as the storm raged, Mower's troops surrounded the camp of the 2nd Louisiana Cavalry, Richard Taylor's principal mounted unit. Helped by their guides — Confederate deserters who knew the Louisiana troopers' countersign — the Federals seized the pickets and walked into the camp, capturing about 250 men, most of their horses and a battery of four guns without firing a shot.

Mower's raid, which deprived Taylor of his cavalry scouts, forced the Confederate leader to retreat to the area of Natchitoches, another 40 miles up the river. But Banks was unable to take advantage of this opening. Despite recent rainstorms, the Red's annual spring rise had yet to take place, and the river was abnormally low. Porter had often boasted that he could take his ships "wherever the sand was damp," but the 50-year-old admiral refused to risk them by trying to run the Alexandria rapids. When at last the river began to rise, the first ship to attempt the rapids, the powerful ironclad *Eastport,* ran aground, blocking the channel for almost three days. Unwilling to advance without the fleet's firepower, Banks stayed put.

While enduring the frustrating delays, Banks on March 26 received a peremptory message from General Grant. If it appeared he could not take Shreveport in the next month, Grant wrote, he must return A. J. Smith's 10,000 men to Sherman by April 15.

Time was running out, but just as Banks's timetable seemed on the verge of ruin another rise of the river freed the *Eastport.* Though a hospital steamer was wrecked, 12 more gunboats and 30 other ships safely passed the Alexandria rapids. The rest of the fleet was left below to protect the Federal line of communication and supply.

The combined force continued up the Red, Banks's men riding and walking along rough riverbank trails while A. J. Smith's troops lounged on the decks of the laboring, chugging transports. By April 3, ships and men had cleared Natchitoches, which Taylor and his Confederates had abandoned, and proceeded to Grand Ecore, a village about 50 miles upstream from Alexandria, where most of Smith's troops came ashore.

Shreveport was now only four days' march ahead, but the deadline for releasing Smith's troops was only a week and a half away. To meet the stringent schedule, Banks decided to march the bulk of his army by what he thought would be the fastest route, the stagecoach road that ran from Grand Ecore to Shreveport. It was a decision that would cost Banks and his men dearly.

The stage road had two salient drawbacks. Unlike the little country roads that ran along the river, the stage route struck off westward away from the Red. This meant that the army marching along it would no longer be

Confederate Major General Richard Taylor *(above)* spent much of the Red River Campaign berating the inactivity of his superior, General Edmund Kirby Smith *(right)*. "Action," Taylor demanded in a letter to Kirby Smith, "prompt, vigorous action is required. While we are deliberating, the enemy is marching."

protected by the guns of Porter's fleet. Also, as it turned out, the stage road provided neither a wide nor a swift route of march. But ignoring the first drawback and ignorant of the second, Banks on April 6 led his army west from Grand Ecore. The men turned their backs on the gunboats and supply vessels, which steamed and tooted reassuringly in the rust-colored river, and they plunged down the forest-hemmed turnpike. If all went well, Banks and his troops would reestablish contact with Porter and the fleet in less than a week's time at Loggy Bayou, about 110 miles farther up the winding Red — and only 30 miles from Shreveport.

For an army that was intending to move swiftly, Banks's force was encumbered with a huge supply train — 1,000 wagons that creaked and rattled over the rutted and increasingly hilly stage road. The country itself became more and more forbidding — a "howling wilderness," as one Massachusetts trooper called it, of red-clay and sand hills covered by gloomy pine forests. The narrow trace, closely bordered by trees, threaded over hillocks and through ravines. Clouded with dust when it was dry, the road turned to gumbo when it rained — "a broad, deep, red-colored ditch," according to one soldier. Drinking water was almost nonexistent.

Banks's order of march added to the army's difficulties. At the head of the long column, properly enough, rode Brigadier General Albert Lee's cavalry division. But following immediately behind the cavalry and crowding the road was Lee's lumbering supply train of 300 wagons. Then came three divisions of infantry of XIII and XIX Corps and a brigade of 1,500 black infantrymen recruited in Louisiana and led by Colonel William H. Dickey. Following the infantry were 700 more wagons. Far behind, chafing at the slow pace of the supply trains, marched the two divisions of A. J. Smith's XVI Corps. On the confined road, the Federal column was strung out for more than 20 miles, with Smith's experienced troops a day's march from the vanguard.

Smith's men would soon be needed desperately because up ahead, near the town of Mansfield, Richard Taylor had decided that at last he was strong enough to make a stand. A Louisianian and an impatient man at the best of times, Taylor was frustrated by his 200-mile retreat and angry at his superior, Kirby Smith, for not sending reinforcements quickly enough. "Had I conceived for an instant that such astonishing delay would ensue before reinforcements reached me," Taylor wrote to Smith's headquarters in Shreveport, "I would have fought a battle even against the heavy odds. It would have been better to lose the State after a defeat than to surrender it without a fight."

Kirby Smith, for his part, had been watching both Banks and Steele, trying to decide which one was the more dangerous. When Pap Price's Missouri and Arkansas infantry divisions reached Shreveport, Smith still hesitated to commit them to attacking either Federal army. Only on April 6, during a visit to Taylor's camp at Mansfield, did the Department commander, finding that Banks was approaching rapidly, at last agree to send along Price's troops. Even then, he told Taylor to be careful about risking a battle.

But Taylor, with substantial reinforcements now at hand or nearby, was in no mood for caution. Walker's Texans and a division of infantry under a Louisiana brigadier general named Jean Jacques Alexandre Alfred Mouton were already with him. Units of Texas cavalry led by Thomas Green had come riding in, giving Taylor a fighting force of about 8,800 men. In addition, the Missouri and Arkansas infantry, 4,400 troops under Brigadier Generals Mosby M. Parsons and Thomas J. Churchill, were now at Keatchie, only 20 miles away. The Confederate commander was ready to fight.

During Banks's advance, Alfred Lee's cavalry had grown used to light encounters with small groups of Taylor's men, who skirmished briefly as they fell back. But on April 7, Lee ran into something different: Three miles beyond Pleasant Hill, on the road to Mansfield, four regiments of General Green's cavalry suddenly attacked, yelling as they charged. Reinforcements drove the Texans away, but Lee was worried by the Confederates' abrupt show of strength. Answering Lee's appeal, Banks ordered General Franklin to send a brigade of infantry forward, bypassing Lee's long line of supply wagons, to support the cavalry's advance.

Soon after sunrise on April 8, the Union army was again on the road, moving slowly. Three miles southeast of Mansfield at Sabine Crossroads, named for an intersecting road that led to the Sabine River, the Federals suddenly ran head on into Taylor's main force. Taylor had selected the best site he could find for a battle, a clearing about 1,200 yards long and 800 yards wide, into which the forested stage road emerged. His men could sweep the clearing from the woods at the far end.

As Taylor posted his small army at the edge of the trees on both sides of the road, he called to General Polignac, leading a brigade in Mouton's division. "Little Frenchman, I am going to fight Banks here if he has a million of men!" In fact, Taylor was outnumbered by more than 2 to 1, but he counted for success on the sort of furious attack he had learned from Jackson in the Shenandoah. He counted, too, on Banks to make a mistake — or perhaps a number of them.

Taylor's troops were in high spirits, eager to stand and shoot after their long, humiliating retreat. "If I am to die for my Country I hope it will be in a blaze of glory that will shine upon my wife and children," one of Walker's officers, Captain Elijah P. Petty, had written home.

Shortly before noon Albert Lee's Federal cavalry emerged into the clearing in hot pursuit of Taylor's skirmishers. After trying to push back Taylor's left, held by Mouton's division, Lee realized that the Confederates had decided to make a strong stand. Withdrawing to a low hill in the center of the clearing, he continued to skirmish and sent

Carbines and revolvers blazing, Confederate cavalrymen charge from the woods to surprise a Federal wagon train and its cavalry escort near Mansfield, Louisiana, on April 7. Brigadier General Albert L. Lee *(above)*, in command of the Union cavalry, ruefully acknowledged the "great impetuosity" of the raid that cost him 53 men.

for reinforcements. Franklin dispatched Brigadier General Thomas E. G. Ransom, commander of XIII Corps, with a second brigade of infantry to help Lee, and Banks went forward to see what was happening. Though Banks called for more troops to clear away the Confederates, he evidently underestimated the situation, for he told Franklin, "We shall be able to rest here."

Lee's long supply train clogged the stage road and Ransom's brigade had difficulty getting to the clearing, but by 3:30 p.m. about 4,800 Union troops were lined up facing Taylor. In the center, with their artillery, were the two infantry brigades Franklin had sent forward — eight regiments of Colonel William J. Landram's 4th Division of Ransom's corps. Covering their flanks were Lee's cavalry brigades. The rest of Banks's infantry units were still on the road, threading their way through the wagons.

Across the clearing, Taylor, whose troops outnumbered the men Banks had gotten to the field, waited impatiently for the Federals to attack. Then at 4 o'clock, when Banks's men did not move, Taylor ordered an assault with Mouton's men moving forward on the left. Emerging from the woods, the Confederates charged across the open ground toward Landram's line. As they came within range, they met a hail of musketry and cannon fire that tore great holes in their ranks. The Louisianians and Texans fell back, then went forward again. "The balls and grape shot crashing about us whistled terribly and plowed into the ground and beat our soldiers

Lousiana's Red River winds southward in the map at right from Confederate-held Shreveport to Simsport, near the Mississippi, where the Federal advance up the river began. Contemporary engravings below and opposite, illustrating some of the key events of the campaign, are shown next to their locations on the map.

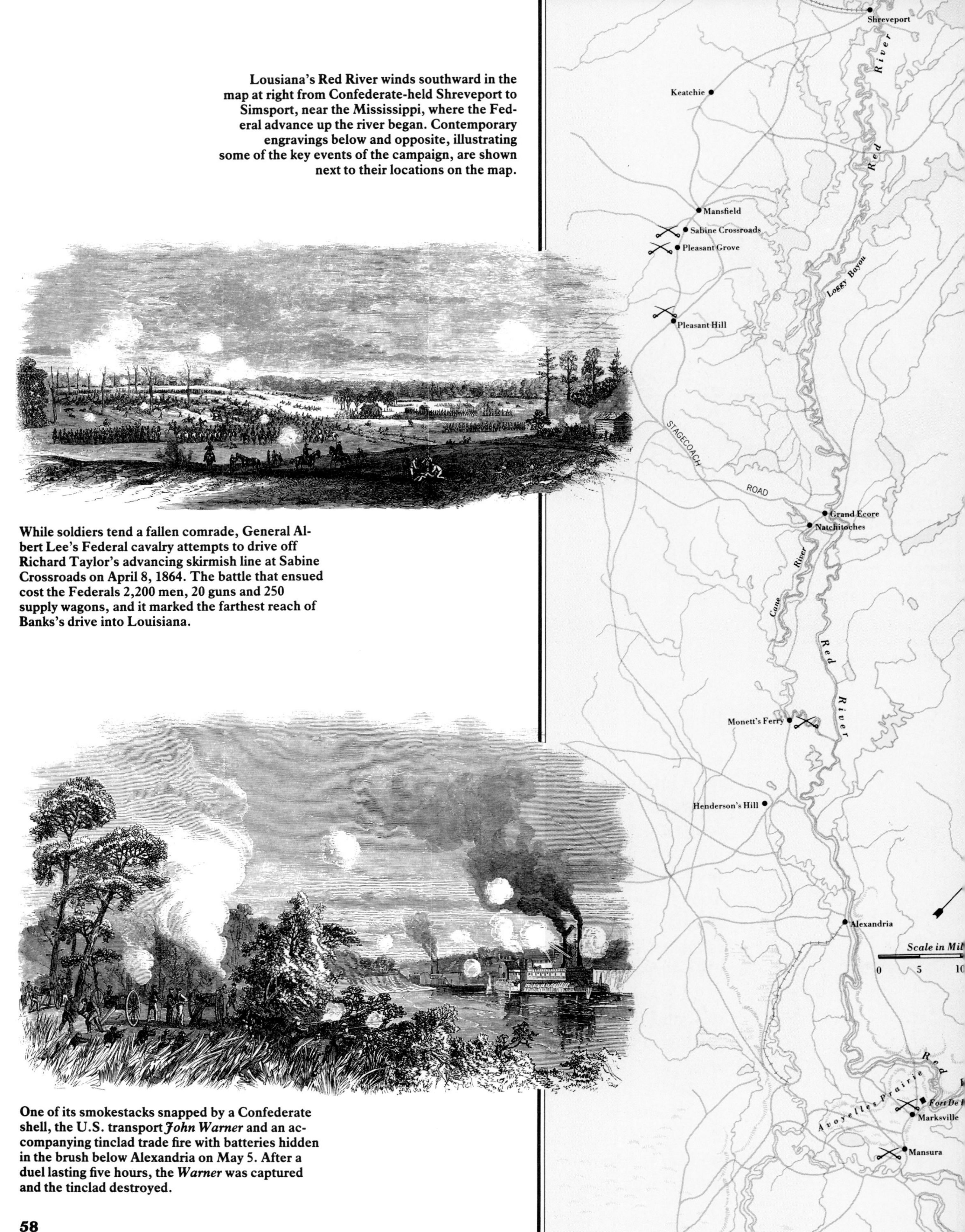

While soldiers tend a fallen comrade, General Albert Lee's Federal cavalry attempts to drive off Richard Taylor's advancing skirmish line at Sabine Crossroads on April 8, 1864. The battle that ensued cost the Federals 2,200 men, 20 guns and 250 supply wagons, and it marked the farthest reach of Banks's drive into Louisiana.

One of its smokestacks snapped by a Confederate shell, the U.S. transport *John Warner* and an accompanying tinclad trade fire with batteries hidden in the brush below Alexandria on May 5. After a duel lasting five hours, the *Warner* was captured and the tinclad destroyed.

Union steamers land their cargoes of salt pork, beef, hardtack and other rations at Grand Ecore, a depot on the Red River. It was here that Banks made the fateful decision to split his army from Admiral Porter's fleet and strike inland.

Climbing over a treacherous abatis, Union forces under General Andrew J. Smith storm the recently completed Fort De Russy on March 14, supported by a bombardment from Porter's fleet. The fort's Confederate garrison of only 300 men put up a spirited defense but was soon overwhelmed.

down even as a storm tears down the trees of a forest," said one Louisiana soldier.

In the murderous fire, General Mouton and many of his officers were killed. In half an hour, the division lost more than 700 men, one third of its strength. Camille Polignac — inevitably called "General Pole Cat" by his men — took command and led the survivors forward again and again, but Landram's men continued to fend them off.

Then in the late afternoon, Taylor ordered the rest of his troops forward. On Polignac's left, some of Green's dismounted cavalry advanced and began to turn Landram's right. At the same time Walker's infantry and units of Green's cavalry led by Brigadier General Hamilton Bee struck at Landram's left. Gradually, they flanked the Federal line. Faced with encirclement, Landram's regiments became confused. "In twenty minutes our line was just crumbling everywhere and falling back," General Lee later reported. When Walker's Texans captured three Union guns and turned them on Landram's men, the Federal withdrawal became a rout.

A half mile to the rear, 1,300 men of Brigadier General Robert A. Cameron's 3rd Division had come up and established a line in the woods. Landram's beaten regiments fled through it, and in about an hour that line, too, collapsed before Taylor's superior numbers. Throwing away their arms and equipment, Banks's soldiers retreated in disorder back up the forested road.

The mob quickly collided with Lee's supply train and spread panic among the teamsters, who abandoned their wagons and joined the flight. With Taylor's troops pressing them and capturing wagons, guns and prisoners, the frightened Federals scrambled past the supply train for two miles, fi-

A Hiding Place Close to the Heart

Facing capture at Sabine Crossroads on April 8, 1864, Color Sergeant Isaac Scott of the 48th Ohio used his last minutes of freedom to tear down and hide his regiment's colorful silk flag. Determined to save the flag from his captors, Sergeant Scott took it with him, concealed in his haversack, to the Confederate prison at Camp Ford, Louisiana. There Scott turned the flag over to the officers of his regiment, who buried it in their shanty. Soon, however, word of the flag's presence spread through the camp, and a grim game of hide-and-seek ensued between Confederate guards eager to claim the prize and the captive officers of the 48th Ohio, who were equally resolved to keep the regiment's banner from them.

Fearful that repeated burials would damage the delicate silk, Captain Daniel Gunsaullus (*right*) hit upon the idea of sewing the flag inside the blouse of his uniform. There it remained, undetected, for several months, while the guards continued to dig holes and search diligently through the possessions of prisoners. Late at night, Gunsaullus would sometimes slip the precious flag from its hiding place and furtively show it to fellow prisoners — some of whom had been in captivity for nearly two years. "Their eyes," an officer later wrote, "glistened at the sight of that emblem of freedom."

In October, Gunsaullus was among a group of exchanged prisoners put on a steamer headed North to freedom. As he stepped aboard, Gunsaullus ripped the flag from his blouse and hastily tied it to a staff. A Union band on the steamer struck up the "Star Spangled Banner" as Gunsaullus proudly raised the flag in the breeze. Ashore, the thwarted prison guards watched as the prize slipped away, while on the deck, exuberant Federals cheered. "No words of tongue or pen," wrote a witness to the scene, "can convey the emotions of that hour."

nally coming upon Brigadier General William Emory's 1st Division of XIX Corps, which had been heading to the front. The fugitives poured through Emory's ranks. "Men without guns or accoutrements," a New Yorker in one regiment described them, "cavalrymen without horses, and artillerymen without cannon, wounded men bleeding and crying at every step, men begrimed with smoke and powder — all in a state of fear and frenzy, while they shouted to our boys not to go forward any farther, for they would all be slaughtered."

Emory, a tall, unruffled West Pointer and a veteran of several campaigns, quickly formed a line near a stream on the side of a wooded ridge called Pleasant Grove. In a fierce 20-minute fight he finally checked the Confederates. Excited by their victory, Taylor's men had become disorganized in their long pursuit through the woods. Charging Emory's fresh troops piecemeal, they were thrown back with heavy losses. As darkness descended, the battle ended with the weary, parched Confederates in possession of the stream, from which they could drink.

Banks had behaved bravely under fire, several times trying to rally his panicked troops. He wanted to maintain his position. Reinforced by A. J. Smith's XVI Corps, which was still well to the rear, he was sure that he could overwhelm Taylor the next day and continue to Shreveport. But his army had been severely mauled. He had lost 2,200 men, 20 guns and more than 200 supply wagons. At a night council, Banks's officers persuaded him to withdraw 14 miles to the village of Pleasant Hill, where he could join A. J. Smith, find water for his men and regroup. During the night, the army retreated, reaching Pleasant Hill and meeting Smith's command early the next morning.

Taylor discovered Banks's withdrawal at dawn and immediately started after him. He sent Price's Missouri and Arkansas infantry divisions, which had arrived after a night march, off on the road to Pleasant Hill, following Green's cavalry. Behind them marched Walker's Texans and Mouton's division, now commanded by Polignac.

The pursuit was so swift that by 9 a.m. Taylor's cavalry had arrived on a plateau a mile short of Pleasant Hill — and there found Banks prepared to renew the fight. The Federal lines extended across open land from a wooded height on their right to a hill on their left. In front of their position was a deep, dry slough, bordered by pines and fallen timber and occupied by advance units. The dozen buildings of the village lay in their rear.

The Arkansas and Missouri troops, who had marched 45 miles in two days, began to arrive shortly after noon. All of the Confederate infantry were tired and thirsty, and as they came in Taylor gave them two hours to rest. At 3 o'clock he began organizing them for the attack. An hour and a half later the Confederates opened fire with 12 guns — including the brass howitzers captured at Valverde in the New Mexico fighting of 1862 — against a New York battery atop a hill on the right side of the Union line. The Federal artillerymen returned the fire, but soon they had to withdraw. Under cover of the bombardment, Missourians and Arkansans led by Thomas Churchill moved through the pine woods on the Union left, intending to flank Banks's line. They never got far enough to the right, however; when they emerged from the woods, they found one of Emory's brigades under Colonel Lewis Benedict ahead of them. With a roar, the Confederate divisions charged Benedict's outnumbered men.

The noise of Churchill's attack was the signal for Walker's Texans to assault Banks's center. At the same time, Thomas Green ordered Bee's cavalry to cross the open ground and charge the Union right.

Bee's horsemen were caught in a deadly flanking fire from a hidden unit of Federal troops, and the regiment led by Colonel August Buchel, a former Prussian Army officer with a flowing white mustache, drew back. "A courier came flying across the field as fast as his horse could carry him from General Green," wrote Levi Wight of Buchel's regiment. The man approached Buchel and reported, "It is Green's orders for you to charge the enemy."

Colonel Buchel, Wight continued, replied that he could "effect nothing but a sacrifice of men in a charge." But when the order to advance was repeated, Buchel led the attack, saying: "Boys, we cannot disobey."

"From one single volley one half of our men fell," Wight subsequently recalled. "The Colonel fell mortally wounded and died three days later."

On the right, Thomas Churchill and his Arkansas and Missouri troops were having a better time of it. Their attack managed at last to flank and cut up Benedict's brigade, forcing it to retreat toward Pleasant Hill village. Benedict himself was killed and his unit's collapse uncovered Banks's left center. Walker's Texans, supported by Polignac and some of Green's dismounted cavalry, poured through the gap.

With his center crumbling and Churchill's troops entering the village at his rear, Banks was facing disaster. But Churchill, in his rush forward, had failed to notice the long blue lines of A. J. Smith's veterans of the Army of the Tennessee hidden in the woods on his right. Smith ordered his entire line to charge. Pivoting on Brigadier General James McMillan's brigade, which held the village, the Federals fell hard on Churchill's flank and drove the Confederates into Walker's brigades at the center of the line.

The Southerners resisted stubbornly, but by dusk panic had seized some of them. As the Union line continued to advance, many Confederates fled into the woods at their rear. Some of the troops became confused

A Federal battery with infantry support repulses General Taylor's attack at Pleasant Hill. "The air seemed all alive," wrote a Federal soldier, "from the spiteful, cat-like spit of the buckshot, the 'pouf' of the old-fashioned musket ball and the 'pee-ee-zing' of the Minié bullet, to the roar of the ordinary shell and the 'whoot-er-whoot-er' of the mortar."

and began firing at each other. To avoid a rout, Taylor ordered his entire force to withdraw. Most of his units retreated six miles through the forest to a small stream. Others remained with Taylor close to the battlefield, throwing themselves down under the trees in utter exhaustion. The Confederates had lost more than 2,600 men at Sabine Crossroads and at Pleasant Hill. Among the dead left on the plateau the second night was Elijah Petty, who had wanted to die in a blaze of glory.

A little before midnight Kirby Smith, who had ridden from Shreveport, joined Taylor in the woods. "Our repulse was so complete," he later wrote, "and our command was so disorganized that had Banks followed up his success vigorously he would have met but feeble opposition to his advance on Shreveport."

There was no need for the Confederates to worry. Immediately after the battle, Banks rode up to the stern-looking A. J. Smith. "God bless you, general," he said gratefully. "You have saved the army." Banks then held a council of war with Franklin and two of his brigadiers. These officers, all West Pointers, unanimously opposed resuming the offensive. The army, they noted, had lost another 1,400 men — 3,600 in all. Much of the Federal supply train had been destroyed, and they had little water. The indecisive Banks abruptly decided to abandon the battlefield with its uncollected dead and wounded and retreat to Grand Ecore.

A. J. Smith objected angrily. To him the Battle of Pleasant Hill had been a victory despite what he considered Banks's incompetent troop deployments. In his fury, he went to Franklin, nominally second in command, proposing that Franklin arrest Banks and take command of the army. "Smith," Franklin replied, "don't you know this is

At 5 p.m. on April 9, 1864, Gen
Thomas Churchill's Confederate
vision charged across the grassy
cline at Pleasant Hill, Louisiana,
rolled up the Federal left-flank
gade, killing its commander, Col
Lewis Benedict (*top map, rig*
Though Dwight and Shaw held
Federal right against the assault
Walker and Bee, the center of
Federal line continued to weaken
the next hour, until a spirited co
terattack (*bottom map*) led by Ge
al James McMillan's brigade en
oped Churchill's right and preve
a Confederate breakthro

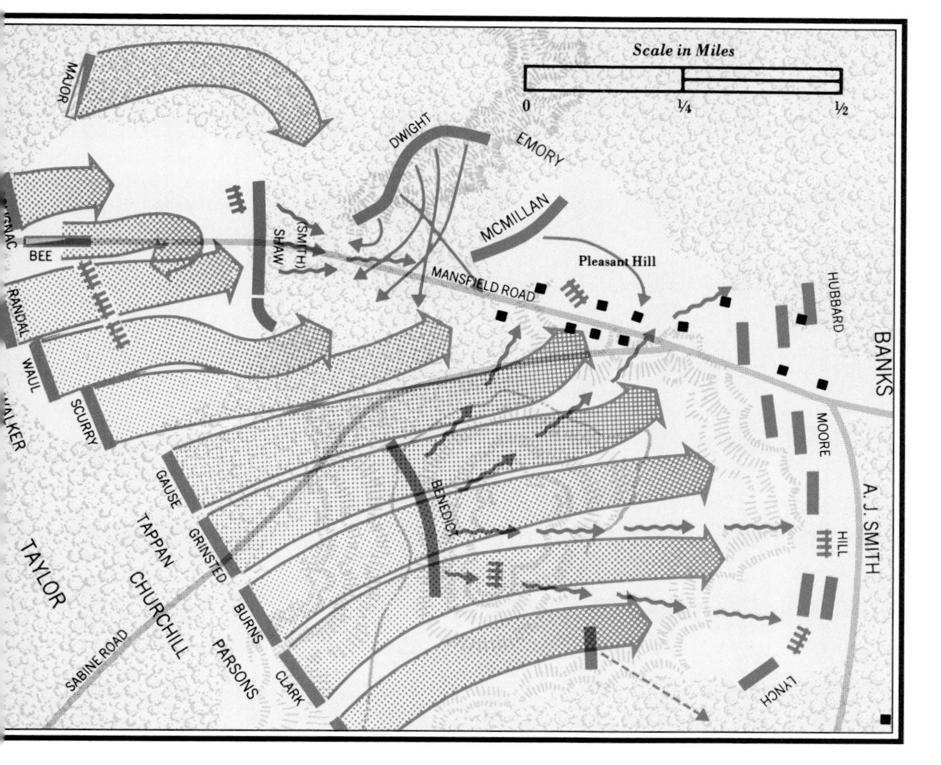

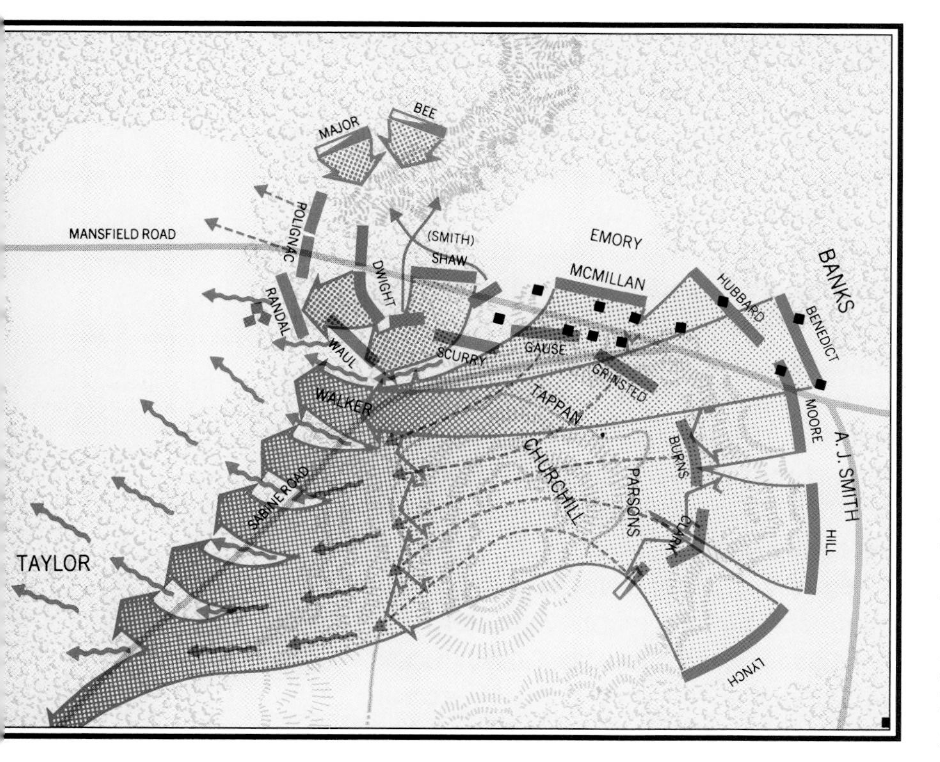

mutiny?" The thought sobered Smith, and the subject was dropped.

That night, Banks's army began its withdrawal, and by the evening of April 11 the last of the men streamed into Grand Ecore. They were weary and disconsolate, but most of all they were contemptuous of their commander, whose grandiose campaign now seemed to make no sense.

Banks was badly in need of provisions and fresh troops. He had sent a message to Porter, whose gunboats were far up the Red River with XVII Corps, asking Porter to turn around and come back. Then he established a semicircular line of entrenchments and breastworks at Grand Ecore to protect his position and settled down along the river to await the fleet.

Back in Mansfield, Taylor and Kirby Smith argued over what to do next. Taylor was sure that an aggressive pursuit by his entire force could trap Banks's army, as well as Porter's fleet, before either of them could get out of the Red River country. But Kirby Smith overruled him. Deciding that the time had come to stop Steele, Kirby Smith sent the infantry divisions of Walker, Churchill and Parsons to join Pap Price in Arkansas, then rode after them himself on April 16. This left the disgruntled Taylor with only the Texas cavalry and Polignac's infantry — about 5,000 men — to harry Banks.

Steele was having his own difficulties. He had not left Little Rock until March 23, a week and a half after he had been ordered to move by General Grant, and he would soon suffer further delays. His route to Shreveport traversed a largely barren country that made supply problems acute. And when he reached Arkadelphia, about 70 miles southwest of Little Rock, he wasted three days waiting for Brigadier General John M. Thayer and his Army of the Frontier — 5,000 Federals coming from their base at Fort Smith, Arkansas — who were supposed to join Steele for the next move to the Little Missouri River. Giving up on Thayer, Steele marched southwest toward the crossroads town of Washington, Arkansas.

On the march, the situation momentarily improved. Steele's troops beat off attacks by elements of Price's Confederate cavalry led by a dashing brigadier general named John Marmaduke and crossed the Little Missouri on a pontoon bridge. There Thayer's force belatedly joined up.

But the newcomers arrived without supplies, and Steele was forced to send back to Little Rock for more rations. Then, as the Federals were crossing the undulating grasslands of Prairie D'Ane, they were attacked again by Confederate cavalry, led this time by the flamboyant Kentucky-born Brigadier General Joseph Shelby and by another able commander, Brigadier General Thomas P. Dockery. After much feinting and maneuvering followed by a night attack, the Confederates withdrew, but the fight had cost Steele three more days as well as about 100 men killed and wounded. The chance of reaching the Shreveport area in time to draw off any defenders fighting Banks seemed increasingly remote.

Still more time was lost as Steele, desperate for supplies, detoured southeast toward the sizable town of Camden on the Ouachita River. Heavy rains turned the road to Camden into a morass that had to be laboriously corduroyed, and the troops had to wade rain-swollen streams and swamps. By now the wily Pap Price was on Steele's trail and striking at his rear guard with five brigades of cavalry reinforced by Brigadier General Samuel B. Maxey's division of horsemen, made up of Texans and Choctaw Indians.

The dilatory nature of Major General Frederick Steele's overland movement from Little Rock to aid Banks's column did not match his reputation as a firebrand, which was known even to the Confederates. "Steele is bold to rashness," wrote Kirby Smith, who would oppose the Federal advance. "He will probably push on without thought of circumspection."

Despite these attacks, Steele and his men reached Camden by April 16. But once there, the Federals suffered one blow after another. The first occurred when Steele sent a train of 198 wagons foraging through the countryside for corn and other food. The escort of about 1,000 men, half of whom were black troops from General John Thayer's 1st Kansas, did a good job of filling the wagons with much-needed provisions. But on April 18, while returning to Camden, the Federals were attacked by a force three times their number under Marmaduke and Maxey at a site named Poison Spring. The Confederates captured or burned all the wagons. They were later accused of murdering some of the wounded blacks, and Maxey's Choctaws were charged with taking scalps.

Steele was reeling from the loss of men, wagons and supplies when he got word that Banks had been repulsed in Louisiana and had withdrawn to Grand Ecore. Uncertain what to do, Steele remained at Camden —

where, on April 23, matters grew worse. The Confederate cavalry was threatening his supply depots and line of communications to Little Rock. Moreover, Churchill's and Parsons' infantry divisions, sent north by Kirby Smith, had arrived outside Camden, with Walker's division right behind them.

Two days later a fresh disaster struck Steele when his entire wagon train, on its way to Pine Bluff for supplies, was captured by 2,500 Confederate cavalrymen after a savage five-hour fight at Marks' Mills. The Union escort had numbered about 1,600 men, and at least 1,300 of them were killed, wounded or captured.

In the crisis, Steele decided to return to Little Rock. Banks had confirmed that the campaign had failed. To march south now was pointless; to linger at Camden meant starvation or capture. On April 26, Steele's much-reduced army crossed the Ouachita River and started north.

The Confederates entered Camden the next day, and on April 28 began their pursuit. Both armies moved quickly, despite pouring rain and muddy roads. On April 29, Steele's army, fighting off Marmaduke at its rear, reached the Saline River at Jenkins' Ferry. The rain continued in torrents and the riverbanks turned to mud. The troops worked all night getting their wagons and artillery through the quagmire and over a pontoon bridge they had cast, but by morning most of the troops still had not crossed.

With the Union force at bay, Kirby Smith, now personally directing the Confederate troops, ordered Churchill's division, the first in line, to attack. The road led down a steep bluff, then across swampy bottom land to a belt of timber along the river. Steele's men had erected a defense of log breastworks and abatis, extending across a constricted area between a creek and an impassable swamp.

Churchill's men moved toward the river, but they were cut down by the Federals' frontal and enfilading fire. In the narrow space, fighting in mud and water with a blanket of fog and smoke obscuring the field, the Confederates could make no progress. After two hours, Kirby Smith threw Parsons' division into the battle, then Walker's brigades, one after the other. As the fighting intensified, every one of Walker's brigade leaders was wounded; two of them — including the veteran of New Mexico, William Scurry — would die of their wounds. Finally, Kirby Smith gave up and withdrew his battered force. The Union troops completed their crossing and destroyed their pontoon bridge behind them. The desperate fighting in what came to be called the Battle of Jenkins' Ferry had cost Kirby Smith about 1,000 casualties, one sixth of his force. Steele had lost more than 700 men.

The Federals, hungry, tattered and begrimed with mud, struggled on through deep swamps and trudged into Little Rock on May 2. To Leander Stillwell, an Illinois veteran of Shiloh, Corinth and Vicksburg who had stayed behind in Little Rock as a provost guard, the returning troops were "the hardest looking outfit of Federal soldiers that I saw during the war, at any time. The most of them looked as if they had been rolled in the mud, numbers of them were barefoot, and I also saw several with the legs of their trousers all gone, high up, socking through the mud like big blue cranes."

The northern arm of the Union's Red River Campaign was no more. On May 3, Kirby Smith ordered his Confederates back to Camden, and six days later he sent Walker's

Texans back to Louisiana to rejoin Taylor. By the time they reached the Red River on May 22, the Federal's southern arm, too, no longer existed.

On April 15, Porter's fleet with XVII Corps had arrived in Grand Ecore to rejoin Banks. It, too, had had a rough time. After receiving Banks's urgent message, Porter had turned his ships around at once and headed downstream; but the narrow river, full of snags and tortuous bends, was falling fast, and the rushing current made navigation doubly difficult. Ships hit submerged stumps, ran aground and collided with each other.

Worse, the high banks overlooking the river swarmed with Confederate cavalrymen, whose muskets and artillery raked the boats every time they got stuck. At Blair's Landing, on April 12, one of the attacks cost the Southerners dearly when a Federal shell decapitated Thomas Green. "His death was

The ironclad U.S.S. *Neosho* glides warily past a mud flat exposed by the receding waters of the Red River. The low-freeboard *Neosho* was among the most powerful warships operating on inland waters, boasting a rotating Ericsson turret at its bow *(left)* and a protective hump on the afterdeck to enclose its paddlewheel.

a public calamity," Taylor wrote, "and mourned as such by the people of Texas and Louisiana." But it was the Federals who generally got the worst of it as Confederate harassment from the wooded shores continued unabated. When Porter's fleet finally reappeared at Grand Ecore, one of Banks's soldiers observed that "the sides of some of the transports are half shot away, and their smoke-stacks look like huge pepper boxes."

Banks faced a familiar dilemma. He still dreamed of capturing Shreveport, but Porter, watching the river grow shallower, was determined to extricate his Mississippi Squadron before the ships were shot to bits or stranded and captured. Banks would not consider starting again for Shreveport without the fleet. A message from Sherman, demanding the immediate return of XVI and XVII Corps, forced a decision. Banks and Porter agreed that they must abandon the campaign, and they notified Sherman that they would need his troops a while longer to help withdraw the fleet.

By April 21 a retreat to Alexandria was under way. The bulk of the troops began to withdraw along the road through Natchitoches. The defeats of the past weeks and the rumor, unfounded but frightening, that Taylor was in pursuit with 25,000 men, gave wings to their heels — the advance guard marching 20 miles in the first 10 hours.

On the river, however, Porter soon had his hands full. The ironclad *Eastport*, barely afloat after colliding with a Confederate torpedo, finally sprang an unstoppable leak and had to be scuttled. Then rear elements of the fleet ran into a force of enemy sharpshooters and artillery. In a wild, two-day battle, in which boats hit snags, lost tiller ropes and became unmanageable under the severe fire from the shore, Porter lost two transports and had three vessels badly damaged. At last he reached the head of the rapids at Alexandria, only to find himself trapped: The river was too low for his ships to navigate.

The marching army soon had troubles of its own. A. J. Smith's angry Westerners, in the rear, plundered and destroyed everything around them, burning all the houses, cotton gins, and barns and other buildings on their route. This further destruction of his home state infuriated Richard Taylor, who made a bold attempt to encircle the Federals at Monett's Ferry, the only practicable crossing of the Cane River.

Taylor had already sent cavalry and artillery well downriver below Banks, ordering them to hold some steep, wooded bluffs that commanded the Cane River crossing from the side opposite Banks's approach. He also told the rest of Green's cavalry, now led by Major General John A. Wharton, to press the Federals from the rear while other Confederate units, including Polignac's infantry, hurried to flank the Union left and right.

When General William Emory and his division, in the van of the Union column, reached the Cane at Monett's Ferry, they found the Confederate position too strong to take by frontal assault. Searching for a solution, both Banks and Emory scouted the canebrake to the left to find a crossing point. Failing at that, they sent some of Emory's troops reinforced by other units two miles to the right, where they waded waist-deep across the muddy, alligator-infested river. The Federals then doubled back through marshes, woods and swampy thickets to hit the Confederate cavalry from the side.

A sharp battle ensued among ravines and hills. But then the Confederate commander,

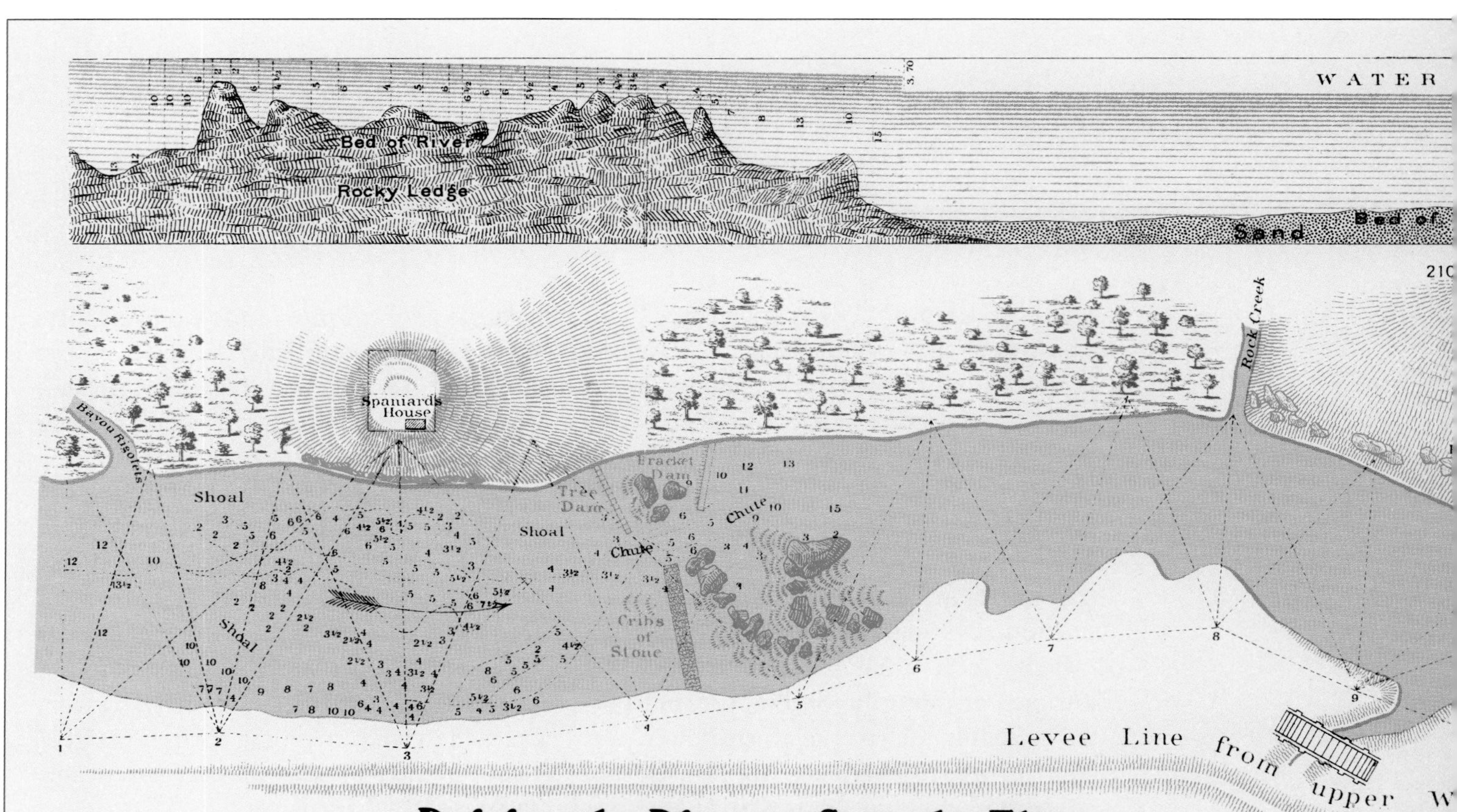

Raising the River to Save the Fleet

As Admiral David Porter retreated down the Red River in late April 1864, he foresaw nothing but "the destruction of the best part of the Mississippi Squadron." Since Porter's fleet had ascended the twin rapids at Alexandria, receding waters had laid bare two ledges of jagged rock, stranding the gunboats in Confederate territory.

Lieutenant Colonel Joseph Bailey, acting chief engineer of XIX Corps, came up with an intricate plan to dam the river and harness its current, creating a chute of water over the rocks. On April 30, a force of more than 3,000 men set to the task, often working in water up to their necks and fighting a current of 10 miles per hour. Using trees, quarried stone and bags filled with dirt, the men created an interlacing network of bracket dams, tree dams and stone cribs (*below*) that extended from both shores.

By May 8, Colonel Bailey had dammed most of the river's 758-foot width, leaving a gap of 150 feet at the center. To narrow this opening, Bailey sank four barges weighted with stone into the river and had them hauled into position alongside the dam wings with tow lines pulled by men on shore, who worked to the spirited accompaniment of an army band.

Just as the river level rose high enough for Porter's ships to attempt the passage, two of the barges broke loose and slammed into a ledge of rocks downstream. Water surged through the opening, lowering the level of the water that had collected above the dam. Admiral Porter, watching from horseback on shore, ordered the U.S.S *Lexington* to make a run for it. As thousand of soldiers watched breathlessly fron shore, the *Lexington* steamed at full spee into the churning waters of the gap. Rollin wildly, the gunboat swept over the falls an caromed off a crippled barge before sweep ing into the deeper waters below. The othe boats followed safely, to the wild cheers o the watching army.

Buoyed by this success, Bailey bega damming the lower rapids, and by May 1 Porter's fleet was on its way to the Missis sippi. The admiral called Bailey's rescu operation "the best engineering feat" h had ever seen. "To an ordinary mind," h said, "the whole thing would have appeare an utter impossibility."

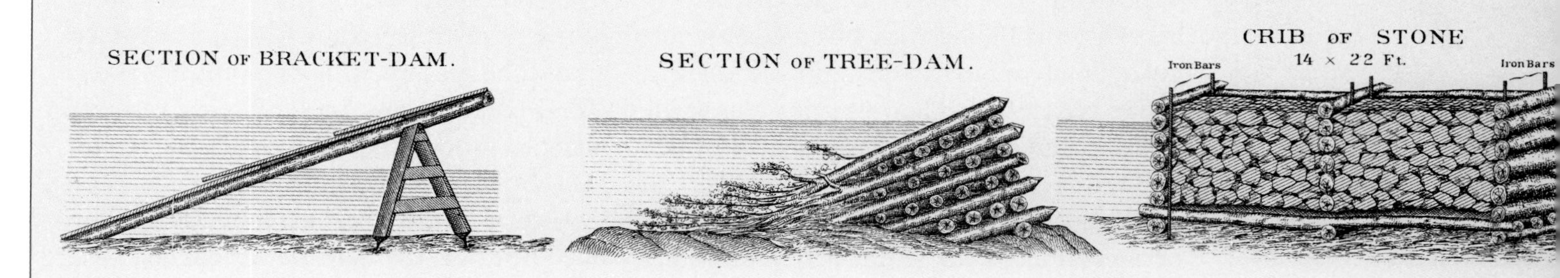

This contemporary chart shows the placement of the Red River dams designed and built by Colonel Joseph Bailey *(left)* to allow Admiral Porter's stranded fleet to pass. Below, workers wade into the river to fill wooden cribs at the upper rapids with stone.

Hamilton Bee, pressed hard on one side, took a Federal feint at face value and thought he was also being flanked on the opposite end of his line. Fearing that his 2,000-man force might be wiped out, Bee ordered a retreat. This gave the Federal column the chance it needed. Despite continued attacks by Wharton's cavalry on the Union rear, Banks's army, much to Richard Taylor's disgust, managed to get across the Cane River and slog on to Alexandria.

The persistent Taylor moved his troops close to town, forcing Banks to establish two rings of defense to protect his men and the fleet, which was in great peril. The Red was lower than ever, and there was no telling how long it would be before the river rose.

Help for Porter came not from the Navy, but rather from Lieutenant Colonel Joseph Bailey, an Army engineer on Franklin's staff who proposed freeing the fleet by building dams much of the way across the Red. He maintained that the dams would raise the water level in the rapids. The idea seemed a long shot at best, but with more than 3,000 troops working first on one set of dams and then a second, the water began to rise. By May 13 all of Porter's remaining vessels had moved safely through the gap and were steaming down the river.

Once Porter was on his way, Banks evacuated Alexandria, but his trials were far from over. On May 16, at Mansura, the retreating Federals found Taylor's valiant little army drawn up in a long, thin line across an open prairie, determined to oppose their further progress. Banks formed his larger force in a line facing them, and for almost four hours, while the men in the ranks watched each other, the two armies engaged in an exchange of artillery fire. Then Banks ordered A. J. Smith to advance, and Taylor quickly retired before the superior force.

Ignoring the setback, Taylor's units pressed the Federal rear guard until the combative Vermonter, General Mower, struck back near Yellow Bayou on May 18. After hours of hard fighting during which the thickets caught fire and obscured the field in smoke, the Confederates again had to withdraw. Losses were heavy on both sides. Thomas Green's original outfit, the 5th Texas Mounted Volunteers, which he had first led into New Mexico with Sibley, came out of the engagement with only seven men left.

Two days before the Yellow Bayou battle, May 16, the van of the Union army had ar-

As a section of the newly built dam at Alexandria gives way, the Federal gunboat *Lexington* races through the churning break. "She entered the gap with a full head of steam on," Admiral Porter wrote, "pitched down the roaring current, made two or three spasmodic rolls, hung for a moment on the rocks below, and then was swept into deep water by the current and rounded to, safely into the bank."

rived at Simsport on the wide Atchafalaya, across which lay safety. Again Lieutenant Colonel Bailey, the dam builder, demonstrated his ingenuity. At his suggestion, Admiral Porter's transports were lashed side by side from one shore to the other, creating a bridge over the river. A plank roadway was laid across the ships' bows to accommodate the artillery, cavalry and wagons, and the army began to cross.

Mower's rear guard caught up two days later, and by May 20 the entire Union army had crossed the river. The disastrous campaign, which had cost the Union more than 8,000 men, nine ships and 57 guns, was over.

During their withdrawal from Alexandria, Federal soldiers had vented their feelings about the wasteful campaign by hooting and hissing Banks. At Simsport the Union commander was met by Major General Edward R. S. Canby — who in 1862 had driven the Confederates from New Mexico. Canby brought news that further humiliated the former Massachusetts Governor. Lincoln and Grant had not dismissed him outright, but they had placed Canby over him as commander of a new, enlarged Military Division of West Mississippi, combining Banks's Gulf Department with that of Arkansas. Banks was relieved of field command and, returning to New Orleans, was relegated to political and administrative duties. The failure of his campaign ended Banks's presidential aspirations; although in 1865, after he had left the army and returned to Massachusetts, he was again elected to Congress.

Taylor, who had suffered more than 4,000 casualties in the campaign (another 2,300 Confederates had been lost in the Arkansas fighting), sent his men down the Atchafalaya and the Teche, reestablishing Confederate control over much of western Louisiana.

The Red River country remained in Confederate hands until the end of the War. With the Union army driven off, the Texas cavalry units were furloughed back to their homes. Long afterward, Levi Wight remembered the farewell address given by his unit's last commander as the battle-worn Texans prepared to leave Louisiana: "We have occasion to drop a tear of regret," said Brigadier General Arthur Bagby. But, he continued, "the army of which I with my associate officers have commanded on many fields of battle with pride have quit themselves with the highest honors of bravery."

Minnesota's Season of Terror

"If we get through this war, and I live, this Indian system shall be reformed."

PRESIDENT ABRAHAM LINCOLN

The town of New Ulm, in the verdant Minnesota River valley, was clamorous with excitement shortly after dawn on August 18, 1862. Even at that early hour a brass band was tooting and many of the village's 900 inhabitants were crowded in the main street. They cheered loudly as a recruiting party, led by a young merchant named Henry Behnke, set off in five wagons to enlist volunteers for the Union Army. It was a glorious summer morning with a great red sun "tingeing all the clouds with crimson, and sending long, scarlet shafts of light up the green river valley and upon the golden bluffs on either side," wrote 14-year-old Mary Schwandt, daughter of one of the many German-immigrant families that had recently established farms on the prairie nearby. All seemed joyous, peaceful, secure. The men in the wagons were seeking volunteers to fight in the civil war that was racking the nation; but the sounds of battle were far away, in distant Kentucky and Virginia.

Patriotic fervor gripped the German-speaking burghers of New Ulm. Minnesota had become a state only four years earlier, and much of its land was still raw frontier, dotted here and there with isolated trading posts, Army forts, and villages of Sioux, Chippewa and Winnebago Indians. But Minnesota's 200,000 white settlers, a third of them foreign-born, yielded to the people of no other state in Unionist enthusiasm. When the War had begun the year before, Minnesota's Alexander Ramsey had been the first Northern governor to wire President Lincoln offering to send troops. Since then, Minnesota had raised five regiments of infantry and more than 5,000 of these volunteers had gone off to fight the Confederates. Now Lincoln had called for 300,000 additional Union soldiers, and the Minnesotans were determined to contribute more than their share.

In a jovial mood and full of their patriotic mission, Henry Behnke and his fellow recruiters rattled westward past pioneer homesteads on the prairie. But five miles out of New Ulm they hauled their wagon teams to an abrupt halt. Before them in the road lay a man who had been shot. As the recruiters jumped down to aid him, several Sioux, stripped to the breechcloth and painted for war, opened fire from the brush. Two members of Behnke's party fell dead, and others were wounded. The survivors, without arms to defend themselves, scrambled back into the wagons, driving two of them crazily at the Indians to run them down. Having scattered the attackers, Behnke's companions piled the dead and wounded in another wagon and raced back to town.

New Ulm was alerted before they got there. A lone rider had galloped through the village shouting, "The Indians are coming — they have murdered the recruiting party!" First to respond was Sheriff Charles Roos, who gathered 30 men with rifles and shotguns and started up the road taken by Behnke. As the two groups joined up, the county militia turned out, armed with a collection of weapons ranging from rifles to

Chief Little Crow reluctantly led the Sioux uprising in 1862, warning his men that troops would descend on them "like the locusts."

pitchforks, and other townspeople frantically began barricading the streets with wagons, boxes and barrels.

No one could believe what was happening. The Sioux of the river valley, led by chiefs friendly to the whites and watched by troops at Fort Ridgely 20 miles northwest of New Ulm, had lived as peaceful neighbors of the settlers for years. True, there were stories that the Sioux had been complaining of ill-treatment by government agents appointed to administer Indian affairs. But no one dreamed that the tribe was plotting violence. The unprovoked attack on the recruiting party came as a harsh surprise. Evidently something both unexpected and unspeakable was afoot.

New Ulm's worst fears were soon confirmed. Throughout the morning and afternoon of August 18, dozens of terrified refugees straggled into town, telling of murders, mutilations, rapes, and the burning of homes and farms. Evidently, much of the Sioux nation had risen and seemed bent on killing every white settler in the valley. Frightened by the reports, many of New Ulm's townspeople joined the refugees on their flight to St. Paul, the state capital, and to Fort Snelling, both located more than 100 miles to the northeast, near the confluence of the Minnesota and Mississippi Rivers.

That night, as pickets patrolled near signal fires and residents continued to build barricades, Henry Behnke and New Ulm's other leading citizens gathered to plan the town's defense; they sent a message to Governor Ramsey asking for 1,000 troops plus wagonloads of ammunition. Then, because St. Paul was too far away to get help to them quickly, a weary Henry Behnke mounted a horse at midnight and set out for the nearer town of Traverse des Sioux to ask the valley's leading citizen, Judge Charles E. Flandrau, to hurry to the rescue with local volunteers.

The first alarms from the valley reached St. Paul the following afternoon, informing Governor Ramsey that the largest Indian massacre in the nation's history had struck his state. More than 350 people, among them five members of Mary Schwandt's family, were already dead and an unknown number, including young Mary, were captives of the Indians. Whole counties were being depopulated; dozens of towns and settlements were in deadly peril.

Two days later, when word of the outbreak reached the East, many Northerners jumped to the conclusion that Confederates were somehow to blame for the tragedy. Horace Greeley, editor of the New York *Tribune*, angrily denounced the massacre as a dastardly conspiracy conceived and directed by Confederate agents. Others agreed with Greeley and worried that the massacre heralded the start of a violent Confederate-fomented uprising by all the Western tribes.

Such suspicions were unfounded. No Confederate agents were roaming Minnesota; no plot was being brewed to stir up the Western tribes. But the Civil War nevertheless had much to do with the massacre of August 18 and the months of violence that were to follow. The Confederate military victories of 1862 had convinced many Indians that the U.S. government — which these native Americans had come to loathe — not only was vulnerable but was doomed to defeat. The root of the Minnesota uprising was the Indians' bitterness; they felt, quite rightly, that during the prewar decades they had been robbed of their ancestral lands and re-

Federal recruits drill below the walls of Fort Snelling at the confluence of the Mississippi and Minnesota Rivers. The task of organizing troops here to fight the Confederates was disrupted in August of 1862 as newly formed Minnesota regiments were dispatched westward to counter the Sioux uprising.

peatedly cheated by the government and its appointed agents. The Civil War seemed to many Indians to provide a golden opportunity to avenge themselves on the white man and all his works. "We understood that the South was getting the best of the fight, and it was said that the North would be whipped," one of the most prominent Sioux chiefs, Big Eagle, later said. "It began to be whispered about that now would be a good time to go to war with the whites and get back the lands."

The Indians who had struck so suddenly were members of bands of Eastern, or Santee, Sioux, which included four subgroups: the Mdewakanton, Wahpekute, Sisseton and Wahpeton. The Santee had roamed the great game-filled forests and prairies of Minnesota for centuries. But in 1851 the government had forced them to cede their ancestral villages and hunting grounds — 24 million acres in all — and move onto a narrow strip of land 20 miles wide that extended for 150 miles along both sides of the upper Minnesota River. In return, the Santee, who were expected to settle down and become farmers, were promised annuities in the form of cash and provisions.

Almost immediately the government's graft-ridden system of managing Indian affairs gave the Santee cause for resentment. During the treaty negotiations, the traders, greedy for illegitimate profit, tricked the Indians into signing an agreement that immediately put them $400,000 in "debt" to the traders. In the following years, the traders continued to divert money promised the Santee into their own pockets to settle debts that the traders claimed — often falsely — the Sioux owed them. "We were deceived, misled, imposed upon and wronged," the chiefs protested in vain.

Other grievances accumulated. Treaty goods and provisions sent to the Indians frequently turned out to be shoddy or rotten — or were stolen by traders and other unscrupulous whites. Even the well-meaning missionaries who established churches on the reservation caused trouble. Santees who clung to their old beliefs and customs despised those Sioux who accepted Christianity, became farmers, and adopted the white man's clothing, haircuts and frame houses.

Worst of all was the pressure exerted by the constantly growing numbers of immi-

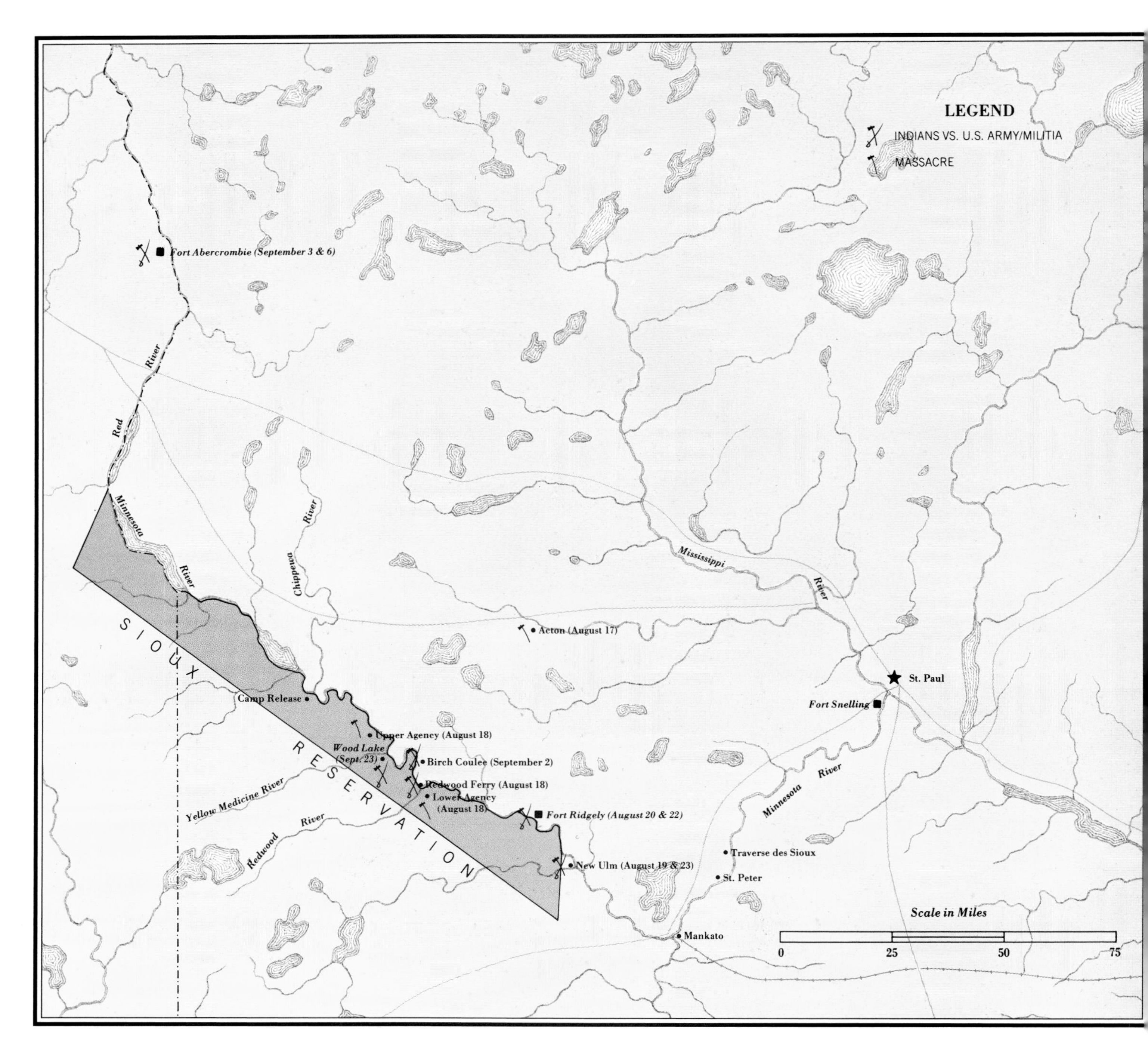

In August 1862, disaffected Sioux in Minnesota rose up to massacre settlers and attack Federals. The violence began with an isolated assault on a farm at Acton on August 17; it became general the next day when the Sioux raided the Lower and Upper Agencies — the administrative centers of their two reservations — and ambushed soldiers at Redwood Ferry. Sharp battles ensued, pitting Federals and civilian militia against a loosely organized but determined foe.

grant settlers, who coveted what little land the Indians still owned. In 1858 the settlers' demands induced the government to invite Little Crow, the most influential Santee spokesman, and several other chiefs to Washington — where they were browbeaten into giving up half of the already cramped reservation. The chiefs were promised $266,880 for 889,600 acres, or 30 cents an acre. But again the bulk of the money appropriated by Congress went to the traders.

Frustrated and angry, the Sioux were nevertheless held in check by Little Crow and the other chiefs. Little Crow was high-handed, vain and the hereditary chief of only one of the Mdewakanton villages, but he possessed oratorical powers that had won him a disproportionate influence over many of the other Sioux. Recognizing the power of the whites, he professed warm friendship for them, cut his hair to shoulder length and lived in a two-story frame house. Although not a Christian, he often attended services at one of the mission churches, garbed in a black frock coat with a velvet collar.

But even Little Crow and his fellow chiefs lost their patience in the summer of 1862 when a newly appointed government agent, Thomas J. Galbraith, appeared determined to starve their people. Most of the Indians' crops had failed the previous year, and many of their villages were in dire straits. Despite the crisis, Galbraith announced that the annual distribution of government provisions and annuities, scheduled for June, would be delayed. Congress, debating whether to make Indian payments that year in gold or in the new wartime greenbacks, had held up the delivery of $71,000 due the Santee. To simplify his bookkeeping, Galbraith had decided to keep the provisions locked up in his warehouses until the money arrived and then distribute everything at once.

The famished Indians seethed with resentment, and on August 4 some of them stormed the warehouse at the more northerly of the two government posts, the Upper Agency, looting sacks of flour. Order was restored only when the commander of the infantry detachment overseeing the distribution persuaded the stubborn Galbraith to issue some provisions and annuity goods.

Little Crow, who was present at the altercation, asked Galbraith to make a similar preliminary distribution to the half-starved Indians of the Lower Agency. Galbraith agreed, then went back on his word. This angered Little Crow and he became even angrier when, during a council at the Lower Agency on August 15, some traders assembled there refused to sell their stock on credit pending the arrival of the Indians' $71,000. "We have no food, but here are these stores filled with food," Little Crow yelled at Galbraith. If no provisions were forthcoming, he added, "we may take our own way to keep ourselves from starving. When men are hungry they help themselves."

At this point Galbraith sought the traders' advice. After a consultation, their leader, a trading-post operator named Andrew J. Myrick, turned to leave. "So far as I am concerned," he snapped, "if they are hungry, let them eat grass or their own dung." Myrick's ruthless remark was translated to the hundreds of Indians standing nearby. After a moment of shock, they dispersed, some making angry gestures and threats.

Nevertheless, all seemed peaceful two days later, on Sunday, August 17. Galbraith, fearing no trouble, left the Lower Agency for Fort Snelling with a semimilitary company he had recruited of halfbreeds and agency employees. Little Crow, dressed in his best Sunday clothes, attended services in the Lower Agency's Episcopal chapel.

But that afternoon an unforeseen and violent event took place that would shatter the peace of hundreds of settler and Indian lives. It began as four Wahpeton youths, returning from a deer hunt north of the Minnesota River, came upon the white farming settlement of Acton. There one of the youths stole some eggs that belonged to a local farmer. A second youth objected that the theft would get them all in trouble—and was immediately accused of cowardice. Stung by the taunts, the second young Indian boasted that he was not afraid to steal eggs or even, if the opportunity arose, to kill a white man.

The opportunity came all too soon. Before leaving Acton, the young Indians became involved in a target-shooting contest with some of the townspeople. Suddenly and for no evident reason, the Indians shot five of the whites, including two women.

Arriving back at their own village, the young Wahpetons announced what they had done. Some of the villagers were shocked, fearing that troops would be sent to punish all the Santees. But the angrier villagers approved of the youths' actions, arguing that the time had finally come for a war of extermination against the whites.

A prime target of Indian outrage at the Lower Agency was trader Andrew Myrick, who refused to give the hungry Sioux provisions on credit with the taunt: "Let them eat grass." Three days later, warriors raided his store, killing two clerks; Myrick leaped from a second-story window, but was shot dead before he could reach cover.

News of the murders traveled fast. Late that night the head warriors of the Lower Agency villages, flushed with excitement, assembled at Little Crow's home to decide what to do. At first Little Crow, sitting on blankets on the floor of his large downstairs room, was surly. "Why do you come to me for advice?" he demanded. Sure that the Indians could not defeat the settlers and the U.S. Army, he opposed a conflict. But gradually, as the resentments of a decade were voiced, those who argued for war gained the upper hand. Little Crow, afraid of losing his authority, suddenly reversed himself and agreed to lead an uprising. "Braves," he warned, "you are little children — you are fools. You will die like rabbits when the hungry wolves hunt them in the Hard Moon." Nevertheless, he declared: "Little Crow is not a coward; he will die with you!"

Word spread quickly among the Santee villages; at dawn on August 18, swarms of painted Indians swept across the countryside. Among the first victims, along with the dead and wounded of Henry Behnke's recruiting party, was trader Myrick. His corpse was found later with grass stuffed in its mouth. Some Indians refused to participate and others risked their lives hiding white friends, but several hundred Sioux were on the warpath, releasing their pent-up hatred in an orgy of murder and pillage.

It was not long before Santee braves clashed with uniformed troops. The revolt had barely begun when the commander of Fort Ridgely's 78-man garrison of Minnesota volunteers, a young captain named John S. Marsh who had had no experience fighting Indians, rashly set off with a detachment of 46 soldiers and an interpreter for the Lower Agency, which was under attack. Despite the evidence of tomahawked bodies and the warnings of refugees whom he passed on the road, Marsh boldly went on to Redwood Ferry. The crossing was about one mile below the agency, which lay on the opposite side of the Minnesota River.

The ferryman had been killed, but his boat was on the shore. An Indian on the far bank, indicating friendship, called to the soldiers to cross. But before the troops could move, they were hit by a volley fired by Indians hidden in the woods across the stream. An instant later, other Indians, who had crept up behind Marsh's men, attacked their rear. "About one-half of our men dropped dead where they had been standing," report-

mong the whites who earned the re-
ect of the Sioux on the Minnesota
ontier was Dr. Thomas Williamson,
physician and missionary. Seen be-
w in a broad-brimmed hat, he is sur-
unded by some of those he served
the Upper Agency. When the up-
sing seemed imminent, friendly In-
ans warned Williamson, and he fled
safety with his family.

ed 19-year-old Sergeant John F. Bishop.

The remnants of Marsh's command took flight through the tall grass that lined the riverbank. Some of the troops made a stand in a thicket, but they were running out of ammunition. Marsh urged his men to escape by swimming the stream. When they hesitated, he jumped in first; but halfway across he suffered a cramp and drowned. "I will never forget the look that brave officer gave us just before he sank for the last time — will never forget how dark the next hour seemed to us, as we crouched underneath the bank of the Minnesota River, and talked over and decided what next best to do," reported Sergeant Bishop, who had taken command.

Bishop and the survivors straggled back to Fort Ridgely during the night. Twenty-five soldiers had lost their lives and five more had been wounded in the ambush. Only one Indian had been killed.

Reacting swiftly to the disaster, Lieutenant Thomas P. Gere, whom Marsh had left in charge of the fort, alerted his tiny garrison of 22 effectives, then dispatched a message to Fort Snelling and Governor Ramsey asking

Hd. Qrs. Fort Ridgely Minn
Aug 18th 8 P.M.
Comdg Officer
Ft Snelling
Capt Marsh left this post at 10 a.m. this morning to prevent Indian depredations at the Lower agency — some of the men have returned from there & I learn that Capt Marsh is killed and only thirteen of his company remaining — The Indians are killing the settlers and plundering the country — Send reinforcements without delay.
Respectfully
Thomas P. Gere
2d Lieut
Fifth Minn Vols
Commanding Post
Please hand this to Gov Ramsey immediately

Lieutenant Thomas P. Gere, the 19-year-old officer left in charge of Fort Ridgely by Captain John Marsh on August 18, scrawled an urgent plea for help *(far left)* to both the commander of Fort Snelling and Minnesota Governor Alexander Ramsey after learning that Marsh had been ambushed. Gere would later distinguish himself against a different foe, seizing a Confederate flag during the Battle of Nashville in December 1864, to earn the Medal of Honor.

for reinforcements. Gere's courier, Private William J. Sturgis, made the 125-mile trip in 18 hours, changing horses frequently on the way. During his headlong dash he overtook Galbraith and the agent's small company of irregulars, known as the Renville Rangers, turning them back to assist Gere.

The inexperienced 19-year-old lieutenant found himself with daunting responsibilities. If the Indians overran Fort Ridgely, the way would be open for them to destroy every downriver settlement as far as St. Paul. Further, more than 200 refugees, mostly frightened women and children, were crowded into the fort's log hospital, surgeon's quarters and stone barracks. And now a stagecoach arrived from St. Paul carrying $71,000 in gold — the Indians' long-delayed annuity money. Gere told no one about the kegs of gold coins, and with the help of the stagecoach guards, he hid them in a building.

Compounding Gere's problems was Fort Ridgely itself. A mere cluster of detached buildings undefended by a stockade, it was an easy target. The lieutenant disposed the few defenders as best he could. He was aided by a massively built artillery sergeant named John Jones, who had stayed at the fort to look after some guns left there when the Regulars were withdrawn in 1861. Jones had taught some of Gere's Minnesota volunteers to load and fire his artillery pieces, which included a 24-pounder howitzer, two 12-pounder mountain howitzers and a six-pounder field gun. He had trained enough men to form three small gun crews, which he now posted at three of the fort's corners.

The fort might easily have been overrun the next morning, August 19, when a large Sioux war party appeared on the prairie. Instead of attacking, however, the Indians held a long, animated council. The leading chiefs — Little Crow, Mankato and Big Eagle — understood the fort's strategic importance and argued for an immediate assault. But they were overruled by a majority of the warriors, who thought it would be easier and more rewarding to attack and loot

New Ulm. Everywhere in the valley, Indians were enriching themselves with plunder. At New Ulm there were shops to be pillaged and women to be captured. The soldiers at the fort could wait, the warriors insisted. With dissension splitting their ranks, the Indians rode away, most of them heading toward New Ulm. The rest, including the chiefs, who wanted no part of an attack on women and children, returned to their villages.

The soldiers and civilians in Fort Ridgely had no idea why the Indians had left, but they nevertheless were relieved. Their mood brightened further during the day as reinforcements arrived: 50 men of Company C of the 5th Minnesota under Lieutenant Timothy J. Sheehan, who had marched through the night and covered 42 miles in nine and a half hours; about four dozen members of Galbraith's Renville Rangers; and a small group of armed citizens from the town of St. Peter. As the senior officer, Lieutenant Sheehan took command at the fort, whose defenders, including those refugees who had guns, now numbered about 180.

The people of New Ulm had also been preparing themselves for attack. On the 19th, when 100 Sioux warriors began shooting from a bluff overlooking the town, the Indians received a warmer reception than they expected. While the women and children huddled in buildings and behind barricades, the town's militiamen under their elected leader, Jacob Nix, effectively returned the Indians' fire and kept the Santees at a distance. None of the reinforcements for whose help Henry Behnke had ridden the previous night had yet appeared; but lacking their chiefs' leadership, the Indians made no concerted attack and did little damage other than burning a few of the town's outlying buildings. A late-afternoon thunderstorm dampened the Indians' ardor, and with the arrival of 16 mounted men — the first to respond to Behnke's appeal — the fight ended. Seventeen townspeople had lost their lives, 11 of them members of a hapless party whom the Indians had trapped on the prairie outside town. The Sioux losses were not known.

That night, Judge Charles Flandrau, whom Behnke had awakened before dawn at Traverse des Sioux, marched in with 125 volunteers. Other citizens' units continued to arrive, and eventually Flandrau, who was elected overall commander, had almost 300 men ready to defend New Ulm should the Indians return.

By the next afternoon, August 20, Little Crow and the other chiefs had persuaded about 400 warriors to move against Fort Ridgely. Following an intricate plan of attack devised by Little Crow, the Indians surrounded the post, then paused while Little Crow sought to distract the defenders by riding back and forth on the prairie west of the fort as if seeking a parley. Then at a signal, Indians on the east side launched a sudden charge. At the same time, other Sioux crept up wooded ravines toward the northeast and the southwest corners of the post.

Musket fire crackled and the Indians occupied some log huts on the fort's north side. But Jones's gun crews, supported by the infantry's steady fire, drove them back. Canister charges ripped into the ravines, halting the Indians there, and the battle settled into long-range firing and ineffectual attempts by the Indians to set the buildings aflame with burning arrows. Afraid of the howitzers, which they had never faced, the Sioux finally withdrew at nightfall.

But the Indians were not through. After a

Sheltered behind a hastily built log breastwork in New Ulm on the afternoon of August 19, settlers fire on the charging Sioux in this scene painted on a barrelhead by a resident of the town. The first person slain at New Ulm was a 13-year-old girl, Emilie Pauli, who was hit by a bullet as she ventured across a street behind the barricade.

day of heavy rain, Little Crow's Santees reappeared at the fort on August 22. This time there were almost twice as many warriors, including 400 Sissetons and Wahpetons who had come from the Upper Agency villages to join the fighting. Wearing camouflage of grass, leaves and clusters of wildflowers in their headbands, the Indians crept up the ravines and among trees and bushes until they were almost upon the buildings. Then, with what Lieutenant Gere called "demoniac yells," they sprang forward.

Musketry from the defenders, firing from behind barricades and from windows in the buildings, checked the Indians everywhere except at the fort's southwest corner, where the warriors seized the stables and the sutler's store. Artillery shelling soon dislodged them but also set the buildings on fire. At the same time, Indian attempts to set fire to other buildings failed; the roofs were still damp from the previous day's rain, and the fire arrows fizzled out.

The battle raged through the afternoon. "The hail of bullets, the whizzing of arrows, and the blood-curdling war-whoop were incessant," Gere wrote later. "The fire in front of Jones's gun became so hot and accurate as to splinter every lineal foot of timber along the top of his barricades."

Little Crow was wounded slightly and the Indians massed around Chief Mankato for a final charge against the vulnerable southwest corner. Simultaneous shots from a mountain howitzer and the 24-pounder landed among them. The "ponderous reverberations" of the cannon, Gere said, "echoed up the valley as though 20 guns had opened, and the frightful explosion struck terror to the savages." The Indians fled and the battle was over. Despite the intensity of the struggle, only six whites had been killed and fewer than 20 wounded in the two fights at the fort. But it was a costly reversal for Little Crow. About 100 of his men had been killed and many more wounded.

The next day brought a second attempt by the Indians to take New Ulm. Smarting from their repulse at the fort, the Sioux appeared west of the town about nine in the morning. "Their advance upon the sloping prairie in the bright sunlight was a very fine spectacle," Judge Flandrau related. "When within about one mile and a half of us the mass began to expand like a fan, and increase in the velocity of its approach. Then the savages uttered a terrific yell and came down upon us like the wind."

Flandrau had deployed a number of his citizen-soldiers on the prairie to meet the charge. They broke and ran, allowing the Indians to occupy some buildings in town. But the defenders rallied and fought back bravely. For a time the Sioux had the upper hand. Many of the houses caught fire and the Indians advanced behind dense clouds of

Weary mission workers and their children pause in their flight from the rampaging Sioux on August 21, two days after they set out across the prairie from the Upper Agency seeking safety to the east. Word of the massacres caused thousands of settlers to abandon their homesteads, virtually depopulating 23 counties in southwestern Minnesota.

smoke. To meet the crisis, Flandrau concentrated 60 of his men for a countercharge. They went forward at a run, cheering loudly, and their assault broke the attack. By nightfall the Sioux had given up. In two days of fighting at New Ulm, the defenders had lost 36 dead and about 23 wounded. Indian losses once more could not be ascertained.

The battle was won, but in the process much of New Ulm had been destroyed, with 190 houses reduced to ashes. The next day Flandrau and his officers ordered the settlement evacuated. The long confinement of the townspeople and refugees, Flandrau explained, "was rapidly producing disease among the women and children, who were huddled in cellars and close rooms like sheep in a cattle car." Guarded by 150 recently arrived reinforcements, about 2,000 refugees left New Ulm and made their way safely to Mankato, 30 miles down the river.

The Indians had expected to rush down the valley to the Mississippi; but the stout defense of New Ulm and Fort Ridgely, according to Chief Big Eagle, "kept the door shut." Veering from that direction, groups of Santees, joined by war parties of sympathetic Yankton and Yanktonai Sioux from the eastern Dakota prairies, moved to the north and northwest, looking for plunder and more whites to attack.

One battle developed near the town of Acton, where the murder of five whites had sparked the uprising. There, about 55 fresh recruits of a company of Minnesota volunteers, heading north to protect settlers, blundered into Little Crow's warriors and another group of Indians led by an elderly chief named Walker Among Sacred Stones. On September 3, the troops and about 20 refugees they were guarding were surrounded by the two Indian bands. Captain Richard Strout, the officer in charge, elected to fight his way out, ordering his green troops to charge Little Crow's braves with bayonets. The attack succeeded, although almost half of Strout's men were killed or wounded, and the troops and settlers retreated to the partially fortified town of Hutchinson.

The Indians also attacked Fort Abercrombie, far to the northwest on the border of the Dakota Territory. The few buildings of that post were unfortified, but the small garrison, Company D of the 5th Minnesota, quickly built breastworks of logs and earth and, aided by fire from three howitzers, successfully withstood attacks by 400 warriors on the 3rd and 6th of September. The Indians continued, however, to ambush and kill other whites in the area for several weeks.

While violence and terror gripped his state's villages and farms, Governor Ramsey began organizing a relief expedition. His first move was to appoint a friendly political rival, Henry Hastings Sibley, colonel of the state militia, directing him to assemble all the recruits he could find and head for the Minnesota River. Sibley, 51, had no military experience, but as a longtime fur trader in the region, he knew the Sioux and the frontier country well. Taking charge of four newly

In a view of the battle at Fort Ridgely on August 22, painted by a soldier who was there, Indians lie between two outbuildings — a stable *(far right)* and a sutler's store — set ablaze by shellfire from the fort. The two sides fought for six hours, an officer said, over ground "alternately lit up by the flames of burning buildings and darkened by whirling clouds of smoke."

Lieutenant Timothy Sheehan *(below)*, the 26-year-old Irishman in command at Fort Ridgely on August 22, held out against superior numbers with the help of Sergeant John Jones *(bottom)*, who commanded a gun crew in an exposed position against the Indians' heaviest onslaughts. Chief Big Eagle, a leader of the attack, conceded, "The soldiers fought so bravely we thought there were more of them than there were."

formed companies of the 6th Minnesota Infantry at Fort Snelling, Sibley had started for Fort Ridgely on August 20.

Sibley's expedition did not go smoothly. Almost from the start, rations were short, as were clothing, weapons and wagons. Artillery caissons held the wrong caliber of ammunition. The green troops marched so slowly that impatient citizens and Minnesota newspapers complained bitterly, calling Sibley a coward, a snail and "the state undertaker with his company of gravediggers."

Gradually, the column made progress. Reinforced by six more companies of the 6th Minnesota and by several small militia units and groups of volunteers — bringing Sibley's total strength to about 1,400 — the army reached beleaguered Fort Ridgely on August 27, five days after the Indians had last attacked it. Sibley put more than 300 additional refugees in wagons and sent them down the valley. Then on August 31, seeing no Indians about, he incautiously dispatched Major Joseph R. Brown and Captain Hiram P. Grant with Company A and 50 volunteer cavalrymen, together with a 20-man fatigue detail, to bury the massacre victims and reconnoiter the Lower Agency.

The men carried out their grim burial task. On the night of September 1 they bivouacked within a circle of their wagons about 16 miles northwest of Fort Ridgely and across the river from the burned remains of the Lower Agency. Inexplicably, Captain Grant chose to establish the camp near the head of Birch Coulee, a deep, wooded ravine that would give any attacking Indians a perfect hidden avenue of approach. Perhaps the captain, having seen no Indian war parties, thought the outbreak was over. But a group of Sioux led by Chiefs Gray Bird, Red Legs and Mankato spotted the camp and, creeping close during the night, surrounded the soldiers. At dawn they attacked.

Many of the Minnesotans, caught half asleep, were killed before they could take shelter. The survivors wriggled beneath the wagons and behind dead horses, returning the fire and driving the Indians back.

At Fort Ridgely, Sibley heard the faint sounds of the battle and sent Companies B, D and E of the 6th Minnesota along with 50 mounted rangers and a section of artillery — 240 men in all, under the command of Colonel Samuel McPhail — to find out what was happening. Just short of the battle site, a small party of Indians intercepted McPhail. The nervous colonel, fearing that he was about to be surrounded, stopped, drew his force into a defensive circle and sent back to the fort for reinforcements.

Sibley left at once with the rest of his command but marched so slowly that it was after midnight before he joined McPhail. Then he delayed another three hours before moving toward the embattled camp near Birch Coulee. About 11 a.m. on the 3rd, having scattered the Indians with artillery fire, he finally rescued the survivors of Brown and Grant's party, who for 31 hours had each subsisted on one quarter of a hard cracker and one ounce of raw cabbage. Their wagons and tents were riddled with bullet holes; sobbing men, red-eyed from lack of sleep, cried for water. The air was foul with the stench of dead horses and men. Altogether, Birch Coulee had claimed the lives of 19 soldiers, and many more had been wounded.

Sibley returned to Fort Ridgely and again drew criticism for failing to press after the Indians. But Birch Coulee had taught him two lessons. First, his officers and his men

Sioux warriors attacking New Ulm o August 23 are met by fire from the town's civilian defenders, who have rallied around their bearded commander, Charles Flandrau *(at right, with sword upraised)*. Raging from house to house, the fighting grew desperate and disorganized. Flandra reported: "Every man did his own work after his own fashion."

needed more training in the techniques of Indian fighting; second, he needed more cavalry, without which the task of pursuing mounted Indians was impossible.

The state adjutant general rushed ammunition, provisions and clothing to Sibley, and Governor Ramsey wired Secretary of War Henry Stanton and the President, asking them to authorize the purchase of 500 horses for use against the Sioux. "This is not our war," Ramsey telegraphed Lincoln sharply on September 6. "It is a National War."

The reply from Washington was unexpected but welcome. Lincoln created the Military Department of the Northwest, to be commanded by Major General John Pope with headquarters at St. Paul. Pope's reputation had suffered from his recent defeat in the Second Battle of Bull Run, but he remained an energetic officer. Hurrying westward by rail, he assumed his new command at St. Paul on September 16.

Before Pope arrived, a chance seemed to emerge for a peaceful solution to the Sioux uprising. Sibley, experienced in Indian ways, thought that Little Crow was tiring of the war. Writing out a message that offered negotiations, Sibley had it placed in a split stake at Birch Coulee. On September 7, a halfbreed messenger arrived with a reply from the chief, listing the Indian grievances that had led to the uprising and stating that the Indians were holding a great many prisoners. Sibley replied that he would talk with Little Crow after the prisoners were freed.

Several other messages were exchanged, but no agreement was reached. Unknown to Little Crow, on September 12 the halfbreed intermediary also gave Sibley a letter from two other chiefs, Wabasha and Taopi, who had consistently opposed the war. Revealing the dissension within the Indian camp, they offered to take possession of the captives and deliver them to Sibley if he would name a place where they could meet. Sibley replied that he soon would begin a march north and would look for them and the prisoners on the prairie, assembled under a white flag. The danger now, Sibley realized, was that any sudden movement against Little Crow might compromise the safety of the captives. "I must use what craft I possess to get these poor creatures out of the possession of the red devils, and then pursue the latter with fire and sword," he wrote his wife.

Sibley started north on September 19 with a considerably reinforced army — now totaling 1,619 men — and three days later he set up camp on the eastern shore of a small lake just below the Upper Agency. By then most of the Sioux were camped with their captives a few miles farther north near the mouth of the Chippewa River.

Despite the dissension in the ranks of the Sioux, Little Crow managed to persuade 700 or more warriors to make another attack on the white troops. Leaving camp at dusk, Little Crow and his followers stole southward during the night and set up an ambush in tall grass and in a ravine along the road the troops would take the next morning. Confident that they would annihilate Sibley's army, the Sioux waited in hiding as the dawn of September 23 broke.

But again the Indians' plans miscarried, this time because their trap was accidentally discovered before it could be sprung. At 7 a.m., before the army moved, several wagonloads of troops from the 3rd Minnesota started out, apparently without permission, to dig potatoes in the abandoned gardens of the Upper Agency. Their wagons came straight on, said Chief Big Eagle, and "would have driven right over our men as they lay in the grass. At last they came so close that our men had to rise up and fire."

As the soldiers jumped down from the wagons to fight back, other members of their regiment hurried forward. In a few moments a vicious little fight — later called the Battle of Wood Lake — was in full cry. Initially the Indians deployed in a wide semicircle whose wings seemed to threaten Sibley's flanks; then they attacked the 3rd Minnesota in the center. The 3rd withdrew in confusion, but reinforced by Galbraith's Renville Rangers, the Minnesotans made a stand on a plateau. At the same time, some Indians started toward the camp through a ravine. They were thrown back by canister from a six-pounder gun and by a charge by members of the 6th and 7th Minnesota Regiments. Another Indian attack was halted near the lake. Finally, simultaneous charges by the 3rd in the center and by parts of the 6th and 7th on the right drove the Indians through the grass and out of the ravine, ending the two-hour conflict. The Sioux fled, having lost more than 25 killed and many wounded. Some of the dead Indians were later scalped by the victorious troops, an action that drew a contemptuous rebuke from Sibley. The army's casualties were seven killed and 34 wounded.

Lacking sufficient cavalry, and still concerned for the safety of the captives, Sibley did not pursue the Indians. But the battle proved decisive. Most of Little Crow's warriors had had enough fighting, and they scattered with their chiefs and families, some going as far as Canada, others joining Yanktonai and Teton bands farther west, still others traveling on to Devils Lake in present-day North Dakota to spend the winter beyond reach of the troops.

While the warriors dispersed, a Sioux chief from the Upper Agency named Red Iron, who had opposed the uprising, helped the other peace-minded chiefs, Wabasha and Taopi, to protect the captives. On September 26, when Sibley appeared with a troop escort at Red Iron's camp near the mouth of the Chippewa River, the chiefs turned over 91 white prisoners and about 150 mixed bloods; in the next few days they released

The Ravages Recalled

Minnesotans who survived the Sioux uprising of 1862 would never forget it. More than 30 years later, three residents of New Ulm — Anton Gág, Christian Heller and Alexander Schwendinger — drew on the recollections of soldiers and settlers to create a panorama of the upheaval, four scenes from which are presented here. The two paintings below illustrate in lurid detail the plight of civilians; those opposite depict troops in desperate straits. Together, they offer a vivid account of the survivors' searing memories, rekindled on canvas.

Armed Sioux fire away while others use their rifles as clubs to finish off a party of settlers. In one such incident on August 19, 1862, two dozen civilians were slain.

In a sensationalized rendering of the attack at the Lower Agency on August 18, women and children are butchered by the Indians. In truth, only men were killed.

urprised by the Sioux at Birch Coulee on September 2, soldiers fight back from behind a breastwork of dead horses. Not one of the defenders' 87 horses lived.

mbushed near Acton on September 3, recruits and citizens under Captain Richard Strout fight back with bayonets fixed, losing 20 men before reaching safety.

Chief Red Iron, one of the so-called friendlies who helped liberate the settlers captured in the uprising, had learned firsthand the price opposing the whites. In 1852, when he protested financial claims made against the Sioux by traders, he was arrested and stripped of his authority until other Indians were induced to honor the claims.

about 30 more captives for a total of 269. The site became known as Camp Release.

Many of the whites and halfbreeds were in pitiful mental and physical condition, but young Mary Schwandt, protected by a kindly family of missionary-influenced Santees during most of her 39-day ordeal, was well. At least one white woman vocally objected to her own liberation. She "had become so infatuated with the redskin who had taken her for a wife," Sibley huffed angrily, that "she declared that were it not for her children she would not leave her dusky paramour."

Sibley established a bivouac near the Chippewa River and, during the succeeding weeks, rounded up hundreds of families of hungry and dispirited Santees who were wandering through the countryside. By the end of October he had nearly 2,000 Indians under guard. Determined to punish those responsible for the uprising and the atrocities committed against the settlers, he appointed a five-man military commission to take evidence against the Indians from the freed captives. Eventually the board sentenced 307 Indians and halfbreeds to be hanged. The list was cut to 303 before it was sent to President Lincoln.

The verdicts received enthusiastic approval throughout Minnesota, but they were held up by the President until he could review the evidence. Lincoln had been visited by the Episcopal Bishop of the Missionary District of Minnesota, Henry B. Whipple, one of the state's few tolerant voices for the Indians. Discussing the evils of the Indian system that had angered the Santee, the clergyman, according to Lincoln, "talked with me about the rascality of this Indian business until I felt it down to my boots."

Lincoln, who had once fought Indians and had been a frontier lawyer himself, was determined to separate the murderers and rapists from those who had simply joined in battles. He found much of the evidence against the condemned Indians unconvincing or deficient. Despite appeals from Ramsey, Pope and others, he narrowed the list to 39, and pardoned one of that number shortly thereafter. On December 26 — in America's largest public mass execution — 38 Indians and halfbreeds were hanged at Mankato. Even

Colonel Henry Hastings Sibley, a former fur trader who had profited handsomely in his dealings with the Sioux, now held all Indians as potential adversaries. Notified by friendlies that the prisoners had been separated from their captors, he marched with colors flying to the camp, demanding that "all the captives should be delivered to me instantly."

with the list reduced, at least three of the executed men turned out later to have been hanged by mistake.

To assuage Minnesota's anti-Indian hysteria, Congress abrogated all treaties with the Santee in February and March 1863 and ordered the tribe's removal from Minnesota. About 1,300 Sioux, mostly women and children, who had been incarcerated after the Wood Lake battle in a crowded and unhealthy stockade near Fort Snelling, were sent to Crow Creek, a bleak, isolated site on the open plains along the Missouri River in present-day South Dakota. About 2,000 Winnebago Indians, a few of whom were suspected of having helped the Santee during the outbreak, also were driven from Minnesota and placed near the Sioux at Crow Creek. So many died there of starvation and disease that the Winnebago soon fled to Nebraska Territory, where in 1865 the Omaha Indians gave them part of their reservation. It was not until 1866 that a peace commission allowed the suffering Santee to move to a better location farther south on timbered land at the mouth of the Niobrara River.

Neither executions nor exile solved the Indian problem on the Minnesota frontier. Sporadic killings and rumors that Little Crow was rallying the fugitive Santee to strike again convinced Pope that new troubles were brewing. So did reports that bands of Yanktonai Sioux on the Dakota prairies, supplied with arms by Canadian traders, and some powerful Teton Sioux from the Missouri River valley were about to join the Santee.

To counter the threat, Pope planned a two-pronged preemptive campaign. With a brigade of almost 3,000 men, mostly infantry, Sibley would march northwest from the Minnesota River, scouring the prairies and pushing Indians westward from the Devils Lake area and the eastern Dakota grasslands to the Missouri. A second column of about 1,200 cavalry and a battery of four howitzers would move north along the Missouri from Fort Randall, neutralizing the Teton Sioux and trapping the hostile Santee and Yanktonai whom Sibley was forcing west. The Missouri River brigade would be led by 43-year-old Brigadier General Alfred Sully, a

Smoke from campfires shrouds the tepees at a stockade erected in November 1862 at Fort Snelling to hold 1,700 captured Sioux, among them the families of the men facing trial for their part in the uprising. The compound was fenced as much to shield the Indians as to confine them: While being escorted to the camp, they had been attacked by an armed mob.

At the Lower Agency in late 1862, a few of the 392 Indians brought before a military commission sit huddled in blankets outside the log house where many of the cases were heard. The man standing guard at left may be one of the mixed-blood soldiers who had been recruited to fight the Confederates, only to be pressed into service against the warring Sioux.

veteran of several prewar campaigns against the Western tribes and more recently of Civil War battles in Virginia. The sometimes irascible son of the celebrated painter Thomas Sully, he was unhappy over his transfer—and was resented by Pope, who had asked Secretary of War Stanton to send him a less eccentric officer.

Pope's elaborate campaign turned into a primitive expedition. Sibley reached the area of Devils Lake easily enough—to find that the rumors about Little Crow fomenting fresh troubles had been false. The unhappy chief was dead, shot and killed by two farmers while he picked berries in a field. He had then been scalped and his body had been thrown on a pile of entrails at a slaughterhouse in a nearby town.

Sibley did encounter a large party of Indians moving toward the Missouri River. They turned out to be Sissetons and Wahpetons led by Standing Buffalo and other chiefs who had not been involved in the uprising. Heading another group of Sissetons and Yanktonais was Inkpaduta, who had been a fugitive since 1857 for leading the so-called Spirit Lake Massacre in Iowa that had taken 30 lives. Although it was evident that most of the Indians wanted nothing more than to hunt buffalo, Sibley expected Inkpaduta to fight. He deployed his troops for battle near a spot called Big Mound; when one of Inkpaduta's young men suddenly shot and killed an Army surgeon, the troops opened fire. In the ensuing battle, the Indians held off the soldiers until their women and children got safely away, then retreated skillfully. The troops pursued them until nightfall, but finally Sibley returned to camp.

Inkpaduta and his warriors, joined by a hunting party of Hunkpapas and Blackfoot Teton Sioux, vowed to fight back. They attacked Sibley twice, at Dead Buffalo Lake on July 26 and at Stony Lake on the 28th. Both times the Indians were routed by counterattacks and by Sibley's howitzers.

Thwarted both in battle and in their yearly buffalo hunt, the Indians retreated to the west side of the Missouri. Sibley followed them to the banks of the big river and waited for a while, searching unsuccessfully for Sully's column. He then returned across the prairie to Minnesota.

Sully's brigade, delayed because shallow water in the Missouri had stalled its supply-carrying steamboats, finally reached the rendezvous point nearly a month after Sibley had decamped. Sully was not to be cheated of his share of the action, however, and when he learned from a captured Indian that Inkpaduta and his hostile band were still camped nearby, he ordered his 1,200 cavalrymen to search for them.

The battle Sully hoped for began on September 3 when an advance group of four cavalry companies rode down a ravine and came upon Inkpaduta's entire party of several thousand Sioux camped by a lake in rocky country near Whitestone Hill, northeast of present-day Ashley, North Dakota. According to white accounts, Inkpaduta thought he had Sully's advance guard trapped in the ravine and delayed attacking while his warriors painted themselves for battle. The Indians maintained that they were preoccupied only with securing and drying meat for the winter and had no intention of fighting.

At any rate, the delay was fatal for Inkpaduta's people. Soon Sully's entire cavalry brigade appeared and charged the Indian camp. Driven into a ravine themselves, the Sioux fought back fiercely until darkness, when many managed to escape.

But Sully and his troopers killed more than 200 Sioux, took more than 150 prisoner, and destroyed all the Indians' possessions, including 400,000 pounds of dried buffalo meat. "To show the extent of their loss in a measure," reported Sergeant J. H. Drips of Company L of the 6th Iowa, "I will

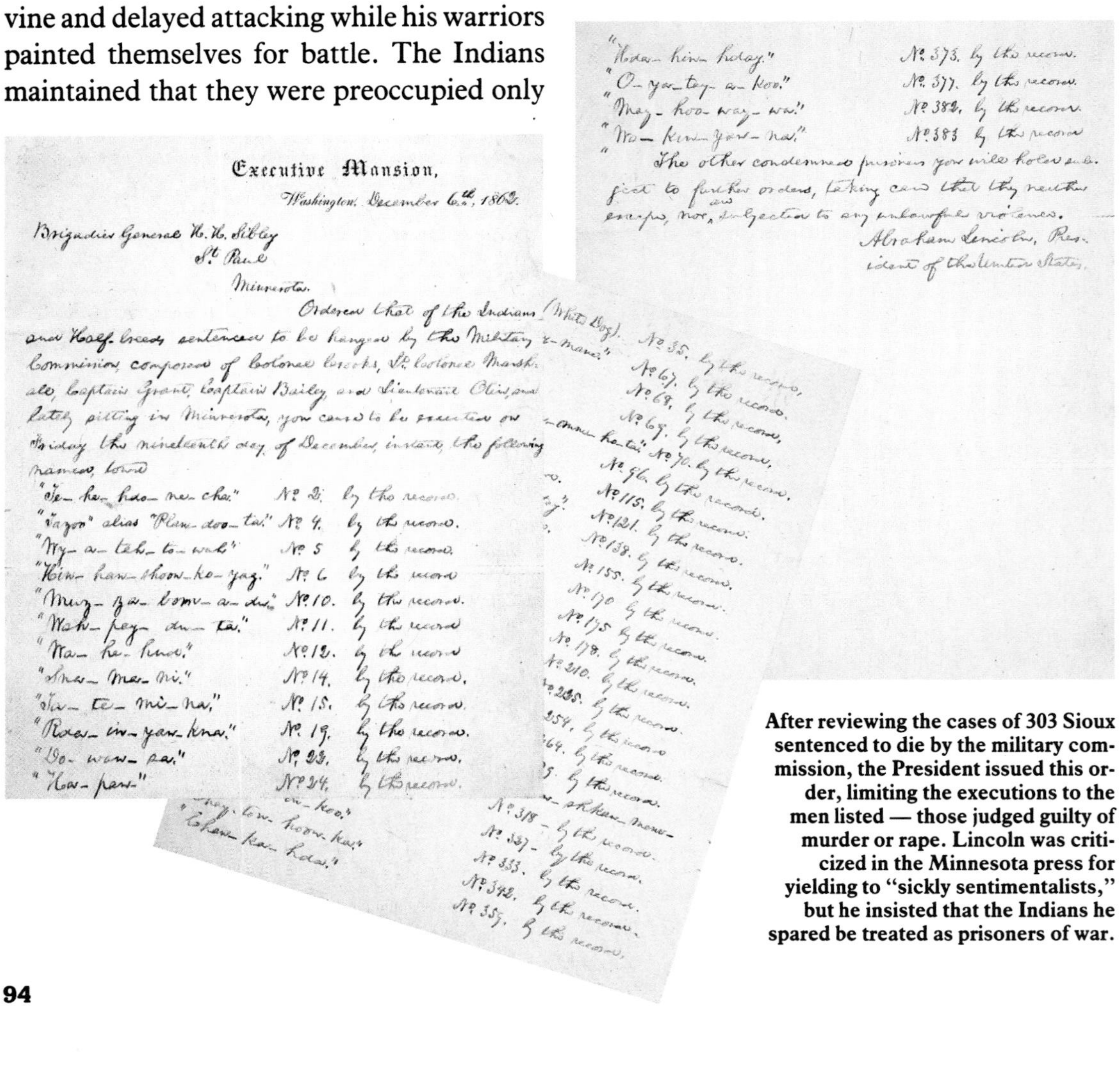

Executive Mansion,
Washington, December 6th, 1862.

Brigadier General H. H. Sibley
St. Paul
Minnesota.

Ordered that of the Indians and Half-breeds sentenced to be hanged by the Military Commission, composed of Colonel Crooks, Lt. Colonel Marshall, Captain Grant, Captain Bailey, and Lieutenant Olin, and lately sitting in Minnesota, you cause to be executed on Friday the nineteenth day of December, instant, the following names, towit

"Te-he-hdo-ne-cha." No. 2. by the record.
"Tazoo" alias "Plan-doo-ta." No. 4. by the record.
"Wy-a-teh-to-wah" No. 5 by the record.
"Hin-han-shoon-ko-yag." No. 6 by the record.
"Muz-za-bom-a-du." No. 10. by the record.
"Wah-pey-du-ta." No. 11. by the record.
"Wa-he-hna." No. 12. by the record.
"Sna-ma-ni." No. 14. by the record.
"Ta-te-mi-na." No. 15. by the record.
"Rda-in-yan-kna." No. 19. by the record.
"Do-wan-sa." No. 23. by the record.
"Ha-pan." No. 24. by the record.

(White Dog) No. 35. by the record.
No. 67. by the record.
No. 68. by the record.
No. 69. by the record.
No. 70. by the record.
No. 96. by the record.
No. 115. by the record.
No. 121. by the record.
No. 138. by the record.
No. 155. by the record.
No. 170 by the record.
No. 175 by the record.
No. 178. by the record.
No. 210. by the record.
No. 225. by the record.
No. 254. by the record.
No. 264. by the record.
No. [illegible]5. by the record.
No. 318. by the record.
"-ay-tow-hoon-ka" No. 327. by the record.
"Chan-ka-hda." No. 333. by the record.
No. 342. by the record.
No. 359. by the record.

"Hda-hin-hday." No. 373. by the record.
"O-ya-tay-a-koo." No. 377. by the record.
"May-hoo-way-wa." No. 382. by the record.
"Wa-kin-yan-na." No. 383 by the record.

The other condemned prisoners you will hold subject to further orders, taking care that they neither escape, nor are subjected to any unlawful violence.

Abraham Lincoln, President of the United States.

After reviewing the cases of 303 Sioux sentenced to die by the military commission, the President issued this order, limiting the executions to the men listed — those judged guilty of murder or rape. Lincoln was criticized in the Minnesota press for yielding to "sickly sentimentalists," but he insisted that the Indians he spared be treated as prisoners of war.

just say that it took a party of 100 men two days to gather up the stuff and burn it." While the Indians who had fled faced starvation and cold, Sully subjected his prisoners, many of them women and children, to a grueling march across the prairies to Crow Creek, where the Santees from Fort Snelling had been exiled.

Yet the 1863 campaign had not fulfilled its purpose. The war had been widened onto the Dakota plains, inflaming more Sioux tribes, and although the fighting had been pushed westward, many Minnesota Santee tribes were still at large and many white settlements were still insecure. Pressed for men and supplies for the war against the South, Washington urged Pope to seek treaties that would end the frontier conflict. But raids by angry Sioux continued, forcing Pope to plan a new campaign in the spring of 1864.

Again, a Federal brigade, led this time by Colonel Minor T. Thomas, was to march across the Dakota prairie from the Minnesota River to the Missouri. A second brigade, ascending the Missouri, would as before be commanded by the combative Sully. But when the two brigades rendezvoused in late

fore an assemblage of citizens and ldiers, the 38 condemned Sioux et their fate at Mankato, Minneso- on December 26, 1862. Their ex- ution had been delayed a week to ow time for the complex prepara- ns. A witness reported that just be- e the drop on which the bound n were standing fell away, the con- mned had chanted and tried to join nds: "Their bodies swayed to and , and their every limb seemed to be eping time. The drop trembled and ook as if all were dancing."

Ancient Weapons for a Doomed Defense

The Indians attacked by General Alfred Sully's Federal troops near Whitestone Hill on September 3, 1863, fought back with an assortment of arms. Some of the warriors in Chief Inkpaduta's band carried rifles similar to their enemy's. But as shown at right in Sully's own painting of the battle — with a sampling of weapons found at the site — many of the Indians relied on more primitive tools of war, such as bows, clubs and lances.

Inkpaduta's people had come to Whitestone Hill on the trail of buffalo, a resource endangered even then by overhunting; and their reliance on the great beasts was evident in the crafting of their arms. Braided buffalo sinews formed the string for a warrior's bow; a snug binding of buffalo hide secured the stone head of his war club to its wooden handle; a similar hide wrapping, adorned with a lock of buffalo fur, held the blade of his lance to its shaft.

Such sturdy implements had served the Sioux well against their ancestral rivals. But the weapons proved less formidable against Sully's well-equipped men, who fought with sabers, carbines and cannon. "The Indians made a very desperate resistance," Sully wrote, "but finally broke and fled, pursued in every direction by bodies of my troops."

The Federals then turned their attention to the fruits of the hunting party's labor, destroying the entire store of meat the Indians had set by for the coming winter and scores of the tepees they had fashioned from the hides of their prey. "I believe I can safely say I gave them one of the most severe punishments that the Indians have ever received," boasted Sully.

It was an ominous episode for the Sioux, one that called to mind the somber words Chief Little Crow had uttered to his warriors a year earlier as the uprising began: "We are only little herds of buffaloes left scattered; the great herds that once covered the plains are no more."

General Alfred Sully's painting of the battle at Whitestone Hill, based on a sketch by one of his officers, details the varied armament of the Sioux — including a war club, wielded against a trooper at far right; a bow, drawn by an Indian kneeling at center beside two comrades with raised rifles; and a lance and shield, lying near a fallen warrior at left. Federal cannon are on the hill in the distance.

BOW WITH
BROKEN STRING
WAR CLUB WITH
STONE HEAD
LANCE WITH
METAL BLADE

Engaged at Killdeer Mountain on July 28, 1864, General Sully's troops face fore and aft to cope with the swarming Sioux, whose tepees are visible in the background. Shell-fire from Federal artillerists — at work in the middle distance at right — proved crucial in scattering the Indians, who detested the projectiles they called "rotten balls."

June at Swan Lake on the east side of the Missouri, Sully was disgusted to discover that Thomas' men were escorting a train of about 200 men, women and children traveling to the Idaho gold mines in 123 ox-drawn wagons — and that the troops would be obliged to see the emigrants safely as far as the Yellowstone River.

Despite the impediment of the wagon train, Sully ferried the army and the emigrants across the Missouri and hurried on to meet any Indians that might be in the area. Learning that an Indian force was near the head of the Heart River in Teton territory, he combined the two brigades and, leaving the emigrants under a strong guard, set off with 2,200 officers and men to do battle.

On July 28, in rugged country beneath the wooded slopes of Killdeer Mountain near the Dakota Territory's Little Missouri River, Sully found the Sioux. Sixteen hundred mounted warriors — Hunkpapas, Sans Arcs, Blackfoots and Minneconjou Tetons, as well as Yanktonais and Santees — were drawn up, waiting for him. Prevented by the broken terrain from launching a cavalry charge, Sully had his men dismount and form a large square, with sides more than a mile long. Placing the artillery and horses in the center, he ordered the square forward. The Indians counterattacked against all its sides, but the men held, driving back some of the Sioux thrusts with fire from the howitzers. Gradually, the Indians withdrew to wooded ravines on the mountainside, again holding off the soldiers while their women and children

A complex figure, Brigadier General Alfred Sully waged harsh campaigns against the Sioux in 1863 and 1864 yet remained sensitive to their grievances. "Make them peaceable," he advised Congress after the conflict, "but don't send Indian agents and traders among them to rob them of what the Government appropriates."

struck the camps in the timber and hurried to safety. Sully launched a mounted charge up the slope, which drove the Indians to cover; then he settled down to raking the mountainside with artillery fire. At nightfall the Indians departed, abandoning large stores of food and equipment, and the fighting ended. Sully had lost five men killed and 10 wounded. He thought that he had slain 150 Indians, but the Sioux later said the figure was 31.

Rejoining the emigrants at the Heart River, Sully moved west toward the Yellowstone, crossing the desolate Badlands of the Little Missouri. It was a tortuous passage. Harassed part of the way by hundreds of Tetons, the caravan threaded through the wild, deeply eroded maze of gullies and buttes, which Sully reputedly described as "Hell with the fires burned out." Emerging from the nightmarish terrain, the expedition was beset with other hardships. Food supplies dwindled, water was scarce and there was little forage. Horses and oxen died from the alkaline water and from the absence of grass. Finally the party reached the Yellowstone, where two supply steamers were waiting.

Deterred from continuing up the Yellowstone by short provisions and by the lack of forage, Sully moved his men instead down that river to Fort Union on the Missouri. There he bid farewell to the Idaho-bound emigrants, who hired a guide to lead them up the Missouri, and made his way back to Fort Rice on the west bank of the Missouri.

The 1864 expedition had accomplished little. The Indians had been chastised at Killdeer Mountain, but the punitive war that had been started against the Santee in Minnesota had been carried far west across the Missouri and now enveloped almost all the powerful Sioux tribes.

In the autumn of 1864, the 1st U.S. Volunteers, the first of six regiments of Confederate prisoners of war recruited by the Union for duty at Western posts, arrived in St. Paul; its men were distributed to the Minnesota and Dakota forts. Some of them, under Colonel Charles A. R. Dimon, an inept 23-year-old Massachusetts protégé of General Benjamin Butler, spent a miserable winter at Fort Rice, harassed by Sioux, numbed by the frigid plains climate and decimated by disease. Before the spring of 1865, one in 10 of them had died of scurvy and diarrhea.

The newcomers' trials were the prelude to a new chapter in the West. Once more, in 1865, Pope planned expeditions against the still-unconquered Sioux. By that time, the government's difficulties in Minnesota and the Dakota Territory had merged with other conflicts with Western tribes that were rooted in the Civil War and had set the entire plains afire. At the heart of these conflicts, too, was the Indian system that had caused the costly war in Minnesota and that Lincoln did not live long enough to reform.

Moving Pictures of the Settlers' Ordeal

In September 1862, as fugitives bearing chilling tales of the Sioux uprising streamed into Rochester in eastern Minnesota, a local sign painter named John Stevens resolved to bring the calamity before the public in bold detail.

Stevens had been enthralled by panoramic travelogues of life on the Mississippi — so-called moving-picture shows in which scenes painted on a canvas strip were unwound between hand-cranked rollers and were described by a narrator. Stevens used this technique to expose what he called the "blood-thirstiness of the savages," highlighting the carnage with a "liberal use of red paint."

Stevens' finished work contained more than 30 panels, each measuring six by seven feet; 10 of the panels are reproduced on these pages. Widely exhibited in the midwest, the traveling show proved especially popular in isolated settlements like those ravaged by the Sioux. The version of the uprising it offered its rapt viewers was not without error and embellishment. Yet it drove home the lesson that the settlers of western Minnesota had learned at great cost: The frontier, for all its bounty, remained a land charged with danger.

cene from the Stevens panorama set near the of St. Peter, a farmer stands on a horse- red thresher, oblivious of an approaching war party. "The Indians came sweeping over airie as silent as death and as swift as the " the narrator intoned as this panel was dis- d. Such assaults led settlers to organize an l band — the St. Peter Frontier Avengers.

e of the attacks that devastated homesteads d Lake Shetek (*background*) on August 20, an n shoots farmer Andrew Koch as others sur- d his wife in the field beyond. The Sioux ed Mrs. Koch, and she set off through the h that fringed the lake to inform her stunned bors that her husband lay dead in the barn- "his face in the mud."

A figure identified by the narrator as a "full-blooded African" raises his tomahawk to strike a girl, whose distraught mother has already seen two of her children cut down. The scene was based loosely on charges against Joseph Godfrey, a mulatto married to an Indian at the Lower Agency. Godfrey was condemned to death by the military commission for "participation in the hostilities" but was spared after he testified against others.

A Family's Race with Death

A compelling scene in Stevens' panorama focused on the plight of the Eastlick family, whose farm on Lake Shetek was menaced by the Sioux on August 20. Warned of the danger, John and Lavina Eastlick rushed with their five children to a neighbor's house determined t make a stand. "I started barefooted, Mrs. Eastlick recalled, "with quite load of powder, shot, and lead. I was s frightened that I could hardly run." Th grim chase that ensued is detailed here

Fleeing from the oncoming Sioux, Lavina Eastlick stands at the front of a wagon wielding a branch as a whip. The settlers had abandoned a nearby house for fear the Indians would set fire to it, and now they found the overloaded wagon a liability: "We urged the horses on as fast as they could go, but did not get them off a walk. The Indians soon came so close that the men thought we had better leave the wagon."

Hidden in the grasses of a slough b the lake, men of the Eastlick party ready their muskets for use against the Sioux while the women and chi dren lie low. Lavina Eastlick *(with hand to her head at center)* was among the first hit by Sioux fire, ye she implored her husband to stay a his post: "I told him not to come to me; but if he had any chance of sho ing an Indian, to stay and shoot hin for he could not do me any good."

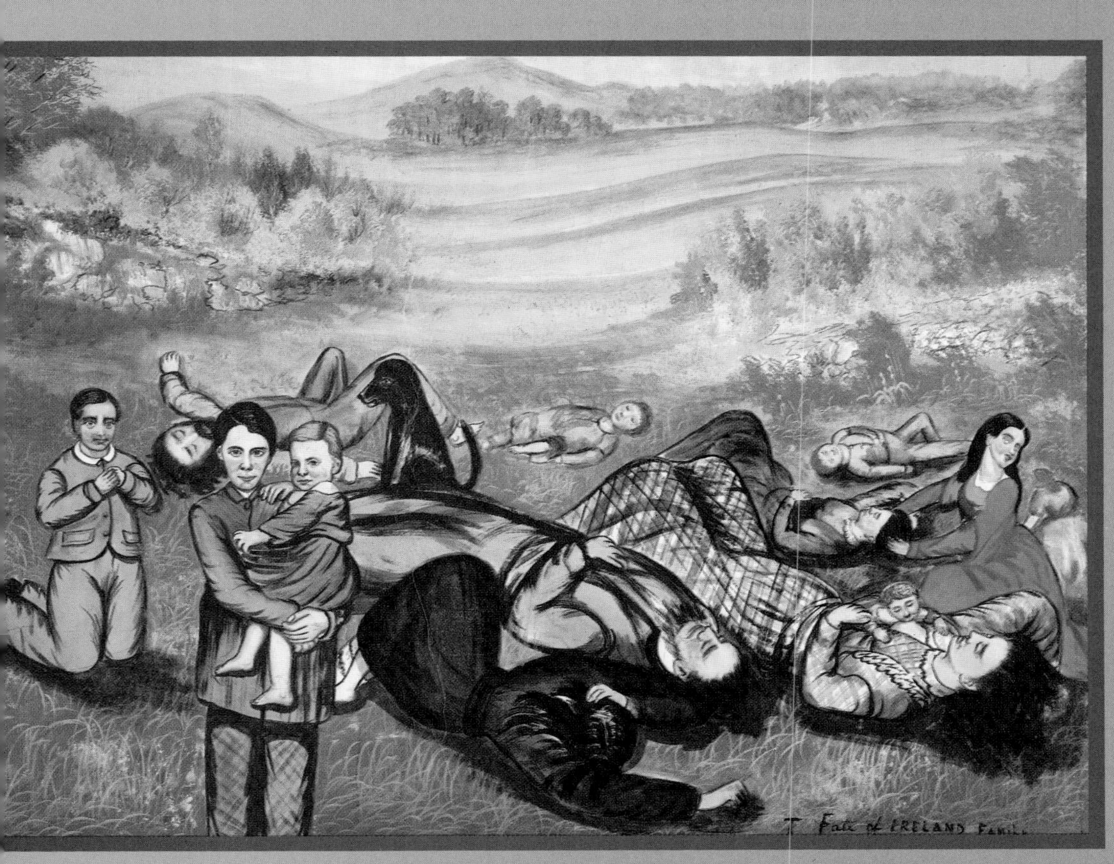

Eleven-year-old Merton Eastlick carries off his 15-month-old brother, Johnny, in the wake of the attack that claimed the lives of their father and three siblings. The infant had been entrusted to Merton by his mother *(center foreground)* before she collapsed from her wounds. She later revived to find a neighbor woman *(right foreground)* lying dead nearby with her two-year-old child asleep at her breast.

/olves menace the slumbering Eastlick boys, huddled together on the prairie. Awakening to the threat, Merton dispersed the pack and continued his trek, carrying his brother 50 miles in five days before joining their mother near New Ulm. The astlicks' ordeal had a special immediacy during one of the show's tours hrough Minnesota: Merton himself narrated and took part of the proceeds home to his widowed mother.

A single shot takes the lives of two of the Indians' captives: a woman identified as Mrs. Smith *(far right)*, the intended victim, and her daughter Julia, who threw herself in its path. The shooting was said to have occurred after a Sioux claimed the daughter for his own.

Arriving at Camp Release on September 26, General Henry Hastings Sibley meets Chief Red Iron with sword raised — a flourish added by the artist to lend an air of conflict to what was in fact a voluntary surrender of the prisoners *(background)*.

An Indian writhing on the ground portrays a victim of the Sioux as others exultantly perform a war dance witnessed by captives — among them a white woman in fanciful Indian dress *(far right)*. Several prisoners told of being made to wear "squaw garments," but at least one young woman stoutly resisted any further impositions: "They wanted to paint my face, and put rings in my ears; but I refused, and they did not insist."

The Captives' Dire Plight

For many settlers caught in the path of the hostile Sioux, the end came swiftly. But the fate of the captured women and children was less certain — as seen here in the Stevens panorama. A few were slain. Yet most survived a bewildering indoctrination, dressing like Sioux when their captors demanded it and witnessing tribal rituals. When released to General Sibley *(below)* in late September, these survivors brought back haunting glimpses of an alien culture.

A Merciless Campaign of Suppression

"As the whites are at war among themselves, you think you can now drive the whites from this country; but this reliance is false. The Great Father at Washington has men enough to drive all the Indians off the plains, and whip the rebels at the same time."

COLORADO GOVERNOR JOHN EVANS TO THE CHEYENNE

The Sioux uprising in Minnesota was only one of a score of explosive conflicts between Indians and whites that took place in the trans-Mississippi West during the Civil War. Seldom if ever was there more bloodshed on the frontier. Violence spread across the entire region, from the Kansas prairies into the Rocky Mountains, from the Dakota Territory to New Mexico. It crested in one of the worst atrocities in American history, the Sand Creek Massacre.

The clashes were rooted in the same causes that had made trouble between whites and Indians in the decade before the War and that would continue to do so for almost 30 years afterward. Prospectors and settlers — indifferent to the battles being fought between North and South or fleeing from them — flooded westward in ever-increasing numbers during the 1860s, overrunning the homelands of the native American.

Inevitably the Indians, often driven to the brink of starvation by the loss of their hunting grounds, raided the settlements and wagon trains of the westering whites. Just as inevitably, the whites demanded military protection. They received it, not from experienced U.S. Army Regulars, most of whom had been transferred East to fight the Confederates, but rather from volunteer forces hastily raised by the Western states and territories. These Western troops often fought with an extra viciousness. Restless for action and filled with tales of Indian atrocities — many of them true — they were spoiling to kill any Indian they saw, hostile or not. Their officers, both professionals and volunteers, often turned out to be Indian-hating zealots who did little to quell the violence.

Most of the Western volunteers were raised in New Mexico, Colorado, and the rough-and-tumble mining communities and brash new towns of California, already a burgeoning state of 380,000 people. Before the War ended and the Regulars returned, California would raise 17,000 volunteers — eight regiments of infantry, two of cavalry and a number of smaller units for specialized duty. No other Western state or territory came close to raising so large a force.

California recruited these troops primarily to protect its communication links with the rest of the nation — the great overland trails that snaked westward 2,000 miles across prairie, mountain and desert from such embarkation points as Atchison, Independence and Kansas City. Especially vulnerable to Indian attack were the emigrant trails that followed the Humboldt River across the desert and grassland stretches of Nevada and the mail and telegraph route farther south, where the Western Shoshone and Paiute tribes had been angered by intrusions on their lands and assaults on their people. In Utah and parts of present-day Wyoming, hungry Northern Shoshone, Bannock and Ute tribes, who had been driven from their

A pair of *cartes de visite* made at Mathew Brady's Washington studio shows California mountain man Seth Kinman and a unique gift he presented to Abraham Lincoln to demonstrate his state's fealty to the Union. Kinman had become so indignant when Eastern newspapers questioned California's loyalty that he traveled 3,000 miles from San Francisco to give the President a chair made entirely of California elk horns.

hunting grounds by Mormons and by other settlers, were raiding emigrant trains as well as ranches and stagecoach stations when the War began.

Before the California volunteers could march eastward across the mountains to protect the trails, however, they had their hands full policing their home state. One Californian in three had migrated from states in the Old South. These pro-Southern Democrats had so dominated California's prewar politics that the building used for government offices in San Francisco was jokingly called "The Virginia Poorhouse." A burst of pro-Northern enthusiasm was ignited by the news of the firing on Fort Sumter — the dispatch was brought by the famous Pony Express — and the state legislature declared California loyal to the Union. But for months afterward, rumors abounded that the dissident Southerners were plotting to capture Federal arsenals, sabotage coastal defenses, and even separate Southern California from the state and declare it part of the Confederacy.

When these alarms subsided — in large measure because hundreds of the Southern-born Californians headed East to join the Confederate armies — many of the volunteer troops were dispatched into the state's mountainous interior to try to settle minor Indian uprisings there. In some areas lawless miners had been killing the natives for sport and seizing their women for concubines. To cope with the resulting Indian reprisals, all 10 companies of the 2nd California Infantry spent 18 months marching and countermarching across 20,000 square miles of rugged mountains and redwood forests — and even then they failed to pacify the area completely.

With the California troops mainly preoccupied at home, the difficult task of guarding the trails in Nevada and Utah fell in part to the newly enlisted 11th Ohio Volunteer Cavalry, one of the very few units sent from east of the Mississippi to the Far West during the War. Commanded by a 51-year-old lieutenant colonel named William O. Collins, the greenhorn Ohioans were guided through the Rockies by the famous old mountain man, Jim Bridger. Arriving at South Pass in present-day Wyoming in the summer of 1862, they found the mail stages were abandoning the dangerous Oregon Trail in favor of the somewhat safer Overland Trail, which ran across the southern part of present-day Wyoming. But some emigrants still trudged westward along the Oregon Trail. As a result, Collins and his four companies had to guard both of the embattled routes. For a while some Kansas volunteers and two understrength companies of Regular cavalry assisted the Ohioans. But even with these reinforcements Collins' men, dispersed in small, vulnerable detachments across a vast and hostile landscape, found it virtually impossible to halt the hit-and-run raids of the Ute, Shoshone and Sioux.

The determined Collins, described by one trooper as "rather old for military service, but finely preserved, energetic and soldierly," returned to Ohio and recruited four more companies. While Collins struggled to meet the Indian menace along the transcontinental trails, units of California volunteers at last started eastward in May 1862 to join the fight. Marching out of Stockton to the strains of "The Girl I Left behind Me," seven companies of the 3rd California Infantry, commanded by a combative 42-year-old former Regular, Colonel Patrick Edward Connor, proceeded across the Sierra Nevada to Nevada. The red-whiskered and hot-tempered Connor, born in Ireland on St. Patrick's Day, 1820, had come to the United States as a child; he enlisted in the Army at the age of 19 and fought in the Seminole and Mexican Wars.

Connor's ultimate destination was Salt Lake City, almost 600 miles east of Stockton. He had been ordered to establish his base there — and, some thought, keep an eye on the Mormons, whose loyalty to the Union was in doubt. On the way, he was to erect forts that would protect the western legs of the transcontinental trails.

On August 1, 1862, Connor reached Fort Churchill in Nevada, where his small army was increased to more than 1,000 men by the addition of several companies of the 2nd California Cavalry. Leaving a company of infantry and one of cavalry at Fort Churchill, Connor moved 250 miles farther east across the desert. At Ruby Valley in eastern Nevada he halted again, building Fort Ruby to help protect the trails and the settlers in that part of the Great Basin. He then turned his attention to Salt Lake City.

Seeking quietly to assess the loyalty of the Mormons as well as to find the best location for his base, Connor left his troops at Ruby Valley, changed into civilian clothes and took an eastbound stagecoach to the Mormon capital. There he found a festering hostility between Nevada's federally appointed Territorial officials and Brigham Young. The Mormon leader and his followers fiercely resented being governed by non-Mormons. The officials for their part detested the Mormons' polygamous and theocratic society, which they considered both sinister and immoral.

Connor, who immediately decided that he, too, disliked the Mormons, did not help the situation. Returning to Fort Ruby, he left two companies of infantry to garrison the place, then marched 700 of his men toward Salt Lake and established a fort in the foothills just three miles east of the city. He named the new installation Camp Douglas — in honor of the late Senator Stephen A. Douglas of Illinois, who had once reviled the Mormons as a "pestiferous, disgusting cancer." And he mounted one of the fort's cannon so that it aimed directly — and insultingly — at the Mormon capital.

Much as he disliked the Mormons, Connor detested the Indians more. When a large number of Shoshones under a chief named Bear Hunter began raiding wagon trains and Mormon settlements in the Cache Valley and on the Bear River north of Salt Lake City, Connor himself went on the warpath.

His first move was to send an expedition led by Major Edward McGarry to the Cache

Bristling Defense on the Pacific

The onset of war transformed the Pacific Coast into a military bastion intended not only to fend off Confederate attacks but also to discourage possible invasion by a European naval force. Giving first priority to the region's most important city, San Francisco, and its gold-filled mint, the Federals mounted huge guns on Alcatraz Island and established a network of bristling coastal defenses like those at Fort Point *(below)*. In commissioning the U.S.S. *Camanche (right)*, the first modern armored warship to sail Pacific waters, Secretary of the Navy Gideon Welles late in the War acknowledged the importance of California and its gold supply to the Union. "Gold is truth," Wells declared. "Irredeemable paper and flimsy expedients are not."

Workmen put the finishing touches on the U.S.S. *Camanche*, an ironclad built to patrol California's coast. The *Camanche* suffered an inauspicious launching in January 1865 when the ship's engineers, after failing to crack a champagne bottle across her prow, sent the ship prematurely into the water — where she hit her own pier and killed a state senator.

Eight-inch columbiad guns line the stone walls of Fort Point, one of several strongholds on San Francisco Bay designed to guard against any raiding warships. During the first months of the War, when it was feared that Confederate sympathizers in the California population might assault the fort, the barrels were pointed inland.

Valley to rescue a white boy being held captive by Bear Hunter's people. After a two-hour fight, in which several Indians were killed, Bear Hunter surrendered the boy.

A week later, Connor heard that the same Indians had stolen stock from emigrants on Bear River. Again, McGarry went north. Although he captured and executed four Indians, he failed to find Bear Hunter's main band or to recover the stock.

Far more serious fighting followed in January 1863, when word arrived that Bear Hunter was attacking parties of miners coming from present-day Idaho and Montana to Salt Lake City for supplies. The troubles centered on Bear River, where the chief and his Shoshones had established a winter camp. Having made up his mind to eliminate Bear Hunter's band once and for all, Connor prepared to make a surprise attack on the encampment.

The campaign was one of the most agonizing that Federal troops ever undertook — a 140-mile trek through weather so frigid that, one soldier recalled, "whiskers and mustache were so chained together by ice that opening the mouth became most difficult." Connor first sent out a small party of 40 infantrymen with two howitzers, ordering the men to march toward Bear River by day so that Indian scouts would think they constituted the entire force coming to attack them. At sundown three days later, Connor set off with a second group, four companies of the 2nd California Cavalry. The mounted men rode through the bitter night, covering 68 miles before stopping to rest at dawn. "The sufferings," recalled one of the troopers, "can never be told in words." Many of the cavalrymen, he said, "were frozen and necessarily left behind."

The flag of the 6th California retains its bright, crisp colors because it was left safely behind in San Francisco while the regiment fought Indians in northwest California and Nevada in 1861. The troops endured the difficult campaign "with the greatest cheerfulness," wrote Brigadier General George Wright, commander of the Pacific Department, despite "hardships and exposures, amidst the snows and rains."

Nevertheless the march continued for a week, the infantry moving by day and the larger force of cavalry traveling by night. The Indians finally became aware of the advance party as it neared Bear River, and withdrawing to their camp, they prepared to put up a fight. At the site of present-day Preston, Idaho, the cavalry passed the infantry and at dawn on January 29 reached the river opposite the Indian encampment.

Bear Hunter had chosen a strong position — a ravine 40 feet wide with steep banks up to 12 feet high. The Indians had cut steps in the embankments from which, concealed behind piles of intertwined willow branches, they could fire across the open plain that lay between themselves and the river.

When Connor's California troopers appeared on the far bank, a number of warriors ran forward, daring the horsemen to ford the river and fight. Connor obliged them, ordering Major McGarry and the cavalry to cross the stream and surround the camp. It was no easy task: The river was high and full of floating ice. Once on the other side McGarry, believing it impracticable to surround

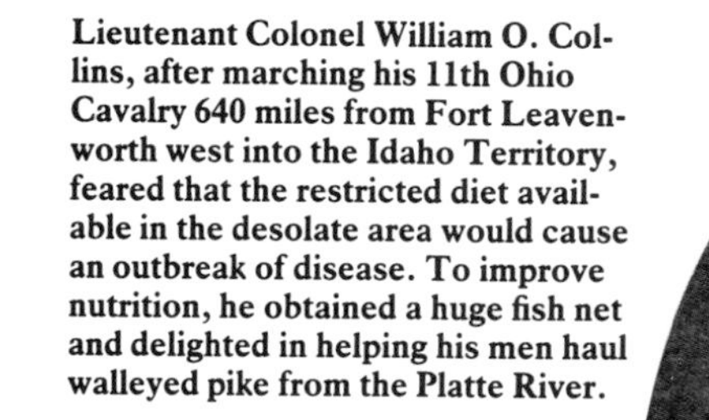

Lieutenant Colonel William O. Collins, after marching his 11th Ohio Cavalry 640 miles from Fort Leavenworth west into the Idaho Territory, feared that the restricted diet available in the desolate area would cause an outbreak of disease. To improve nutrition, he obtained a huge fish net and delighted in helping his men haul walleyed pike from the Platte River.

A sketch by Lieutenant Caspar Wever Collins, who served with his father's cavalry, shows Sweetwater Station, one of the forts built by the Ohioans in the Idaho Territory. At lower left, a soldier returns from hunting, one of the few diversions at the remote outpost.

Sweetwater Station Idh. Ter.

the Indians, dismounted his men and immediately launched a frontal attack across the open plain. A fusillade from the Shoshones felled many of his men and brought the attack to a halt.

Connor next ordered McGarry and some of his cavalrymen to turn the Indians' left flank. Connor then sent the infantry across the river and around the Indians' right flank. This tactic worked. Having successfully surrounded the camp, the Californians closed in and gained the ravine.

With that the battle became a slaughter. Yelling wildly, the Californians leaped on the Indians, engaging them in hand-to-hand fighting. Bear Hunter's people tried to flee, but many were killed as they scrambled among the trees along the river or attempted to swim the icy stream.

Four hours after it had begun, the fight was over. Bear Hunter was dead, along with an estimated 250 members of his band, including some women and children. A few Indians escaped; about 160 women and children were taken prisoner. Several Mormons who had accompanied the troops later reported that some of the Californians went around the battlefield killing the wounded "by knocking them in the head with an axe." Connor, whose casualties totaled 21 killed and 42 wounded out of the 200 men who had been engaged, left the surviving Indian women and children in the camp with a small supply of food and headed back toward Salt Lake City.

Grateful for what had been done, Mormons along the way aided the wounded and welcomed the freezing soldiers into the warmth of their homes. The settlers in Cache Valley, freed from fear of Bear Hunter's Shoshones, praised Connor's success as an intervention of the Almighty.

Promoted to brigadier general for his victory, the implacable Connor kept pressure on the Shoshone, Bannock, Ute and Paiute, sometimes merely threatening them, sometimes routing them in clashes that cost the Indians severe casualties and losses of food and property. One by one, the bands concluded that they had had enough. In a series of treaty councils during the summer and fall of 1863, Connor and Utah's Superintendent of Indian Affairs, James D. Doty, persuaded them to end their hostility and settle on reservations. Although the peace was tenuous and raids continued sporadically, Connor and Doty optimistically informed the Overland Mail Company in October, "All routes of travel through Utah Territory to Nevada and California, and to the Beaver Head and Boise River gold mines, may now be used with safety."

In Salt Lake City, meanwhile, Connor and the Territorial officers had feuded so vehemently with the Mormons that an armed clash seemed to be in the making. The crisis blew over only when President Lincoln replaced the undiplomatic officials, naming as governor the mild and inoffensive Indian Superintendent, James Doty. The last tensions evaporated when Major General Irvin McDowell, who in July 1864 took command of the Department of the Pacific in San Francisco, toned down Connor's belligerency, warning him that it was "the course of true patriotism for you not to embark on any hostilities." Connor accepted McDowell's counsel, and gradually adopting a more amicable attitude toward Brigham Young and his followers, he turned his formidable energies in a more peaceful — and profitable — direction. With the aid of the many California miners in his command, Connor developed a number of silver mines in Bingham Canyon, 25 miles southwest of Salt Lake City, erecting a smelter and forming several mining companies.

While Connor and his men suppressed the Indians in Utah, another group of California volunteers had been embroiled with Indians several hundred miles away in the southwest. These were the troops under Colonel James Carleton who had arrived too late to help repulse the Confederate invasion of the New Mexico Territory in 1862. The Indian trouble had begun when Carleton's men, marching eastward across the Territory from Southern California, had encountered Apaches, perhaps the most feared warriors on the continent.

Separated into many independent bands, the Apache dwelled in the harsh mountains and deserts of south central New Mexico and farther east beyond the Rio Grande. Fierce combatants and in some cases expert horsemen, they had preyed for generations on Spaniards, Mexicans and rival Indians alike.

Colonel Patrick Edward Connor, ordered to Utah to settle a possible Mormon revolt, called Salt Lake City a "community of traitors, fanatics, murderers and whores." In time, however, Connor developed a grudging respect for the Mormon leader, Brigham Young; once when Young faced a court action, Connor agreed to pay his $100,000 bail.

At first they had been friendly to American pioneers, but when increasing numbers of prospectors, ranchers and U.S. troops moved into their country following the gold strikes of the 1850s, the Apache launched a series of savage reprisals. When the Regular troops withdrew from their forts in the area in 1861, the Apache decided to rid their ancestral lands of all outsiders.

Carleton's troops first ran into these Indians at Apache Pass, site of an important spring and an abandoned stage station. There a band of Chiricahua Apaches led by the powerful chief Cochise killed two couriers Carleton had sent ahead to alert Colonel Edward Canby, Federal commander in New Mexico, that reinforcements were on the way. The year before, the Army had made an unappeasable enemy of Cochise by trying to seize him during a parley in the mistaken belief that he had been involved in a raid against a white rancher. Cochise escaped and went on a killing spree; the troops in return hanged six of his people, including his brother and two of his nephews.

Cochise was not finished with Carleton's men. A few days after the murder of the couriers, Cochise's snipers picked off three members of an advance reconnaissance group. Three weeks after that, a large Chiricahua war party ambushed elements of the 1st California Infantry led by Captain Thomas L. Roberts, who were traveling as Carleton's advance guard. In a fierce battle among the rocks in Apache Pass, two more Californians were killed and several wounded. Only after two days of intermittent fighting did the Californians' howitzer fire induce the Apaches to withdraw.

Arriving at Apache Pass with his main column, Carleton ordered the troops to build a post, later named Fort Bowie, to protect the road and the pass's vital spring. Then, leaving 100 men to garrison the new fort, Carleton continued to the Rio Grande. On September 18, 1862, promoted to brigadier general, he succeeded Canby as commander of the Department of New Mexico and took over the headquarters in Santa Fe.

With the Confederates in retreat across Texas, Carleton could turn his entire attention to the Indians, especially the Mescalero Apache, who were proving an even greater threat than Cochise's Chiricahuas. A veteran of several prewar Indian campaigns, Carleton had become convinced that the best policy was not to make peace treaties or even to conduct talks with any hostiles. Instead, he believed they should be fought without mercy until they surrendered. Then they should be placed in reservations where they

Colonel James Carleton found it "indispensably necessary" to establish this Federal post at Apache Pass in July 1862 to prevent Indians from ambushing the travelers who stopped to draw water from its spring. Named Fort Bowie in honor of a popular colonel of the 5th California, its garrison for years escorted wagon trains and stagecoaches through the perilous Apache country.

could become Christians and be turned into peaceful farmers.

Ruthless in his determination to tame the Mescalero and the other southwestern bands, Carleton ordered into the field nine companies of troopers — four from his own Californian regiments and five from the 1st New Mexico Cavalry, now commanded by Kit Carson. Carleton's instructions were blunt and stern: "There is to be no council held with the Indians nor any talks. The men are to be slain whenever and wherever they can be found." Should the Indians beg for peace, he went on, "their chiefs and 20 of their principal men must come to Santa Fe to have a talk here; but tell them fairly and frankly that you will keep after their people and slay them until you receive orders to desist from these headquarters."

Carson, an old frontiersman who understood the Indians' culture and thinking, considered the orders too extreme and told Carleton so. He could, he said, control the Mescalero and the other Apaches by more humane methods. The Indians most of all needed food. In the 1850s, the Army had forced them to live in an area almost devoid of resources other than game — and white inroads since then had driven away most of the antelope, elk and deer. Rations supplied by the Army had ceased when Canby's troops abandoned Fort Stanton in

1861. Although Mescaleros had killed and captured a number of settlers since that time, the principal objectives of their raids had been horses, cattle and grain.

Carleton listened to Carson's arguments but brushed them aside. The Indians were to be attacked and killed until the tribes surrendered. Loyal to his commander, Carson entered the Mescalero country east of the Rio Grande and reactivated Fort Stanton. The appearance of the troops alarmed the Indians, many of whom fled south into the Sacramento and Guadalupe Mountains. Others soon streamed into the fort to ask for peace.

Nevertheless, the fighting and killing continued. One company of New Mexico scouts under Captain James (Paddy) Graydon, the veteran of Canby's force who had used mules in an unsuccessful attempt to blow up the Confederate camp at Valverde, met a Mescalero group led by Manuelito, the tribe's most influential chief. The Indians were on their way to Santa Fe to surrender, but Graydon's men ignored Manuelito's signs for peace. They opened fire, gunning down Manuelito and 11 of his companions.

A second confrontation occurred when some of Carleton's California troops under Captain William McCleave, coming up from the south, attacked and defeated a band of about 100 Mescaleros in Dog Canyon, southwest of Fort Stanton. The survivors, including three chiefs, made their way to the fort and surrendered to Carson, who sent the leaders to see Carleton in Santa Fe.

By the end of November, Carleton had refined his plan for pacifying the Indians. He built a new post, called Fort Sumner, in the arid plains country on the Pecos River, far east of the white settlements on the Rio Grande, and decreed that all Indians who surrendered would live near this isolated post. His army would feed the refugees, Carleton said, until they could grow their own food. Those who did not surrender and go to Fort Sumner would be hunted down.

Carleton's promise of food for the Indian families ended the so-called Mescalero war. While a number of the tribespeople evaded the troops and escaped westward or into Mexico, about 400 Mescaleros settled at Fort Sumner under the guns of some of Carleton's soldiers. They dug irrigation canals and attempted to raise crops in a 15-mile strip along the Pecos River. Insects, floods and burning summer temperatures frustrated most of their efforts, and they became almost entirely dependent on government rations.

No sooner had Carleton arranged this dubious solution to the Mescalero problem than he found that other Apaches, the Mimbreño, led by Chief Mangas Coloradas, were spreading terror among miners and settlers from the Rio Grande to Pinos Altos, south of the Gila River, the site of some rich gold mines. The frightened miners, in fact, had all but evacuated Pinos Altos.

Carleton moved to rid the gold fields of the Mimbreño. He ordered Brigadier General Joseph R. West — field commander of the California volunteers now that Carleton was head of the New Mexico Department — to establish a post near Pinos Altos and wage the same kind of war against Mangas Coloradas that Carson had been conducting against the Mescalero.

West sent out an advance company of the 1st California Cavalry under Captain E. D. Shirland. What happened next remains the subject of contradictory reports. The most widely accepted version was that of a prospector named Daniel Ellis Conner, one of several miners in the Pinos Altos area who were trying to get past the Mimbreño to hunt for gold farther west. According to Conner, a mountain man named Joseph Walker, the prospectors' guide, concocted a scheme to seize Mangas Coloradas, who was in a winter camp nearby, and force the chief to allow the white men to travel across the mountains in safety. Walker and his group approached the Mimbreño camp under a white flag, lured the elderly chief away and then took him prisoner at gunpoint.

The prospectors took their captive to Fort McLane, a little-used outpost, where they found General West and the main body of California troops. West took charge of Mangas Coloradas, warning him that if he tried to escape, "his life would be the immediate forfeit." But what West really wanted, it seems clear, was for the guards to kill the chief during the night — which they evidently did. During Daniel Conner's turn at sentinel duty about midnight, as he later wrote, he saw the guards applying heated bayonets to the chief's legs and feet. When Mangas Coloradas could stand the torture no longer and pulled away, they shot him dead.

West followed up with aggressive attacks on the Mimbreño camps, killing members of the dead chief's family and inflicting heavy losses on his followers. When the survivors fled into the mountains, West sent companies of troops after them, hunting down and wiping out the small, scattered groups.

Angry Apache warriors struck back elsewhere, raiding settlements and forts along the Rio Grande. Yet the Apache, under constant harassment, lost such a great number of their people from fighting as well as from hunger and disease that they eventually sent a message asking to discuss peace. Implacable as ever, Carleton's answer to the Indians' request was that they would have to go to the Fort Sumner reservation. The Apache, unwilling to be confined in the barren strip along the Pecos River, resumed their raids.

At this point Michael Steck, the Territory's Indian Superintendent, already furious at Carleton's autocratic usurpation of the management of Indian affairs and his

The Indian fighting of bearded Captain William McCleave, seen above with other officers of the 1st California Cavalry, was interrupted in 1862 when he and a small unit blundered into a remote Confederate outpost near Tucson and were captured. McCleave and his men were soon released in a prisoner exchange.

olonel James Carleton, already own as a fierce Indian fighter when e Civil War began, regarded Indis as little more than a species of ld game. "An Indian is a more tchful and a more wary animal than leer," Carleton once said. "He ist be hunted with skill."

uncompromising Indian policy, complained vehemently to his superiors in the Interior Department. He had already forwarded letters and petitions from others in New Mexico, blaming the continued Apache raids on Carleton. But Washington turned a deaf ear and backed Carleton.

After the death of Mangas Coloradas, Walker's prospectors had made their way westward and had struck gold near the present site of Prescott in central Arizona, which had become a separate territory in February of 1863. The news excited Carleton, who promised to send troops to ensure that the new mining district was secure. That October he created the Military District of Northern Arizona, including all of the Territory north of the Gila River, and dispatched three companies of California volunteers to the mines, where they set up Fort Whipple.

Within months, aggressions by miners and the volunteers had stirred up local bands of Yavapais and Western Apaches. Their retaliatory raids soon had the miners petitioning for the "utter extermination of the ruthless savages who have so long prevented the settlement and development of the Territory." A private group of Indian fighters, led by one of Walker's assistant guides but fed by the Army and accompanied occasionally by California volunteers, campaigned relentlessly against the Yavapai and Apache, destroying settlements and killing dozens of the Indians. One device these vigilantes used was to lure the village chiefs into meetings with offers of tobacco and pinole, a favorite food made of sweetened flour. Then the whites either gunned down the Indians or poisoned them by mixing strychnine with the pinole.

Despite such tactics, the Indian raids went on, and many miners and settlers left Prescott. Farther south near Tucson, other Apaches, including Cochise's Chiricahuas, had continued their attacks against ranchers, miners and travelers using the Southern Overland route to California. By May 1864, Carleton was forced to recognize that all of southern Arizona was unsafe.

Undaunted by the evident failure of his policies, Carleton prepared what was to be "a general rising of both citizens and soldiers" against the Apache and Yavapai. A force of 500 men of the 1st and 5th California Infantry, 1st New Mexico Infantry and 1st California Cavalry would enter Arizona, marching west from Las Cruces on the Rio Grande, and pursue the hostile bands. Other detachments already stationed in Arizona would comb different areas in similar operations.

Miners, friendly Pima and Maricopa Indians and "every citizen of the Territory who has a rifle" would be sent out in additional parties. Even the Mexican Governors of Sonora and Chihuahua were urged to hunt down any Indians who sought safety south of the border.

Carleton's offensive, conducted vigorously through the summer and fall of 1864, was ineffective. After an early victory, in which Californians destroyed an Apache band in the Mescal Mountains, the various columns spent most of their time struggling through mountain passes and across deserts in stifling heat. By late autumn, with the enlistment terms of many of the California companies coming to an end, Carleton suspended the campaign. His troops, wrote a Tucson resident, had only enraged the Indians "without breaking their spirit." Similar campaigns would be mounted against the elusive Apache for many years after the Civil War.

One tribe whose spirit Carleton did crush was the Navajo, who lived in the largely unexplored high desert of northeastern Arizona and northwestern New Mexico. Essentially a pastoral people who tended gardens, orchards and large flocks of sheep and goats, the tribe also boasted ferocious warriors. For generations they had made war on other tribes along the Rio Grande. Efforts by the U.S. Army to end their forays had been interrupted by the Civil War, and when Carleton arrived in Santa Fe in 1862 he found the Navajo raiding white settlements as well as the encampments of rival tribes.

Carleton sent four companies of New Mexico volunteer troops under Lieutenant Colonel J. Francisco Chavez to build Fort Wingate near present-day Gallup, New Mexico, on the edge of Navajo country. Alarmed by the troops' arrival, as well as by reports of Carleton's severe treatment of the Mescalero tribe, leaders of a peace group among the Navajo twice traveled to Santa Fe to meet with the district commander. But Carleton stubbornly informed the emissaries that if they wanted to discuss peace they would have to surrender and go to Fort Sumner with the Mescalero.

The Navajo refused and on June 23, 1863, Carleton sent them a final warning through Colonel Chavez: "Tell them they can have until the twentieth day of July of this year to come in." After that date, he added, "every Navajo that is seen will be considered as hostile and treated accordingly."

Carleton meant what he said. With the Mescalero campaign concluded, he was able to send Colonel Carson and nine companies of the 1st New Mexico Cavalry to establish Fort Canby inside Navajo country. From there Carson, still following Carleton's orders, conducted a series of far-ranging searches for Navajos, killing small groups here and there and systematically seizing or destroying the Navajos' crops, livestock, blankets and other possessions. Most of the Navajo managed to stay out of sight of the troops, but the loss of their food supplies, coupled with unrelenting pressure that kept them constantly on the move, gradually undermined their morale.

Aware of the Navajos' plight, Carleton prepared a decisive blow. He ordered Carson to attack the Indians' principal stronghold at Canyon de Chelly, a Y-shaped canyon with sheer walls up to 1,000 feet high. The Navajo, who considered the place sacred, lived along its rims and also maintained hogans, gardens and peach orchards on the canyon floor. On January 6, 1864, at the head of 389 men, Carson set off across the high, snow-covered country for the canyon's western entrance. Simultaneously another officer, Captain Albert H. Pfeiffer, led two companies toward the eastern entrance. Six days later, Carson reached the canyon, where one of his patrols skirmished with some Navajos and killed 11 of them.

After three days of exploring the canyon's rims in a vain attempt to discover a route down, Carson returned to its western entrance — and found Pfeiffer and his men waiting for him. They had traversed the length of the canyon, running into no opposition except for a few shouting Navajos who had ineffectually rained arrows and rocks on them from places along the rim. Carson had missed seeing Pfeiffer's men, probably because they had come down the Canyon del Muerto, the more distant branch of the Y.

The following morning, 60 Navajos surrendered, explaining, said Carson, that "they are in a complete state of starvation, and that many of their women and children have already died from this cause." Carson ordered two companies to march back through the canyon and destroy the Indians' hogans and peach orchards; then he returned with his command and the prisoners to Fort Canby. On the way, many more Navajos, facing starvation and convinced they could no longer contend with Carson's troops, also gave up. In three weeks, almost 3,000 Navajos surrendered, and by mid-March the number had doubled. Altogether, more than 8,000 Indians, almost three fourths of the tribe, came in.

Surrender did not end the Navajos' suffering, however. Carleton ordered them removed to remote Fort Sumner, a trek of 400 miles. Many of the Indians died during this agonizing Long Walk, which subjected

Enemies More Deadly than Combat

Of the hundreds of California soldiers who lost their lives during the Civil War, relatively few died while engaged in battle. In the sparsely populated states and territories of the trans-Mississippi West, boredom and loneliness proved to be virulent enemies — and the ones less easily conquered than hostile Indians or Confederates.

An alarming number of soldiers stationed in such isolated places as Skull Valley, in the Arizona Territory, and Mad River, California, chose to take their own lives; others died from self-inflicted wounds that officially were ruled accidental. Shooting and stabbing deaths were a common result of brawls with fellow soldiers, who in their turn were subject to death sentences at their courts martial.

The causes of other soldiers' deaths remain mysteriously enigmatic. Private Frank Urebecker of the 1st Veteran Infantry, for example, was found dead of "accidental suffocation," and Private George Howard of the 5th Veteran Infantry succumbed to "softening of the brain." These deaths, recorded by little more than a gravestone similar to the one at left and by a succinct notation entered on the company rolls, sounded a note heard all too frequently in the reports of the California volunteers — the unmistakable cry of despair.

Plunging walls of red sandstone dominate Canyon de Chelly, a citadel of the Navajo where Carson's expedition in January 1864 led to the capture or surrender of 8,000 Indians. One of those who escaped was Manuelito *(above)*, a great chief who for years kept just ahead of pursuing soldiers. "I will not leave my country," Manuelito said. "I intend to die here."

them to starvation, disease and exposure.

The New Mexicans saluted Carleton and Carson for delivering them from the Navajo. Superintendent Steck, however, objected to placing the tribe on the reservation around Fort Sumner, which lacked food to support the 400 Mescaleros already there. Although Carleton refused to listen to him, Steck was proved right. Despite the expenditure of large sums and the imposition of emergency measures — Carleton for a time put his own troops on half rations to provide extra food for the reservation — the Army could scarcely feed all the Indians. When a measles epidemic struck down members of both tribes in November 1865, the Mescalero decided that they had had enough of the overcrowded reservation. They fled to hiding places in the mountains.

Word of the Navajos' scandalous situation did not reach Washington until after the War. In 1868, a year after Carleton's departure from New Mexico, the tribe's ordeal was ended. Following a visit of inquiry by General William Tecumseh Sherman, who was shocked to find the Navajos "sunk into a condition of absolute poverty and despair," the Indians were permitted to return to their Arizona homeland, where a reservation was created for them.

While the War lasted, however, the team of Carleton and Carson continued to go after other Indians. Their next targets were bands of Kiowas and Comanches, some of the ablest horsemen on the plains, who had continued their prewar habit of attacking wagon trains and stealing livestock along the Santa Fe Trail. From camps in the Texas Panhandle, their war bands terrorized ranchers and settlers as far away as southeastern Colorado and southwestern Kansas.

The outbursts alarmed Carleton, who could not allow his Missouri-New Mexico supply line to be cut. When the Indians temporarily gave up raiding in the fall of 1864 to prepare for the winter by hunting buffalo in the Panhandle, Carleton struck. He dispatched Kit Carson with about 400 men and two mountain howitzers to give the Kiowas and Comanches "a severe drubbing." Carson's force included 75 Ute warriors, who had been promised food for their families for joining the expedition.

At dawn on November 25, Carson fell on a

Kiowa Apache village of about 170 lodges. The surprised Indians put up a fight long enough for their women and children to get away, then, still resisting, they retreated down the Canadian River with Carson's men in close pursuit.

Now it was Carson's turn to be surprised. As his troops reached Adobe Wall — the crumbling ruins of an abandoned trading post — they halted abruptly at the appearance of more than a thousand Comanches who streamed from a large nearby village to reinforce the Kiowa Apaches.

Dismounting at the ruins, Carson's men deployed as skirmishers in the tall grass and, with the help of their howitzers, held off the Indians for several hours. But as more and more Comanches arrived, even the stalwart Carson grew worried. Remounting his men, he began a fighting retreat.

What followed was one of the most dramatic running gun battles — and eventual escapes — in the annals of the West. The Indians tried to stop Carson by setting fire to the prairie grass and riding up close to the column, concealed in clouds of smoke. The troops countered by starting fires of their own that hid their movements and enabled them to move safely away.

Shortly before sundown, Carson and his men had retreated to the village they had attacked that morning. Here they stood and fought until their howitzers drove the Apaches and Comanches out of range. Given a little breathing room, Carson seized evidence of the tribes' depredations — including the clothing of white women and children — and then ordered his troops to put the torch to the village, creating bonfires of tepees, wagons, buffalo robes, gunpowder

Under armed guard, resettled Navajos use adobe bricks to construct living quarters at Fort Sumner, in the remote Bosque Redondo region of the New Mexico Territory. When completed, the structures were occupied by Union soldiers; the Indians themselves lived in makeshift hogans.

and stores of dried meat and berries. The Indians pressed their attack no further, and Carson's troops slipped away, thankful to have escaped annihilation.

Carson's aborted campaign was the last engineered during the Civil War by Carleton — who was widely critized then and later for his stewardship of New Mexico as well as for his brutal handling of the Indians. He had come close to establishing a military dictatorship in Santa Fe, fighting Territorial officials, intimidating the judiciary and flouting civil liberties. The only thing he had earned, observed the *Weekly New Mexican,* was "the detestation and contempt of almost the entire population of the Territory." Carleton had broken the Navajo and had diminished the raiding by other tribes. Yet his critics contended that his most positive achievement was to call in question the Army's entire policy toward the Indians, which led to at least slightly more humane procedures in the postwar years.

No less harsh than Carleton in dealing with the Indians was another autocrat, John Evans, the wartime Governor of Colorado. Evans had made a fortune in railroads and real estate — the Chicago suburb of Evanston, Illinois, is named for him — and about the time the Civil War began he went west to Denver, seeking new fields to conquer. His driving ambition was to see the first transcontinental railroad run through his adopted city and to have Colorado as a result emerge as a thriving state.

Evans found his ambitions thwarted, however, by Indians who blocked the Union Pacific's proposed route across the Great Plains. His initial efforts to clear the Indians from the area produced only bitter fruit — savage warfare across portions of all the trails to the West.

The problems with the Plains Indians dated in large measure from February 1861, when fast-talking government agents had tricked some of the more peaceful chiefs of the southern bands of Cheyennes and Arapahos into signing a new treaty. The agreement bound the Indians to move onto a small, arid reservation near Fort Wise in southeastern Colorado that was virtually void of water and game and to relinquish claim to the rest of their huge territory between the Platte and Arkansas Rivers.

The chiefs soon saw they had been hoodwinked and, ignoring the new reservation where they realized their people would starve, continued to hunt wherever the buffalo roamed. Moreover, other Cheyenne and Arapaho bands from northern Colorado had not signed the treaty and refused to do so.

Evans believed that if Colorado were to prosper, he would have to force the Cheyenne and Arapaho to live on the land set aside in the treaty. The 1862 uprising of the Eastern Sioux in Minnesota added urgency to his efforts. Many Colorado settlers became convinced that a general war with the Plains tribes was imminent, and they pressed Evans to get the Indians isolated and under guard with all possible speed.

In the summer of 1863, Evans sent emissaries to all the Cheyenne and Arapaho bands, inviting them to a new treaty council on September 1 on the Arikaree Fork of the Republican River. The wary Indians refused to attend, sending word that they regarded all treaties with whites as swindles. Moreover, they were angered at the recent killing of a drunken Cheyenne by a sentinel at Fort Larned in Kansas. "The white man's hands

An oil painting executed immediately after the Civil War by the well-known Western artist William Cary shows Indian warriors armed with clubs and lances swooping down on an unprotected wagon train making the overland passage to the West. Hundreds of emigrants were killed in such attacks during the war years.

were dripping with their blood, and now he calls them to make a treaty," one of Evans' emissaries was told by a trader.

Despite their resentment, most of the Cheyenne and Arapaho spent the summer and fall of 1863 harmlessly hunting buffalo. Except for a few depredations by "single bands and small parties," Evans conceded, the Indians were peaceful.

But then Evans received a report from a white man who lived among the Indians that all the Plains tribes were combining for war the next spring. The informant was unreliable, but Evans and other prominent Colorado citizens concluded that the only answer was a final showdown with the Indians. One of those urging Evans on was the hero of the 1862 Battle of Glorieta Pass, the former preacher John M. Chivington, who had recently brought his 1st Colorado Volunteers back from New Mexico. Now a colonel, Chivington had been given command of the Military District of Colorado.

Evans and Chivington needed only a provocation, and in April 1864 they found one. Along the South Platte east of Denver, small groups of Cheyenne warriors made off with some livestock. Colorado volunteers immediately took to the field, with orders from Chivington to "kill Cheyennes wherever and whenever found." Attacking Cheyennes indiscriminately, they recovered some cattle, but they also burned peaceful camps, attacked guiltless bands, and killed an important peace-minded Cheyenne chief named Lean Bear, who rode out from his village to greet the soldiers in friendship and was blasted off his horse.

Among the chiefs who tried to keep peace with the white man during the Civil War were Spotted Tail *(left)*, a Sioux, and Little Raven *(below)*, an Arapaho. Little Raven once struck down two of his own braves with a war club rather than allow them to brawl with whites. "He wanted to take a gun and shoot them," reported one of a group of witnesses to the incident, "but we wouldn't let him."

Several bands of vengeful Cheyenne and Sioux warriors struck back almost at once, with raids in Kansas and along the Platte River. Evans of course took this as proof that he had been right all along. He wrote to Major General Samuel Curtis, the commander at Fort Leavenworth, urging him to send back the Colorado volunteers that Curtis was planning to use to fight the Confederates in Arkansas.

An experienced officer, Curtis suspected Evans' alarm was unfounded and sent his inspector general, Major T. I. McKenny, to find out what was going on in Colorado. McKenny concluded first that no general Indian uprising had taken place, and second, that if trouble was brewing, it was the fault of white "scouting parties that are roaming over the country, who do not know one tribe from another and who kill anything in the shape of an Indian."

War with the Indians was closer, however, than McKenny knew. Several days before he reported to General Curtis, a group of four Arapahos had murdered a ranch hand named Nathan Hungate, his wife and their two young daughters. The Hungates' mutilated bodies were brought into Denver in a wagon and put on public display, arousing the citizens to a frenzy of fear and anger. Evans chose that moment to declare war on the tribes. Hoping to separate friendly Indians from hostile ones, he spread the word that any Indian who wanted to remain at peace should go to certain designated forts to avoid "being killed through mistake."

Evans' offer came too late. The rising tension had contributed to other confrontations, and there were few friendly Indians left in the region. One incident involved a drunken commander at Fort Larned who fired on a peaceful band of Southern Arapahos led by Left Hand, a long-time friend of the whites who had labored hard to avoid war. Another was provoked by Brigadier General Robert B. Mitchell, the commander of the District of Nebraska, who summoned

The order of Colorado Governor John Evans *(below)* to "kill and destroy all hostile Indians" was fervently carried out by Colonel John Chivington *(right)* of the 1st Colorado Volunteers. Chivington, a former clergyman, once declared that he "believed it to be right and honorable to use any means under God's heaven to kill Indians that would kill women and children."

Spotted Tail and Bad Wound, two peacefully inclined Sioux chieftains, and imperiously ordered them to keep their people away from the buffalo-hunting grounds in the Platte Valley even though the land was still legally the Indians'. When the Sioux warriors ignored Mitchell's dictum and continued both to hunt and to raid, he sent troops to track them down.

One after another, like firecrackers on a string, the tribes became inflamed. By July 1864 a general uprising of Cheyennes, Arapahos, Sioux, Kiowas, Comanches and Kiowa Apaches had begun, and the war that Governor Evans had started was raging out of control. The southern bands raided the Santa Fe Trail, some settlements along the Arkansas River and scattered points in Kansas on the Saline, Solomon and Republican Rivers. On the main Platte and its southern fork, which led to Denver, Sioux, Cheyennes and Arapahos attacked stagecoaches and wagon trains, burned ranches and stage stations, and murdered scores of people. Hundreds of settlers fled in terror to the relative safety of the forts. By mid-August the Indians had stopped all traffic on the Overland Trail along the South Platte, and for six weeks Denver was cut off and its inhabitants were in danger of starvation.

Despite the summer's alarms, Chivington and Evans had found time for politics, leading the move for Colorado statehood that would benefit both of them. Chivington was nominated for Congress; Evans expected to be named a senator. But their ambitions seemed in peril when, with the approach of autumn, the various Indian bands began to lose their passion for raiding and turned to hunting buffalo for winter meat. As the raids slackened, Black Kettle, a peace-minded Cheyenne, and other chiefs who had opposed the summer's violence regained their influence. After a council, the chiefs dispatched messengers to Major Edward Wynkoop, commander at Fort Lyon, the former Fort Wise, offering to end hostilities. Leaving Fort Lyon, Wynkoop and 130 men of the 1st Colorado met Black Kettle, Left Hand and other Southern Cheyenne and Arapaho chiefs on September 10 along the Smoky Hill River. After convincing Wynkoop of their sincerity, the Indians turned over four white captives, and Black Kettle and six other leaders accompanied Wynkoop to Denver to try to arrange a peace with Evans.

The arrival of the chiefs put Evans and Chivington in an awkward position. Peace would antagonize the population, which was crying for retribution. Moreover, a new regiment of 100-day volunteers, the 3rd Colorado Cavalry, recruited largely from the refuse of Denver's saloons, was spoiling for a fight. And a temporary settlement, many Coloradans feared, would leave the tribes free to raid again the next spring.

At a council with Black Kettle's delegation

Chiefs and Federal officers appear together after the Camp Weld peace council of September 28, 1864, although little accord was reached. "The council," wrote Major Edward Wynkoop of the 1st Colorado Cavalry *(left, kneeling)*, "was divided, undecided and could not come to an understanding among themselves."

at Camp Weld near Denver on September 28, Evans and Chivington spoke ambiguously. Telling the Indians that peace was now a matter for the military, Evans turned responsibility over to Chivington, who said that when the Indians were ready to do so, they could give themselves up to Major Wynkoop at Fort Lyon. Since they had already offered to do just that, the chiefs — and Wynkoop — left the council satisfied that a peace had been made.

But Chivington, driven by his political ambitions, had developed a contempt for ethical and legal restraints. Behaving as though he were accountable to no one, he combined a malevolent lust for power with a self-righteous religious fervor. Assuring the people of Colorado that no peace with the Indians had been made, he soon set off to make war on the Arapaho and Cheyenne.

These Indians, led by Black Kettle, Left Hand and Little Raven, had settled peacefully at Fort Lyon. There Wynkoop's successor in command of the fort, a practical young major named Scott Anthony, had persuaded the Cheyenne and Arapaho to feed themselves by hunting buffalo some distance from the fort, near Sand Creek.

Major Anthony's move set the stage for a disaster. Learning that the Indians were preoccupied with hunting, Chivington prepared his restless 3rd Colorado Cavalry for action. Cloaking his movements in secrecy, he dispatched a column commanded by an ambitious, Indian-hating politician from Denver named George L. Shoup and joined the expedition before its arrival at Fort Lyon on November 28. His men, Chivington announced, were going to attack the unsuspecting bands at Sand Creek. When a number of the officers at the fort argued strenuously that this would violate pledges they had given, Chivington responded furiously, damning "any man that was in sympathy with Indians" and warning that such individuals "had better get out of the United States service."

That same night, Chivington and Anthony left the fort with 700 members of the 1st and 3rd Colorado volunteers, including 125 of the fort's garrison, and a battery of four mountain howitzers. By dawn they reached a ridge above Black Kettle's village on Sand Creek, where 500 Southern Cheyennes, as well as Left Hand and about 50 of his Arapahos, lay sleeping.

As Chivington deployed his men for the assault, letting them know that he wanted no prisoners, the Indians came awake. Black Kettle could not believe what was happening. He tied an American flag and a white flag to the end of a lodgepole and held it in the air in front of his tepee, shouting to his frightened people that the troops would not harm them. Moments later, the Coloradans advanced toward the village at a rapid trot. Gathering speed, some veered off to seize the Indians' pony herd on the south side of the creek. Shoup's wild, shouting mob of cavalry volunteers then crossed the stream and headed straight for the Indians' camp while the others circled its sides and rear to cut off escape.

"All was confusion and noise," recalled a Cheyenne halfbreed, George Bent, who was in the village with his mother's people. "The Indians all began running, but they did not seem to know what to do or where to turn. The women and children were screaming and wailing, the men running to the lodges for their arms and shouting advice and directions to one another."

A group of warriors made a brief stand in front of the tepees, then scattered under howitzer fire. Shooting from all directions, the troops cut down men, women and children, riddling them with bullets and riding after those who tried to run away. Dozens of Indians, dazed and bleeding from wounds, scrambled along the streambed toward the west, leaving a trail of dead and injured behind them. About two miles from the camp, the survivors clustered behind a tall embankment, clawing out hollows and pits in the earthen wall. Surrounded by Chivington's men, who feared going in after them, the Indians fought back all day. Among them were Black Kettle and Left Hand, the latter mortally wounded.

Elsewhere the slaughter continued. In the confusion, many Indians escaped into the hills, but more than 150 were killed. Two thirds of them were women and children. For hours, the Coloradans indulged in an orgy of brutality, hunting down and murdering the wounded, scalping and cutting up the dead. Later testimony by some of the officers and men, as well as by traders and halfbreeds who had been in the village when it was attacked, told of soldiers shooting babies and little children, ripping open the bodies of women who were screaming for mercy, stripping skin from corpses for tobacco pouches, and cutting off the ears, nose and scrotum of a chief.

As darkness fell, the troops gave up trying to overwhelm the pocket of Indians in the bank of the stream and returned to the village. During the night, the surviving Indians escaped. Half-naked, freezing and without food, they headed northeast for the camps of Sioux and other Cheyennes. The Coloradans did not pursue them. In the morning Chivington, whose losses were nine killed and 38 wounded, looted and burned the tepees and set off for the nearby Arapaho village, intending to wipe it out as well. But those Indians had wisely fled south of the Arkansas River toward the Kiowa, and the search for them was unsuccessful. Laden with booty and proudly calling themselves "The Bloody Thirdsters," the 100-day volunteers returned in triumph to Denver, where they were wildly acclaimed. Indian rings and earrings, some still attached to fingers and ears, were displayed in the streets, and scores of Cheyenne scalps were shown in theaters and festooned as decorations above the mirrors in Denver saloons.

News of the treacherous attack and the volunteers' barbarous excesses was received in Washington with shock and revulsion. General Henry Halleck, Army chief of staff, demanded Chivington's court martial, but by that time Chivington had resigned from the Army and was beyond reach. Instead, during 1865, three separate investigations were conducted, two by Congress and one by a military commission.

Meanwhile, word of what had been done to Black Kettle's people swept through all the bands of the central and northern plains. War pipes were smoked and once again angry warriors began to strike in retaliation. On January 7, a combined party of 1,000 Cheyennes and Sioux raided Julesburg, at the junction of the Oregon and Overland Trails. The attacks spread along both forks of the Platte, causing even more devastation than the attacks of the preceding summer. Stages and trains of wagons carrying freight and the U.S. mail were halted, miles of telegraph wire were ripped down, and this time Salt Lake City and San Francisco as well as

hese officers of the 3rd Colorado
valry — a regiment raised in 1864
meet a perceived "Indian crisis" —
ced the challenge of leading troops
cruited almost exclusively from
lorado's saloons and jails. Lack
any other opportunity to fight
ubtless contributed to the ferocity
the regiment's attack on the Indian
mp at Sand Creek.

Denver were cut off from overland communication with the East. On the 2nd of February, Sioux, Cheyennes and Arapahos again fell on Julesburg, ransacking and burning the settlement.

Having avenged the Sand Creek Massacre, all the bands — totaling 6,000 Indians — finally left the Platte and traveled north to the Black Hills, beyond the reach of troops. There Spotted Tail's Brulé Sioux, who wanted to hunt in their own country south of the Platte River, left to make peace at Fort Laramie, and the rest went west to the Powder River to hunt.

To meet the Indian problem, in the meantime, General Ulysses S. Grant had brought about a reorganization of the Western military departments and their leadership. In March, Major General John Pope, transferred from the Department of the Northwest at St. Paul to the command of a new Division of the Missouri, laid plans for a comprehensive campaign that was intended to restore security to all the Western routes, open new ones, especially to the Montana mines, and break the power of the hostile tribes. Three columns would take the field in separate but coordinated expeditions.

One column, under General Alfred Sully, would cross the Dakotas and pacify the Western Sioux, building a post within their Powder River hunting grounds in present-day Wyoming. From Fort Laramie, General Connor, promoted to the command of a new District of the Plains, would march to the Powder River country and join Sully's troops against the Sioux. A third column, under Brigadier General James H. Ford, the new commander of the District of the Upper Arkansas, would march from Fort Larned to strike the Kiowa and other tribes living south of the Arkansas River.

A number of factors delayed, and ultimately frustrated, Pope's grand offensive. Because of bad weather and the belated signing of supply and transportation contracts, the campaign did not get under way until after the Civil War ended in April of 1865. Then, the release of volunteer units whose enlistments had expired, and the time it took to organize Regulars for service in the West, created logistical problems and temporary shortages of troops.

At the same time, Pope and his generals ran into a peace offensive launched in Congress and the East by persons who were revolted by the Sand Creek Massacre and blamed the Army for the Indians' hostility. With support from President Andrew Johnson's Administration, peace negotiations were begun with some of the tribes while Pope's troops cooled their heels. At last, the government made treaties with Black Kettle's Southern Cheyenne, the Arapaho and other southern Plains tribes that extinguished Indian title to most of the disputed central plains.

As a result, Ford's expedition never got

Carbines and pistols blazing, the 3rd Colorado Cavalry drives frantic Cheyennes from their village at Sand Creek, Colorado, on November 29, 1864, heedless of an American and a white flag the Indians had raised in a gesture of friendship. Six hours later, the entire length of the creek bed for which the camp was named was littered with bodies. "All sexes and ages were killed," wrote a witness to the carnage, "women and children and warriors, all ages from one week to 80 years."

under way. Sully and Connor got going, but they accomplished little. Connor's campaign, waged by three columns, was especially arduous, expensive and frustrating. The troops marched around erratically in the poorly mapped country, enduring violent storms, coming close to starvation, losing scores of weakened horses and fighting inconclusive engagements. Pope finally aborted the expedition, ordering Connor to return to command his old District of Utah. The campaign proved worse than a failure. It left the Sioux, Northern Cheyenne, and Arapaho tribes more determined than ever to continue their resistance in the years that followed the Civil War.

Meanwhile, the investigations of the Sand Creek tragedy had been concluded. On May 30, 1865, Congress's Joint Committee on the Conduct of the War issued its report, describing Sand Creek as "the scene of murder and barbarity," Chivington's conduct as disgracing "the veriest savage," and Evans' testimony as "prevarications and shuffling." The report called for the removal from office of those responsible for the outrage. President Johnson demanded and got the resignation of Governor Evans, whose dream of statehood for Colorado was not fulfilled until 1878.

Faces of the Frontier Armies

By the mid-19th Century, the American West had an eclectic population of pioneer farmers, brawling gold seekers and fugitives from one unpleasantness or another back East. When the call to arms came in 1861, these men filled the ranks of the Federal and Confederate frontier armies to fight for control of their sprawling domain.

The portraits on these pages constitute a diverse gallery of Westerners who fought for the Union; their unsmiling faces and dusty attire provide a more striking contrast to their Federal comrades in the Army of the Potomac than to the Western Confederates who appear on the following pages.

Revolver in hand and Spencer rifle at the ready, an 11th Ohio trooper is equipped for patrol duty at Deer Creek Station, Wyoming.

Supported by a cane, Colonel James Leake of the 20th Iowa appears lean and ragged two days after his release from a Confederate prison.

A sergeant of the 1st Oregon Cavalry displays the saber he carried in service in the Washington Territory.

These privates rode in the 7th Kansas Cavalry, a unit called the Jayhawkers after a fictitious bird of prey that was noisy and destructive.

Sergeant Charles Schroeder of the 1st Missouri Cavalry battled Confederates and Indians in Arkansas, Kansas and his home state.

A Kansas cavalryman wears a frontiersman's coonskin hat instead of his regulation forage cap.

Confederates Who Would "Sooner Fight than Eat"

Like their Federal adversaries, the Westerners who fought for the Confederacy were self-reliant individualists. Though only a minority of them owned slaves, most were rankled by a lack of U.S. government protection that left their lands vulnerable to Indian attack. That dissatisfaction, augmented by long-festering parochial feuds that had little to do with national issues, drove many southwesterners to the secessionist cause. These frontier Confederat[e] proved eager and capable fighters wh[o] served with a conviction every bit as deep a[s] that of the men serving in Robert E. Lee['s] Army of Northern Virginia.

His gun casually at his shou[l]der, Lieutenant Jack Swilling, a Texas trooper, manifests his claim that he woul[d] "sooner fight than eat."

Captain Samuel Richardson of the 3rd Texas went to war in jaguar-skin trousers with holsters to match.

Captain William Inge of the 1st Missouri, said his commander, served in a "gallan[t] wise and cautious fashion."

Recruits still wearing civilian attire form up behind kneeling veterans of the 4th Texas Cavalry after being sworn in at Ellis County, Texas.

On December 7, 1862, these Arkansas volunteers fought to a standoff with the Union Army of the Frontier in the Battle of Prairie Grove.

A Clash of Uneasy Alliances

"Remember that the enemy you engage have no feelings of mercy or kindness towards you. His ranks are composed of Pin Indians, free Negroes, Southern Tories, Kansas Jayhawkers and hired Dutch cutthroats."

MAJOR GENERAL THOMAS C. HINDMAN, C.S.A., BEFORE THE BATTLE OF PRAIRIE GROVE, ARKANSAS, DECEMBER 7, 1862

In the first days of March 1862, one of the strangest-appearing armies of the War wound through the wintry hills of northwestern Arkansas. Hunched against the cold and blowing snow, the strung-out column included 200 Confederate cavalrymen from Texas and 1,000 Cherokee Indians from the Indian Territory — today's Oklahoma. The Indians wore feathers in their slouch hats and cloth turbans and were armed variously with tomahawks, war clubs, rifles, shotguns, bows and arrows, and Bowie knives. They were clad in a motley assortment of fringed jackets and pants, calico shirts, buckskin leggings, blankets and moccasins. The faces of many were painted for war.

In a carriage at their head rode their commander, Brigadier General Albert Pike, and his black servant, Brutus. The 52-year-old Pike was a gargantuan man of almost 300 pounds, with a mane of hair and a beard that covered his chest. An eccentric Boston-born lawyer, poet, Freemason, and scholar versed in Indian languages as well as in Latin, Greek and Sanskrit, he was dressed like a Plains Indian in leggings, moccasins and feathers. As an Arkansas landowner, Pike had little military experience, but he knew Indians. In May 1861, the Richmond government had made him its representative to the tribes of the Indian Territory, which lay on the Confederacy's flank just west of Arkansas and sandwiched uncomfortably between Confederate Texas and Union Kansas.

Pike's task was to negotiate treaties of alliance with the Territory's Indian inhabitants, principally members of the Five Civilized Tribes: the Cherokee, Creek, Chickasaw, Choctaw and Seminole. These tribes, native to the southeast, had been forced to move to the Territory in the 1830s; they had long since adopted many of the trappings and institutions of white society. Pike found the Indians seething with dissension. The Chickasaw and Choctaw, who lived close to the Red River border of Texas, were pro-Confederate, but only about half of the members of the other tribes favored the South. By November, when Pike's treaties were ratified by the Confederate Congress, several thousand pro-Union Indians, led by the fierce old Creek chief Opothleyahola, had broken ranks and fled to Kansas.

Pike was not happy to be in Arkansas, and not just because of the blustery March weather. The treaties he had negotiated specifically stated that the Indians were obligated to fight only inside the borders of their own territory; if the Indians were threatened by Federals, white Confederate troops were to be sent to assist them. But now the Confederates needed the Indians to help them outside the Indian Territory.

A crisis in Missouri — the geographical linchpin of the immediate trans-Mississippi area — had forced the Confederacy to break its pledge of protection. The crisis had been brought on by General Sterling (Pap) Price, a prewar Governor of Missouri, who had a fixation with winning his state for the South.

Hands raised, two Indians are sworn into military service by Federal recruiting officers. In the Indian Territory, nearly every able-bodied male fought either for the Confederacy or for the Union — and at different times, many fought for both.

In the early months of the War, Price thought he had Missouri within his grasp. On August 10, 1861, he and Brigadier General Ben McCulloch of Texas, the Confederate military commander of Arkansas and the Indian Territory, had combined forces at Wilson's Creek in Missouri and defeated a Union army. One month later, Price won another victory at Lexington, on the Missouri River. But the Federals recovered from these early defeats and forced Price to retreat to the southwestern corner of the state. In November, when the Federals settled into winter camps at Sedalia and Rolla, Price wanted to renew the fight, but McCulloch refused. Ever since the Missouri and Arkansas armies had joined, the two generals had been feuding. McCulloch, a former Texas Ranger, considered the courtly, silver-haired Price an amateur and thought his raffish, ill-equipped "huckleberry cavalry" little more than an undisciplined mob. Price, in turn, criticized McCulloch for being indifferent to the fate of Missouri.

McCulloch believed a winter campaign would be folly. He had been charged with protecting Arkansas and the Indian Territory; Missouri was outside his bailiwick. Withdrawing his troops into northwestern Arkansas, McCulloch let Price go.

Flying the blue flag of Missouri rather than the Stars and Bars of the Confederacy, Price marched his high-spirited little army up the western portion of the state to Osceola, where he issued a ringing call to Missourians to join him. "Are we a generation of driveling, sniveling, degraded slaves?" his proclamation thundered. "Or are we men?" Price quickly attracted 2,500 enthusiastic recruits. But by mid-December he had achieved little of military importance, and his presence had stirred up the Federals. Again Price appealed to McCulloch for support. But McCulloch was in Richmond, discussing with the Confederate high command his problems in getting along with Price. In late December, Price fell back to Springfield, Missouri, to shorten his supply line.

Concerned by the acerbic rivalry between Price and McCulloch, Jefferson Davis sought a strong-willed officer to put over them and head a new Trans-Mississippi District within General Albert Sidney Johnston's Western Department. The assignment was not an enviable one. From the onset of hostilities, the Missouri-Arkansas-Indian Territory region had been a poor orphan to the Eastern Theater. The geography was remote, the passions of the people

Brigadier General Albert Pike warned the Confederate government against subordinating the interests of Indians in the Indian Territory to those of whites in Arkansas and Missouri. "It is important that our Indians should have our troops by their side," he wrote, "that they may not conclude that they are fighting for us only and not equally for themselves."

intense and partisan, and the military and political leaders accustomed to fending for themselves.

Pro-Price Missourians objected so vehemently to Davis' first choice, Colonel Henry Heth of Virginia, that Heth declined the appointment. Davis' second choice, General Braxton Bragg, also refused. Bragg had no desire to risk his reputation in an area where, he wrote, "so much has been lost, and so little done."

At length, in January 1862, Davis found his man in Major General Earl Van Dorn, the dapper, combative former commander of the Department of Texas. "We Missourians were delighted," wrote Colonel Thomas Snead, Price's adjutant, "for he was known to be a fighting man, and we felt sure he would help us regain our State."

Like Price, Van Dorn had grandiose plans and was eager for action. "I must have St. Louis — then huzza!" he wrote his wife on the day of his appointment. But before Van Dorn could act, the Federals forced his hand. In St. Louis, Major General Henry Halleck, head of the Department of the Missouri who would go on to become President Lincoln's general in chief, ordered Brigadier General Samuel R. Curtis, a somber West Pointer and former Iowa Congressman, to drive Price out of Missouri.

Curtis' offensive would be part of a three-pronged Federal effort to secure the Mississippi River, which in Halleck's words, was the "great central line of the Western theater." While Curtis attacked in southwestern Missouri, Halleck planned for Brigadier General John Pope to assail the strategically located Mississippi River town of New Madrid in the eastern part of the state and Brigadier General U. S. Grant to drive southward into Tennessee. On February 10, Curtis set out from Lebanon, Missouri, with 12,000 men and 50 guns. Outnumbered and outgunned, Price evacuated his camps and beat a hasty retreat toward the Arkansas border.

Looking forward to a decisive battle that would destroy Curtis and open a path to St. Louis, the unperturbed Van Dorn prepared to meet the Federals head on. He called on the governors of the states in his Trans-Mississippi District to rush reinforcements and ordered McCulloch to assemble his troops. McCulloch, in turn, ordered General Pike to join him with his Cherokees.

On February 17, Price's retreating Missourians reached McCulloch's camp at Cross Hollow, Arkansas; the two armies continued the withdrawal together. Determined to leave nothing for the pursuing Yankees, some of the troops looted and burned buildings as they traveled south through Fayetteville. The town had many Union sympathizers; there were many more of them after the Confederates left.

The two generals ended their retreat at Cove Creek, in the depths of Arkansas' rugged Boston Mountains. Behind them, Cur-

Civil War within the Tribes

When Albert Pike *(opposite)* arrived in the Indian Territory in May 1861 to negotiate alliances with the Five Civilized Tribes, the Choctaw and the Chickasaw, whose lands bordered Confederate Texas, quickly gave him their support. But the Cherokee, Creek and Seminole were as bitterly divided as their white neighbors in Arkansas and Missouri. Ever since their removal from their homelands in the South, these tribes had been torn between those who supported removal and those who opposed it. The Civil War rekindled the old hatreds.

Creek and Seminole leaders Opothleyahola *(below, center)* and Billy Bowlegs *(below, right)*, who had opposed resettlement, refused to meet with Pike. When their rivals, Daniel MacIntosh *(bottom center)*, whose mixed-blood father had been slain as a traitor by followers of Opothleyahola for signing the removal treaty, and Seminole John Jumper *(bottom right)* agreed to Pike's terms, Opothleyahola and Billy Bowlegs fled to Kansas with 9,000 supporters.

Cherokee chief John Ross *(below, left)* was a plantation owner only one-eighth Indian, but his support came from the full bloods. He persuaded them to go along with Pike because he thought the North would lose the War and he feared that his pro-South rival, Stand Watie *(bottom left)* might displace him. As the tides of war shifted, Ross's supporters changed their allegiance to the Union.

JOHN ROSS
Cherokee

OPOTHLEYAHOLA
Creek

BILLY BOWLEGS
Seminole

STAND WATIE
Cherokee

DANIEL MACINTOSH
Creek

JOHN JUMPER
Seminole

tis, now more than 200 miles from his supply base at Rolla, Missouri, ground to a halt at McCulloch's abandoned camp at Cross Hollow. Forced to leave men in his rear to guard his supply lines, the Union commander was in need of reinforcements. But Halleck had no men to spare. Instead, he directed Curtis to go no farther. Curtis dispersed his divisions to strategic points and waited.

On March 3, Van Dorn joined Price and McCulloch at Cove Creek, and over a rich breakfast of kidneys stewed in sherry, the three generals prepared their attack. Price had 7,000 men, McCulloch about 8,000. Pike would add another thousand or more. Although Van Dorn thought that Curtis' force was much larger, the Confederate total of 16,000 actually outnumbered the Union army, which had been reduced to about 10,500 effectives.

Van Dorn launched his newly named Army of the West the next morning, heading north for Bentonville, Curtis' most advanced position. The town was held by Brigadier General Franz Sigel and two divisions composed largely of German immigrants and sons of immigrants from St. Louis.

The next day, Curtis learned of the Confederates' approach from scouts. Notifying Sigel to withdraw, Curtis ordered his force to concentrate 14 miles north of Bentonville, on a high bluff along the northern side of Little Sugar Creek. The position was a good one, backed by a chain of cliffs and wooded heights two and a half miles long. Called Pea Ridge, after the wild peas that grew on vines along its slopes, the heights overlooked the Telegraph road, the main route from Fayetteville to Springfield. It was along this road that the Federals assumed the Confederates would have to march. Curtis' men threw up earthworks and felled trees to block the road.

Samuel R. Curtis, shown here after his promotion to major general, pursued Price's Confederates into Arkansas in February 1862 and initiated a propaganda campaign urging the state's pro-South citizenry to renounce guerrilla warfare. "The unfortunate condition of Missouri will be transferred to Arkansas," Curtis warned, "if you allow this complicity of yourselves in the struggle."

Complying with orders, Sigel sent the bulk of his two divisions to join the others at Little Sugar Creek. But he kept back 600 men and a battery of six guns, forming a rear guard at McKissick's farm near Bentonville. By midmorning on March 6, Van Dorn's forces, with Price's Missourians in the lead, approached from the south. Thinking he was facing the main Union army, Van Dorn attempted to encircle Sigel's detachment. After a series of sharp skirmishes in which Missourians fought Missourians, Sigel fell back to Little Sugar Creek. Van Dorn then ordered his army to bivouac for the night and sat down with Price, McCulloch and Brigadier General James McIntosh, McCulloch's cavalry leader, to plan his next step. Late that afternoon Albert Pike's Indian brigade and 200 Texans arrived and went into camp along the Telegraph road.

Hesitant to risk a frontal assault on Curtis' strong position, Van Dorn decided on a bold alternative. McCulloch, who knew the area, had told him of a secondary road that diverged from the Telegraph road close to their campsite. Known as the Bentonville Detour, the eight-mile route circled the western end of Pea Ridge and rejoined the Telegraph road north of Curtis' position. By marching up it that night, the Confederates could flank Curtis. Then, turning south at the intersection, they could come down the Telegraph road in the morning to attack the Federals from the rear and cut their line of retreat.

Unfortunately, Van Dorn never bothered to explain his plan to the newly arrived General Pike. At 9:30 p.m. Pike got a message that merely directed him to follow McCulloch's division. Where, he did not know.

By that time Price's cavalry, in the lead, had already started moving. The horsemen forded Little Sugar Creek, rode up the Bentonville Detour — and swiftly ran into trouble. Earlier in the day, the Federal 4th Iowa under Colonel Grenville M. Dodge had felled bushes and trees to block the road. Price's advance slowed to a crawl as his troopers, already suffering from fatigue, hunger and cold, struggled to clear the way.

A delay developed, also, at the creek, where the infantry could not wade the icy, fast-running stream. Eventually a precarious bridge was fashioned and the men moved across in single file. As they regrouped and trudged northward, Van Dorn, who had fallen sick with chills and fever, rode past them in an ambulance, accompanied by his staff. The weary troops complained bitterly about "General Damdborn" who could ride while they had to walk.

By 10 a.m. on the 7th, Price's division had reached the junction with the Telegraph road, but McCulloch's troops still had many miles to go and Pike's men had just crossed Little Sugar Creek. By now, Curtis was aware of what was happening. Wheeling his troops around, he sent Colonel Eugene A. Carr with a brigade of the 4th Division northward on the Telegraph road to intercept Price. At the same time, he ordered Colonel Peter J. Osterhaus, one of Sigel's division commanders, to move west past the hamlet of Leetown with a force of cavalry, infantry and artillery and attack the Confederates on the Bentonville Detour.

The unexpected appearance of Carr's troops in Price's front forced Van Dorn to change his plans. The delays had cost him the advantage of surprise, and with McCulloch and Pike still on the Detour, Price was in a perilous position. Fearing that Curtis would throw his entire force against Price and overwhelm him, Van Dorn ordered McCulloch to reverse his march, take Pike's force with him and attack Curtis' western flank near Lee town. The assault would take pressure off Price and compel Curtis to fight on two fronts.

Van Dorn's decision to divide his command would prove costly, for it would give Curtis the opportunity to dispose of the Confederate forces one at a time. Moreover, Van Dorn's divisions would be out of touch with each other, widely separated by the rugged wall of Pea Ridge.

The order to countermarch bewildered

This inflammatory engraving, published in the North, inaccurately depicts the Cherokees who were fighting Federals at Pea Ridge as wild savages dressed like Plains Indians. Ironically, the few scalpings and mutilations of dead Federals that did occur at Pea Ridge were mostly the work of Indians who later defected to the Union side.

McCulloch's men; few of them could understand why they were turning around. Sergeant William Watson of the 3rd Louisiana wrote later that the battle was "a mass of mixed up confusion from beginning to end." Pike, trailing McCulloch, had no idea what was expected of him. As his men reached the western end of Pea Ridge, a regiment of General McIntosh's Texas cavalrymen rode past him in the opposite direction, shouting instructions to fall in behind. Pike turned his Cherokees around and blindly followed. At last word came that they were moving to attack a Federal force at Leetown.

About a mile from the Bentonville Detour, Pike's Cherokees collided with Osterhaus' troops. As Union artillery opened up, Pike halted his men along a rail fence in the woods. Facing him, on Osterhaus' left flank, were a battery of three guns and Osterhaus' Missouri and Iowa cavalry. To Pike's left, McCulloch, resplendent in a uniform of black velvet topped by a plumed hat, maneuvered his brigades of infantry and cavalry into position against Osterhaus' main force.

Before the Federals could attack, McCulloch started his division forward. His movement was the signal for a wild charge by Pike's Indians. Filling the air with war whoops, they raced across a field toward Osterhaus' battery. Riding in the lead were Colonel John Drew's full-blooded Cherokee — known as Pin Cherokee for the crossed pins they wore on their coats as a sign of their adherence to traditional tribal customs. Behind them, dismounted, came a regiment of Cherokee mixed bloods, led by a three-quarter Cherokee colonel, Stand Watie. Ironically, until Pike's treaty, Drew's Pin Cherokee, who had bitterly opposed their relocation to the Indian Territory, and Stand Watie's mixed bloods, who had fa-

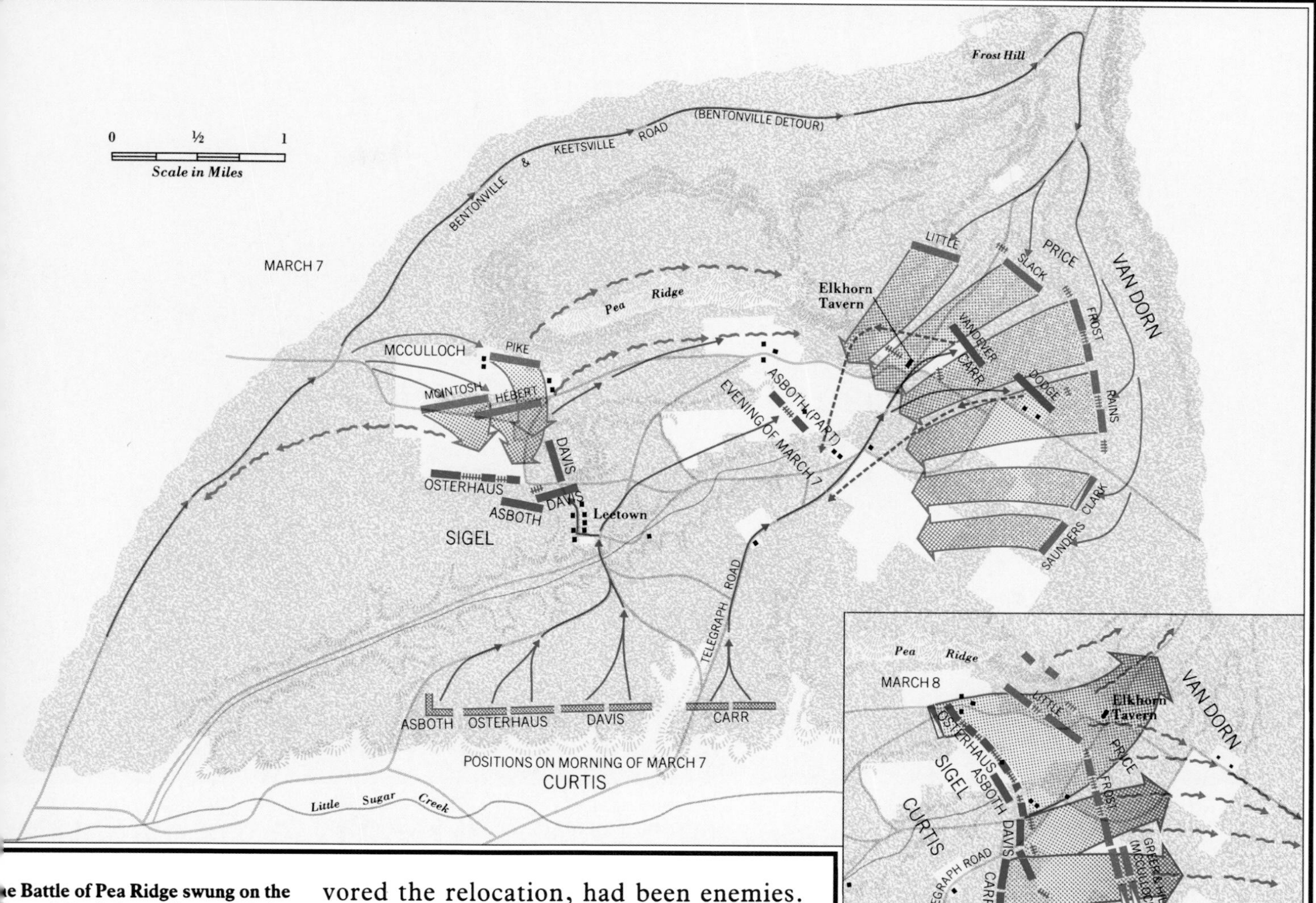

The Battle of Pea Ridge swung on the failure of Confederate General Earl Van Dorn's attempt to rout General Samuel Curtis' Federals by surprising them from the rear. On March 7, 1862, three Federal divisions were able to defeat part of Van Dorn's force under Pike and McCulloch west of Leetown while other Federals under Eugene Carr held off Pap Price's Missourians near Elkhorn Tavern. On the next day *(inset),* Curtis merged his forces to rout Price and complete the Union victory.

vored the relocation, had been enemies.

Panic-stricken, Osterhaus' Federals fled. The Cherokees swarmed over the battery — and lost all semblance of discipline. Ignoring Pike's orders to pursue the enemy, the Indians rode excitedly around the "wagons that shoot," mounting the guns, yelping and whooping in triumph. In the confusion, Osterhaus regrouped his men and opened fire with another of his batteries. Now it was the Indians' turn to panic. As the shells dropped among them, they ran back to the woods.

On Pike's left, McCulloch's infantry, under Colonel Louis Hébert, and his cavalry, led by McIntosh, were slowly driving Osterhaus' main force before them. "We kept advancing and they falling steadily back," recalled a Confederate sergeant. "Our advancing kept us enveloped in the dense smoke, while their falling back kept them in the clear where they could be easily seen."

Suddenly, the tide turned. Colonel Jefferson C. Davis' Federal 3rd Division, coming in from the east to reinforce Osterhaus, hit the Confederates' left flank by surprise. A bullet fired by Private Peter Pelican of the 36th Illinois struck McCulloch, killing him instantly. A short time later, McIntosh also was killed, and the loss of the two leaders plunged the Confederates into confusion. Hébert's brigade quickly fell apart, and Hébert and some of his officers were captured.

In midafternoon, Pike learned that he was now the senior Confederate officer in the field. Hurrying back and forth across the battlefield, he gathered up Stand Watie's Cherokees and his own Texans along with some of McCulloch's battered troops and

His wounded arm in a sling, Genera Sterling Price *(left foreground)* rallie his men as Federals in the distance begin a final advance in this painting of Pea Ridge done by a Confederate At center, artillerists reach to catch their mounted captain, Churchill Clark, the 19-year-old grandson of e plorer William Clark, who has been decapitated by a Federal cannon ba

tried to set up a defensive line. It was too late. The soldiers, too exhausted and beaten to fight any more, streamed past him on their way back to the Bentonville Detour. Reluctantly joining the withdrawal, Pike soon received orders to take his battered troops around to Van Dorn on the Telegraph road.

Price and Van Dorn, meanwhile, had fared considerably better, driving back the elements of Carr's division that Curtis had sent against them in the morning. As more and more of Price's Missourians entered the Telegraph road and turned south to join the battle, Carr's men retreated across the hollows and ridges on both sides of the road and along the wooded slopes of Pea Ridge. Advancing in the rocks and timber east of the road, Price's left wing, under Brigadier General William Y. Slack, captured a gun and drove the Federals from the crest; but Slack was mortally wounded. Price suffered a flesh wound in the abdomen and another in his right arm, but he stayed on the field.

The afternoon brought a lull while Van Dorn and Price prepared a fresh assault. Because of the pressure from McCulloch's division, Curtis had resisted sending more troops to Carr. But he had kept Sigel's 2nd Division, under Brigadier General Alexander Asboth, in reserve at Little Sugar Creek. Now he ordered a portion of Asboth's men forward, and as darkness fell, their guns checked the Missourians' advance.

Price's men believed they had won a victory, but their fighting strength was sapped. Days of marching and fighting, without adequate food or rest, had exhausted them physically and mentally. Long after dark, they were joined by Pike's and McCulloch's equally weary units, who straggled in from the Bentonville Detour.

That evening Van Dorn had a cause for anxiety far greater than the weakened condition of his troops, however. With his men low on ammunition, he had sent for his wagon train, only to discover that through some "strange and criminal mistake," an ordnance officer had ordered it withdrawn beyond Bentonville. Without a replenishment of food and ammunition, the Confederates could not mount another attack.

Early the next morning a Union battery opened fire, setting off an artillery duel that subsided gradually as the Confederate guns, one by one, became disabled or ran out of shells. With elements of all four of his divisions now in position, Curtis attacked.

For a while, the Confederates held. On the right, some of Price's infantry made a gallant stand on the ridge above Elkhorn Tavern before Sigel's artillery and infantry drove them down the slopes and onto the Telegraph road. At the same time, waves of Federal infantry surged against Van Dorn's center and left. Bareheaded, his wounded arm in a sling, Price rode along the line, exhorting his faltering Missourians to hold. But without the artillery, it was useless. As the Confederate left crumbled, Van Dorn gave the order to withdraw. "Gloom spread over the men in an instant," wrote one of Price's cavalrymen in his diary. Discipline quickly collapsed and the retreat became a rout.

Many Missourians fled north into their own state, where they organized guerrilla bands that would fight on against the Federals until the end of the War. Cursing Van Dorn, the main body of Confederates circled around the Federals and, breaking into small groups, retreated deeper into Arkansas. For

embers of Confederate General en McCulloch's staff gathered for is ambrotype shortly after cCulloch's death at Pea Ridge. ieutenant Frank C. Armstrong *tanding, far right),* who was a few et away when McCulloch was lled, and Lieutenant Lindsay Loax *(seated, near right)* became nerals themselves.

days the bone-weary men trudged through the Boston Mountains in pouring rain. "Hunger added its terrors to the misery of the march," a Missouri officer recalled.

Half-dead from cold and starvation, the Confederates straggled into Van Buren, Arkansas, where Van Dorn and Price regrouped them. But Pike refused to join up. Convinced that Van Dorn's army was utterly destroyed, he headed his small force back into the Indian Territory, fearful that the area would now be invaded.

Although each side had lost about 1,300 men and Van Dorn vaingloriously reported, "I was not defeated, but only foiled in my intentions," Curtis had won a decisive victory. Never again would the Confederates muster the strength to seriously threaten Missouri — although the indomitable Price would make another doomed effort in 1864.

For the moment, Van Dorn and Price reequipped their weakened forces — largely with supplies waiting at Fort Smith, Arkansas, for transshipment to Pike's Indians. They then led their forces across the Mississippi to help stem General U.S. Grant's offensive in Tennessee. This reassignment angered the government of Arkansas, since it stripped the state of protection. Van Dorn vowed that he and the troops would return, but it proved a hollow promise. He would serve east of the Mississippi until 1863, when he was shot dead by a jealous husband. Nor would many of the Missouri and Arkansas troops he and Price took East with them ever see their home states again.

Furious with Van Dorn, Pike brooded unhappily in the Indian Territory. Not only had Van Dorn commandeered arms and equipment earmarked for the Indians, but he had abandoned the Territory as well, breaking the Confederacy's vow to protect the tribes there. Worse still, following the battle, Curtis had accused Pike's Indians of having scalped some of the Federal soldiers. The charges were true, but Van Dorn, instead of defending Pike and his men, countered by charging that Sigel's Germans had been equally barbarous in shooting Confederate prisoners. Insultingly, Van Dorn sent Pike orders to restrain the Indians in future actions "from committing any barbarities upon the wounded, prisoners, or dead who may fall into their hands."

Stung by this ill treatment, Pike adopted his own strategy for the Indian Territory. Convinced that he could not defend the exposed northern part of the region, he withdrew toward the Red River, intending to put up a defense there, with Texas as his "base of operations." Joined by some Texas cavalry units, Pike halted in Choctaw country and built a fort that he named for the dead McCulloch. He ordered the Creek and Seminole to defend their own lands and dispatched Drew's and Stand Watie's regiments to the Cherokee country to scout for enemy incursions.

There was substance for Pike's fears. Since the beginning of the War, James H. Lane, the fiery Kansas senator, had wanted to lead a Federal force, composed partly of loyal Kansas Indians, through the Indian Territory to Texas. A tall, cadaverous man, Lane was an antislavery zealot and a veteran of the prewar fire-and-brimstone border fighting. In the first months of the War he had organized a brigade of Kansas jayhawkers that had slashed across the Missouri line, killing and burning indiscriminately. Lane's reckless forays had turned whole counties

ack volunteers of the Kansas Inde-
ndent Battery, U.S. Colored Light
tillery, man two sections of their
ttery of three-inch ordnance rifles
Fort Leavenworth. The battery's
ptain and lieutenants also were
ack, making it one of the few black
its without a single white officer.

against the Union and stimulated the growth of bushwacker and guerrilla bands that harassed the Federal troops.

The Federal victory at Pea Ridge gave Lane his opportunity. By the early summer of 1862, after a winter of suffering in squalid refugee camps, the Indians who had fled to Kansas had become an intolerable burden to the state and were clamoring to return to their homes. Brigadier General James Blunt, a militant abolitionist doctor in prewar Kansas, was ordered to escort them back and secure the Indian Territory for them by crushing Stand Watie's Cherokees, who had been making a nuisance of themselves raiding southern Kansas and southwestern Missouri. Blunt was authorized to enlist several home guard Indian regiments in Kansas. Washington had originally opposed the idea. "The nature of our present troubles forbids the use of savages," the War Department had ruled. But now, because of the shortage of available white troops and the fierce desire of the refugee Indians to help free their homelands, approval was granted.

Blunt stayed at Fort Leavenworth to organize his supply system; the expedition left Baxter Springs, Kansas, on June 28, 1862, under Colonel William Weer. The 6,000-man force included infantry, cavalry and artillery units from Kansas, Wisconsin, Iowa and Indiana; a regiment of Creek and Seminole warriors who had fled north the previous winter; and another of Cherokees, Delawares, Caddos, Osages and Kickapoos.

Aware of Blunt's plans, the Confederate Cherokees angrily demanded help from Major General Thomas C. Hindman, an autocratic, pouter pigeon of a man, five feet one inch tall, who had been sent west to replace Van Dorn. Hindman, who was busy rebuilding Confederate strength in Arkansas, ordered Pike to move north and guard the Kansas border. But Pike refused, adhering to his own strategy. In exasperation, Hindman ultimately sent a single battalion of Missourians led by Colonel J. J. Clarkson to aid the Cherokees.

Entering the Indian Territory in two columns, Colonel Weer's Federals made short work of their outnumbered opponents. On July 3, the 6th Kansas attacked Stand Watie's command, seized his supplies and sent his mixed bloods fleeing toward the Arkansas River. That same morning, at Locust Grove, the 9th Kansas and the 1st Indian Home Guard Regiment, composed principally of Opothleyahola's Creek warriors, thrashed Clarkson's Missourians. The Confederate survivors fled to Tahlequah, the Cherokee capital, spreading panic. Never very firm in their allegiance to the Confederacy, most of Drew's Pin Cherokees at this moment defected to the Union side. Weer used some of them to fill out his 2nd Indian Home Guard Regiment. With the rest he formed a third Indian regiment under the command of Colonel William A. Phillips, a Scotsman who had come to Kansas in 1855 as a correspondent for Horace Greeley's New York *Tribune*.

Weer sent a small force to Tahlequah to arrest John Ross, the 71-year-old principal Cherokee chief. Then, not knowing what to do next, Weer lay in camp on the Grand River, drinking heavily for 10 days. In the idleness and heat, his men's morale plummeted and their supplies ran low. Suddenly a combined force of Texans, Chickasaws and

Colonel Louis Downing, a Cherokee mixed-blood minister in General Pike's Indian Brigade, abandoned the Southern cause after the Confederate defeat at Locust Grove in July 1862. He was among approximately 9,000 Cherokees — about half the tribe — who eventually switched their allegiance to the Union.

Choctaws led by Colonel Douglas H. Cooper — belatedly ordered north by Pike — appeared in their front, across the Arkansas River. With guerrillas in Missouri threatening their rear and Cooper's force in front of them, Weer's officers became restive. Finally, they mutinied. Prussian-born Colonel Frederick Salomon of the 9th Wisconsin Volunteers, a mostly German-born regiment, arrested the inebriated Weer and assumed command.

Salomon left the three Indian regiments to patrol the northern part of the Territory and started his white troops back toward Kansas, taking along John Ross, who rode with his entourage in a caravan of carriages that also held the boxed-up treasury and archives of the Cherokee nation. Many of the refugee Indians, their hopes dashed, trudged along, heading back to more months of miserable exile in Kansas.

Ross's capture plunged the Cherokee country into chaos. In the wake of the Federal retreat, a reign of terror broke out. The shaky alliance between the pro-Confederate Cherokee and the Northern sympathizers his battle flag of the Confederate st Cherokee Mounted Rifles was aptured at Locust Grove on July 3, 362, by a combined force of Kan-ans and refugee Indians led by Colo-el William Weer. About a hundred onfederate soldiers were also cap-ured, and Weer reported "great diffi-ulty in restraining the Indians from xterminating the rebels."

unraveled completely, and each side sought vengeance against the other. Families were murdered, homes burned, crops destroyed and herds of livestock slaughtered. Unable to police the region, the three Union Indian regiments withdrew to Kansas, leaving the Territory once again in the hands of the Confederate Indians. The secessionist Cherokee quickly named Stand Watie in Ross's place, triggering the flight of a new wave of frightened pro-Union Indians to the already crowded refugee camps in Kansas.

In Arkansas, meanwhile, General Hindman was proving to be every bit as ambitious as his predecessor, Earl Van Dorn. Having raised a new force of 20,000 Texans, Arkansans and Missourians, the industrious Hindman was anxious to strike a blow against Federal troops in Kansas and Missouri. Unfortunately, his dictatorial way of dealing with almost everyone — conscripts, businessmen and politicians alike — had turned many Arkansans against him. On July 30, Jefferson Davis superseded him with a 57-year-old North Carolinian, Major General Theophilus H. Holmes. Hindman's offensive, however, went forward.

To augment his forces, Hindman had ordered General Pike to bring his Indians out of the Territory. For Pike, this was the last straw. In a fit of temper, he resigned his commission. Scorned now by Southerners as a traitor and detested by Northerners because of the scalpings at Pea Ridge, this strangest of all Confederate generals, who stated later that he had never wanted "the damned command" in the first place, was out of the War. He was succeeded by Colonel Cooper, who immediately joined Hindman at the Missouri-Arkansas border with his Chickasaws and Choctaws, a small unit of Texans, as well as some of Stand Watie's mixed-blood Cherokees — a total of 2,000 men. Crossing the border into Newtonia, Missouri, Cooper also assumed command of 2,300 Missourians led by Price's dashing cavalry leader, Colonel Joseph O. (Jo) Shelby.

General Blunt, learning of this new threat to southwestern Missouri, sent two brigades under newly promoted Brigadier General Frederick Salomon and a now-sober Colonel Weer — whose dispute had been patched up — to make a reconnaissance in force. On September 30, 1862, probing into Newtonia, the Federals skirmished with Shelby's Missourians and Cooper's Indians and were driven from the town.

Salomon's repulse galvanized the Federal high command. In St. Louis, Curtis, now heading the Department of the Missouri, ordered Blunt to reinforce Brigadier General John M. Schofield, commander of Federal forces in southwestern Missouri and northeastern Arkansas. On October 3, they met at Sarcoxie, Missouri, and the next day they fell on Cooper and Shelby at Newtonia, driving the outnumbered Confederates back to the Arkansas River, where Hindman regrouped them for another attack.

Suffering from illness and thinking the season too far advanced for further campaigning, Schofield returned to St. Louis, leaving Blunt in command of what was now designated the Army of the Frontier. Blunt personally led the Army's 1st Division, with Brigadier General Francis J. Herron commanding the 2nd and 3rd Divisions. Meanwhile, the Confederate hold on Vicksburg, Mississippi, was being threatened by Grant, and Holmes received orders to send 10,000 men to reinforce that strategically critical city. He directed Hindman to bring his army East. But Hindman won permission to eliminate the Federal threat to the Arkansas River valley first.

Hoping to whip Blunt before the Kansan could unite with Herron, Hindman sent two brigades of horsemen — about 2,500 troopers — under Brigadier General John S. Marmaduke to Cane Hill, a long, low ridge north of the Boston Mountains, near Blunt's position in northwest Arkansas. The tall, aristocratic Marmaduke, son and nephew of two Missouri governors, had been educated at Yale, Harvard and West Point. His mission was to draw Blunt away from Herron so that Hindman could defeat the two Federal forces in detail.

Blunt learned of Marmaduke's arrival at Cane Hill, and on November 28, at the head of 5,000 men, he moved aggressively to the attack. Stung by Federal artillery fire, the outnumbered Confederates retreated to the foot of the Boston Mountains. Bold charges by the 11th Kansas Infantry, the 2nd Kansas Cavalry (Dismounted) and Colonel Phillips' Pin Cherokees of the 3rd Home Guard Indian Regiment forced Marmaduke to retreat again to a gorge along a road leading to Van Buren. As night came on, Marmaduke made a final stand. Three companies of the 6th Kansas Cavalry charged wildly into the defile to try to seize the Confederates' artillery. Ambushed by a rear guard made up of Shelby's Missourians, the Kansans were hurled back, fighting their way clear with sabers and pistols. A flag of truce sent by Marmaduke to recover his dead and wounded ended the fighting, and during the night the Confederates withdrew to Dripping Springs, eight miles north of Van Buren.

Only a clever covering tactic by Shelby saved Marmaduke's force from destruction.

During the withdrawal, Shelby divided his companies, stationing them about 250 yards apart along the line of retreat. After each company fired, it mounted and galloped to the rear of the others, then dismounted and took a new position, forcing the Federals to fight through a gauntlet of fire. It was dangerous work, and Shelby himself had four horses shot out from under him. His outfit would soon become known as Shelby's Iron Brigade for its vigor and spirit.

Victorious, Blunt encamped at Cane Hill. But his respite was brief. On December 3, Hindman left Van Buren with 11,300 men and 22 cannon to attack him. Now Blunt was outnumbered, and he sent a message to Herron at Springfield to hurry and join him. Covering an incredible 110 miles in three days, Herron's two divisions of 6,000 men and 30 artillery pieces got to Fayetteville on the 6th and forced Hindman to alter his plan.

Hindman had originally intended to trap Blunt's inferior force by sending part of his troops around to the north to strike the Federals in the flanks and rear, driving them into the main Confederate army arrayed across their front. Now he decided to march his entire army northeast during the night, defeat Herron's force and then turn on Blunt.

Hindman's operation began well. During the night of the 6th, Blunt, assuming that he would be attacked after daylight, had ordered his troops to pull back to a more defensible line. Lighting campfires to conceal their intent, Hindman's army stole away from the Federals, leaving a cavalry regiment to stall any pursuit. In the morning, Herron's divisions deployed on the north side of the Illinois River with Hindman's troops opposite them in a strong, horseshoe-shaped line on a hill in a stand of timber known as Prairie Grove. At 9:30 a.m., the Federal artillery opened up and the battle began. Under cover of the artillery barrage, Herron's infantry crossed the river. Costly attacks and counterattacks followed, with neither side gaining an advantage.

Then Blunt, 12 miles away, realized what was happening and rushed to Herron's aid. Now Hindman had to fight both Union forces along an extended line. As the afternoon wore on, casualties mounted on each side. In one dreadful incident, wounded Federals who had crawled onto mounds of straw in an apple orchard to await treatment died horribly when Union shells accidentally set the straw on fire, burning the helpless men alive. "Two hundred human bodies lay half consumed in one vast sepulchre, and in every position of mutilated and horrible contortion," an observer recalled. "A large drove of hogs, attracted doubtless by the scent of roasting flesh, came greedily from the apple trees and gorged themselves upon the unholy banquet."

At sunset, after 12 hours of fighting, the firing slackened. The Confederates had had enough, and during the night Hindman ordered his army to retreat southward. As at Pea Ridge, each side had suffered about 1,300 casualties; but the Federals held the field. Hindman's army was broken. By the time it reached Dripping Springs, near Van Buren, thousands of troops had deserted.

The Battle of Prairie Grove ended permanently Confederate control of northwestern Arkansas and the Indian Territory north of the Arkansas River. Always considered of secondary importance by both Washington and Richmond, the region now received even less attention as each side diverted men and matériel to the great battlefields farther east. But the killing and destruction did not stop. Instead, the war along the Arkansas-Indian Territory border evolved into a series of bitter raids and counterraids, terrorizing and brutalizing the area's inhabitants.

The Federal victory at Prairie Grove touched off a wave of pro-Union sentiment among the people of northwest Arkansas. Hundreds of men who had hidden from Hindman's conscription agents emerged from the hills. Federal recruiters enlisted these so-called Mountain Feds in two Arkansas regiments that would fight for the Union.

Replaced as Confederate commander of the Trans-Mississippi District, General Holmes hung on as the head of the Arkansas District. Brigadier General William L. Cabell was assigned the thankless task of rebuilding Confederate strength in northwestern Arkansas. Thomas Hindman was transferred to the East, and Sterling Price was ordered back to Arkansas to take command of Hindman's division.

The new assignments did not improve matters. In April 1863 a raid by Marmaduke's cavalry, directed against southeastern Missouri, ended in failure. And on July 4, the day Vicksburg fell, cutting off the trans-Mississippi Confederates from the rest of the South, Holmes and Price suffered a crushing defeat at Helena, Arkansas. Two months later, Little Rock fell to Major General Frederick Steele, leaving the Federals in command of the Arkansas River. In the Indian Territory, the Cherokee country was a shambles. Without effective government, the private civil war between Federal and Confederate sympathizers in the tribes continued to claim lives and lay waste the once-prosperous countryside. Bands of outlaws with no allegiance but to themselves terrorized families on both sides.

In the spring of 1863, the Federals had tried again to move refugee Indians back into the Territory. Gathering up about a thousand Cherokee, Creek and Seminole families from camps at Neosho, Missouri, Colonel Phillips, with a 3,000-man force, escorted them first to Cherokee country, where the Cherokees dispersed to their homes. The lands of the Creek and Seminole were still behind the Confederate lines, so these Indians went on with Phillips to Fort Gibson in the western part of the Territory.

The Federal position at Fort Gibson was soon threatened, however, by a 5,000-man Confederate force led by Douglas Cooper, now a brigadier general. Phillips appealed for reinforcements, and General Blunt hastily ordered the newly organized 1st Kansas Colored Infantry Regiment, the 2nd Colorado Volunteer Cavalry and a section of the 2nd Kansas Battery to the fort, along with a supply train of 300 wagons. Phillips sent out 600 of his own men, including Pin Cherokees and Wisconsin and Kansas cavalrymen, to help guard the inbound train. At Cabin Creek, south of Baxter Springs, the relief column and its escort were ambushed by Cooper's Texans and Confederate Indians led by Stand Watie. After three days of bloody fighting, the Federal troops finally drove off the Confederates and brought the precious supplies safely into Fort Gibson.

A week later, Blunt arrived and took over command from Phillips. Learning that Cabell was moving southwest from Arkansas to join Cooper in an assault on the fort, Blunt decided to hit Cooper before he could be reinforced. Crossing the Arkansas River and making a night march, he fell on Cooper's

After crossing the Arkansas River on a pontoon bridge left behind by retreating Confederates, the 3rd Minnesota Infantry leads Major General Frederick Steele's army into Little Rock on September 11, 1863. The regiment earned the honor for its efficiency and discipline in combat.

camp at Honey Springs on July 17. After a two-hour fight, a sudden rainstorm turned much of the Confederates' gunpowder into a useless paste, forcing them to quit the fight before Cabell's army could get there to help.

At Fort Gibson, Blunt was strengthened by 1,500 Kansas cavalrymen under Colonel William F. Cloud, and on August 22, with 4,500 troops, he recrossed the Arkansas River and resumed the offensive. Within 10 days he pushed the Confederates back into southwestern Arkansas and captured Fort Smith. But one month later his luck ran out. Riding toward Fort Smith with an escort of 100 men, Blunt ran into the notorious guerrilla leader William C. Quantrill and his band of 400 cutthroats, who were attacking the small Federal post at Baxter Springs. The 150-man garrison had holed up and was fighting back successfully when Blunt and his retinue appeared. Because Quantrill's raiders wore Federal uniforms, Blunt thought at first that they were part of the garrison. Realizing the mistake, his escort fired a single volley, then scattered. More than 70 of Blunt's party were overtaken and ruthlessly shot down. Humiliated and shaken, Blunt eventually reached Fort Smith, only to find that he had been relieved of command.

More sensational than Blunt's debacle at Baxter Springs was another Confederate raid into Missouri during September and October of 1863 by 600 members of Shelby's Iron Brigade. Approved by Lieutenant General Edmund Kirby Smith, the new commander of the Trans-Mississippi Department, as a means to recruit Southern sympathizers and tie up Federal troops who might otherwise be sent East, the raid served more as a Confederate morale booster.

Leaving Arkadelphia, Arkansas, on September 22, Shelby's troopers rode north and crossed the Arkansas River. Joined by guerrilla bands that swelled their number to 1,200, they fought and plundered their way to Boonville on the Missouri River, 750 miles north of their starting point, capturing Federal detachments, destroying supply depots, and burning bridges and railroad cars. The Missouri militia finally closed in on them at Marshall and, after almost trapping them, pursued them back to the Arkansas River. In the 41-day raid, the hard-riding Confederates, now wearing captured Federal uniforms and sprigs of red sumac as insignia in their hats, killed and wounded scores of Union soldiers, destroyed almost two million dollars' worth of property and supplies, and brought back several hundred sympathizers to join Sterling Price's army in Arkansas.

A charge by the 6th Kansas Cavalry overruns the Confederate supply depot at Honey Springs in the Indian Territory on July 17, 1863, in this sketch by newspaper artist James O'Neill. Three months later, while accompanying Federal forces in Kansas, O'Neill was killed by the guerrill[a] band led by William Quantrill.

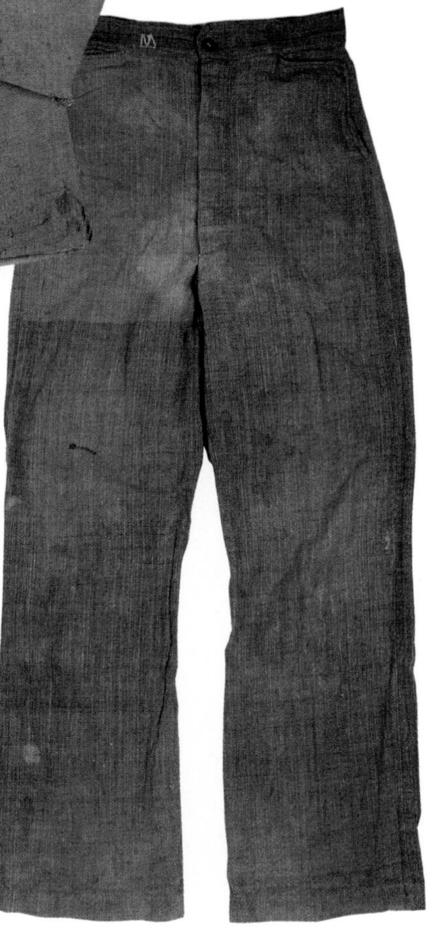

'his homespun butternut jacket, nsey-woolsey shirt and jean trousers vere worn by Private Burton March-anks of the 30th Texas Cavalry, who vas grievously wounded and cap-ured by the Federals at Honey prings. Paroled after the battle, Aarchbanks was allowed to go home o Johnson County, Texas, to die.

Shelby lost 150 of his own men, but the Iron Brigade had enlarged its reputation for verve and daring. "You've heard of Jeb Stuart's Ride around McClellan?" its veterans boasted. "Hell, brother, Jo Shelby rode around MISSOURI!"

At the same time at Fort Smith, problems were bedeviling the Federals. The Arkansas River was too low for boats to reach the post from Little Rock. As a result, the troops there and at Fort Gibson had to rely on ox-drawn supply trains from Fort Scott, Kansas. The area teemed with guerrilla bands who struck the supply trains and terrorized pro-Union families. Soon the Federal garrison at Fort Smith had its hands full protecting and trying to feed more than 1,500 refugees who had fled their homes in northwest Arkansas.

The Confederates had their troubles as well. Roughly 18,000 Cherokees and Creeks, their lands now in Union possession, fled south toward the Red River, where they clustered in wretched refugee camps on the Choctaw and Chickasaw lands. Despite reinforcements of two Texas regiments under Colonel Richard M. Gano, the Indians lacked the strength for an offensive and had to rely on Stand Watie and his Cherokees to conduct raids into their own country. In November, Stand Watie attacked the loyalist Cherokees at Tahlequah, destroying the tribal capital.

Barely a month later, the Federals retaliated by invading the Choctaw country. With 1,500 Union Indians, Colonel Phillips marched from Fort Gibson almost to the Red River, laying waste the countryside in a methodical attempt to break the Choctaws' and Chickasaws' morale. He failed, but he left more than 400 square miles in ruin.

Colonel Richard M. Gano won high praise for destroying a 250-wagon Federal supply train at Cabin Creek in the Indian Territory on September 19, 1864. Wrote Gano's superior: "Not the least of the glorious results of this achievement is the increased goodwill of the Indian and white troops toward each other."

Spring rains reopened the Arkansas River to navigation in 1864, but Confederate ambushes kept the Union garrisons in a virtual state of siege. In addition, the Federals at Fort Gibson had a new problem — the feeding and clothing of 5,000 refugee Indians who had returned to the Cherokee country only to find their homes and lands in ruins. Their needs put an extra burden on the Arkansas River sternwheelers that ran the Confederate gauntlet with provisions for the Union forts. On June 15, Stand Watie shocked Federal commanders along the river by capturing one of the vessels, the *J. R. Williams,* which was loaded with $120,000 worth of supplies. The feat earned the able Cherokee a Confederate promotion to brigadier general.

Three months later, at the head of 800 Indians, Stand Watie participated in a greater coup at Cabin Creek. Cooperating with a force of 1,200 men under Colonel Gano, Stand Watie helped capture a huge Federal supply train of more than 250 wagons carrying $1.5 million worth of food, clothing, and other necessities for the troops and refugee Indians at Fort Gibson.

In Arkansas, at the same time, another Confederate foray was getting started that would eclipse any yet seen along the border. It was a last-ditch effort by Sterling Price to win Missouri. Though Price's plans were imprecise, he proposed timing his invasion to influence the Federal presidential election in November. Price believed that if he could take St. Louis and trigger an uprising of secessionists throughout Missouri, he might help Northern peace advocates defeat Lincoln and force a negotiated end to the War — with Missouri part of an independent South.

Price set to work organizing his force into three cavalry divisions under Marmaduke, Shelby and Major General James F. Fagan. Altogether, Price had 12,000 Missourians and Arkansans and 14 artillery pieces. One third of the men were raw recruits with no weapons, however, and many even lacked horses; they were counting on being able to acquire arms and mounts in Missouri. Price insisted on hobbling himself further with a long train of supply wagons, which was bound to be a drag on the army's progress. In addition, he brought along a clutch of Missouri politicians, including the former Governor, Thomas C. Reynolds, who had been presiding over a Confederate Missouri government-in-exile in Texas. Part of Price's scheme was to reinstall Reynolds in the Missouri capital at Jefferson City.

Price started his force northward from Pocahontas, in Arkansas, on September 19. In St. Louis, Major General William S. Rosecrans, who had taken command of the Union's Department of the Missouri, had received many reports from scouts and spies of Price's preparations. His own forces, about 11,000 men, were scattered throughout the state. Hastily, Rosecrans concentrated his men at strategic points and requested re-

esolute but no longer robust, rmer Governor Sterling Price was nsidered by some better suited issuing political proclamations an to leading the Confederacy's st great cavalry raid into Missouri. ne junior officer described Price having "the roar of a lion, but the ring of a guinea pig."

inforcements. He was given 4,500 infantrymen from Major General Andrew J. Smith's corps of the Army of the Tennessee — veterans of the Red River Campaign — who had been on their way to join General William Tecumseh Sherman in Atlanta before being diverted to St. Louis.

Learning that Smith and his force had moved into position south of St. Louis, Price paused near Pilot Knob, a fortified post defended by Brigadier General Thomas Ewing Jr. and 1,100 Federal troops. Shelby, arguing that the unmounted, outnumbered Federals could not pursue them, advised Price to bypass Pilot Knob. But Price saw a chance for a quick kill. In August 1863 Ewing had been the author of a harsh order that had expelled all civilians from Missouri's pro-Confederate western counties. His purpose was to eliminate havens for guerrillas. The opportunity to bring this hated Union general to justice seemed to him to be reason enough for an attack.

It was a costly error. Though greatly outmanned, Ewing fought from within Fort Davidson, an earthwork protected by 13 cannon and three mortars. Attacking frontally on September 27, the Confederates were ripped to shreds by Ewing's gunners. By nightfall, when Price called off the attack, more than a thousand casualties lay in front of the fort. The defenders had lost only 75 men. Then, during the night, Ewing and his troops slipped through Price's lines and stole away to safety.

The defeat convinced Price that he lacked the strength to attack St. Louis. Instead, he veered northwest toward Jefferson City. Along the way, his men indulged in unrestrained pillaging — filling the wagons with loot and, in the words of Shelby's dismayed adjutant, Major John N. Edwards, adding to their ranks a "rabble of deadheads, stragglers and stolen negroes."

Reaching the hills around Jefferson City, Price wisely concluded again that the Federals were too strong and led his army on toward Boonville. Soon afterward, Major General Alfred Pleasonton, the experienced former chief of cavalry of the Army of the Potomac, entered the Missouri capital and sent 4,000 horsemen under Brigadier General John Sanborn to follow Price. Farther east, more reinforcements were on the way.

Unconcerned, Price moved leisurely toward Lexington, on the Missouri River. He was again in pro-Southern country, and several thousand more volunteers joined his column. In addition, almost all the guerrilla bands that had been plaguing Federal commanders emerged from their hiding places to attach themselves to Price's force. One day, the notorious Bloody Bill Anderson and his followers rode in — with human scalps decorating their horses' bridles. Price made them get rid of the scalps, then accepted a brace of silver-mounted pistols from Anderson and welcomed him into his army. Quantrill's raiders, who had split with their leader and

General Price's division commanders, Major General John S. Marmaduke, Brigadier General Joseph O. Shelby and Major General James F. Fagan *(top to bottom)*, were not on good terms with their commanding officer — or with one another. Shelby quarreled with Marmaduke; Fagan and Marmaduke distrusted Price; and Price considered Marmaduke incompetent.

Thundering out of the prairie south of Westport, Missouri, Confederate Colonel Sidney D. Jackman's brigade overruns the Topeka Battery of the 2nd Kansas militia near the Big Blue River on October 22, 1864. A militiaman who survived the charge remembered it as "Pandemonium turned loose."

were now commanded by George Todd, joined Shelby's division as scouts.

As Federal pursuers closed in on Price from the rear, another army was forming in his front. General Curtis, who now commanded the Department of Kansas, was marshaling a force west of Kansas City. He recalled Blunt from western Kansas, where he had been campaigning against the Cheyenne and Arapaho, and put him in field command. Spoiling for action, Blunt gathered 2,000 troops at Fort Scott, crossed into Missouri and marched quickly to Lexington. On October 19, he was attacked and driven back by Shelby. Retreating to the west side of the Little Blue River, Blunt formed a defensive line with the help of 1,000 reinforcements from Curtis. On October 21, Price's army, with Marmaduke's division in the lead, reached the Little Blue and attacked Blunt. Unable to make headway against the Kansan's firm resistance, Marmaduke was reinforced by Shelby. Their combined force threatened to flank and surround Blunt, who retreated again through the town of Independence to the Big Blue River. Here Curtis was intending to make a stand with Blunt's troops and about 10,000 Kansas militia who had belatedly realized that their own state was being threatened.

The next day, Shelby forced a crossing of the Big Blue and drove through part of Curtis' line, shattering several regiments of Kansans and taking many prisoners. With his other units in danger of being cut off, Curtis fell back to Westport, south of Kansas City.

Thinking his army victorious, Price was actually in great peril. While his van had been crossing the Big Blue, his rear had been struck by Pleasonton's cavalry. Caught between the two forces, Price sent his plunder-laden wagon train south toward Fort Scott while the divisions of Shelby and Fagan turned and attacked Curtis. Marmaduke, meanwhile, was ordered to hold off Pleasonton at the Big Blue.

On Sunday morning, October 23, the two armies — 29,000 men in all — collided in what would be known as the Battle of Westport, the War's largest engagement west of the Mississippi. Although heavily outnumbered, Shelby drove the Federals back. But everywhere else Price faced disaster. At the Big Blue, part of Pleasonton's cavalry trounced Marmaduke's division. At the same time, another brigade of Pleasonton's cavalry moved to intercept Price's wagon train. With the Federal cavalry in their rear and Blunt pressing toward them in front, Shelby and Fagan raced south to the Fort Scott road, where they joined Price and the rest of the Confederate horde in full retreat.

Curtis and Pleasonton took off in hot pursuit. On October 25, Price crossed the Marais des Cygnes River. With Shelby in the lead and Marmaduke and Fagan in the rear, Price continued a few miles across an open prairie to Mine Creek, a tributary of the Marais des Cygnes. Close on his heels came Pleasonton's cavalry, led by two brigades under Colonel John Phillips and Lieutenant Colonel Frederick W. Benteen. Shelby, Price and part of the wagon train got across Mine Creek, but then a few wagons overturned and the crossing became hopelessly clogged. Fearful of being caught in midstream, Fagan and Marmaduke set up a line on the north bank and prepared to defend themselves.

Moments later, Phillips and Benteen, with about 2,600 troopers, appeared and charged without pause. Then, as if swept by a wave of fear, the first line of Federal horsemen fal-

he charge of Colonel James Mc-
hee's Arkansas cavalry *(left)* runs
ad on into a countercharge led by
aptain Curtis Johnson's 15th Kan-
s Cavalry at Westport in this heroic
ural by N. C. Wyeth. In the melee,
e commanders singled each other
t and exchanged shots; Johnson
as wounded in the arm, McGhee
lled by a bullet through the heart.

tered. Just behind, Major Abial R. Pierce of the 4th Iowa screamed at his men to take up the attack. Galloping past the stalled first line, the Iowans thundered toward the Confederates. Pierce's brave action inspired the entire Union force. With a roar they charged as one. Seconds later, 2,600 horses and men crashed into the strung-out Confederate divisions, breaking their line with such fury that, as an Iowa trooper later reported, "it all fell away like a row of bricks."

Approximately 500 Confederates were killed or wounded and 560 were captured, including Generals Marmaduke and Cabell. Riding back to see what had happened, Price found his men "retreating in utter and indescribable confusion."

Price's army never recovered from the charge at Mine Creek. The demoralized Confederates tried to make a stand several more times, only to lose more men, wagons and equipment. As Price crossed into the Indian Territory, most of the guerrilla bands stayed with him for their own safety, freeing Missouri and Kansas at last from the terror of their presence. On November 7, the ragged survivors crossed the Arkansas River and the Federals ended their pursuit. Price led his starving men across the Indian Territory to Texas, then back to Arkansas. By December 15, a mere 3,500 men out of his original 12,000 were still with him.

Price's failure ended the war in the trans-Mississippi West. Although Stand Watie and others would continue to raid along the Arkansas River, neither side had the strength to do more than harass the other. On May 26, 1865, more than a month after Appomattox, General Edmund Kirby Smith surrendered what was left of the trans-Mississippi Confederacy. On June 23, 1865, at Doaksville, the capital of the Choctaw country in the Indian Territory, General Stand Watie surrendered his Indian forces. It was the last formal submission of any sizable body of Confederate troops.

THE LAST ENTRY.

The Harrowing Career of a Kansas Volunteer

Three hundred untested Kansas militiamen marched smartly across the state line into northwest Missouri in October 1864 to help repel the Confederate army of Major General Sterling (Pap) Price. Many of the freshly mobilized citizens looked forward to a merry adventure — and one of them, a 28-year-old farmer from Topeka named Samuel J. Reader, took a pocket diary to record his impressions of soldier life.

Joining a larger Federal force, the Kansans were ordered to guard Russell's Ford on the Big Blue River in Jackson County, at the extreme right of the Union line. That night, spirits were high as the men enjoyed their evening meal around campfires on the nearby Mockbee farm. One wag decorated his coat with epaulets made of pumpkin rind. Another brashly proclaimed: "If old Pap Price runs against our company, he'll regret it the longest day he lives!"

An unfamiliar sound — the threatening boom of artillery — put an end to the jollity. Price's battle-hardened veterans were preparing to attack in the morning. As Reader would recall, "The next 12 hours were to bring more startling experiences and varied emotions than fall to the lot of an individual in the ordinary walks of life in as many years." For Reader, the experiences included terrifying brushes with death, capture and eventual escape. Many years later he illustrated his diary with the watercolors shown here and on the following pages, captioning them with a wry humor made possible only by the passage of time.

Riding in column, the 2nd Kansas State Militia nears the Missouri border on October 21, 1864. A few of the short-term volunteers expressed reluctance to cross the line, fearing it might empower the Federal government to keep them in the field indefinitely. When one man asked Reader *(left)* his opinion, he replied wisely: "We had better follow wherever the commissary wagon goes."

A Mix of "Dread and Curiosity"

Samuel Reader's crude map details the Mockbee farm, where the Kansans were posted. They put their lone artillery piece, a 24-pounder howitzer, in the lane beside the barn. As the enemy approached, Reader related, "I felt a thrill through my frame. My mind was a curious mixture of dread, curiosity and a species of wild enthusiasm."

Reader *(center)* fires one of the two shots he managed to get off. Both missed. Seeing Confederate horsemen approach, he recalled: "I was struck with the absurd idea that they resembled school-boys playing at crack the whip. I could hardly realize that they were hostile men intent on taking our lives."

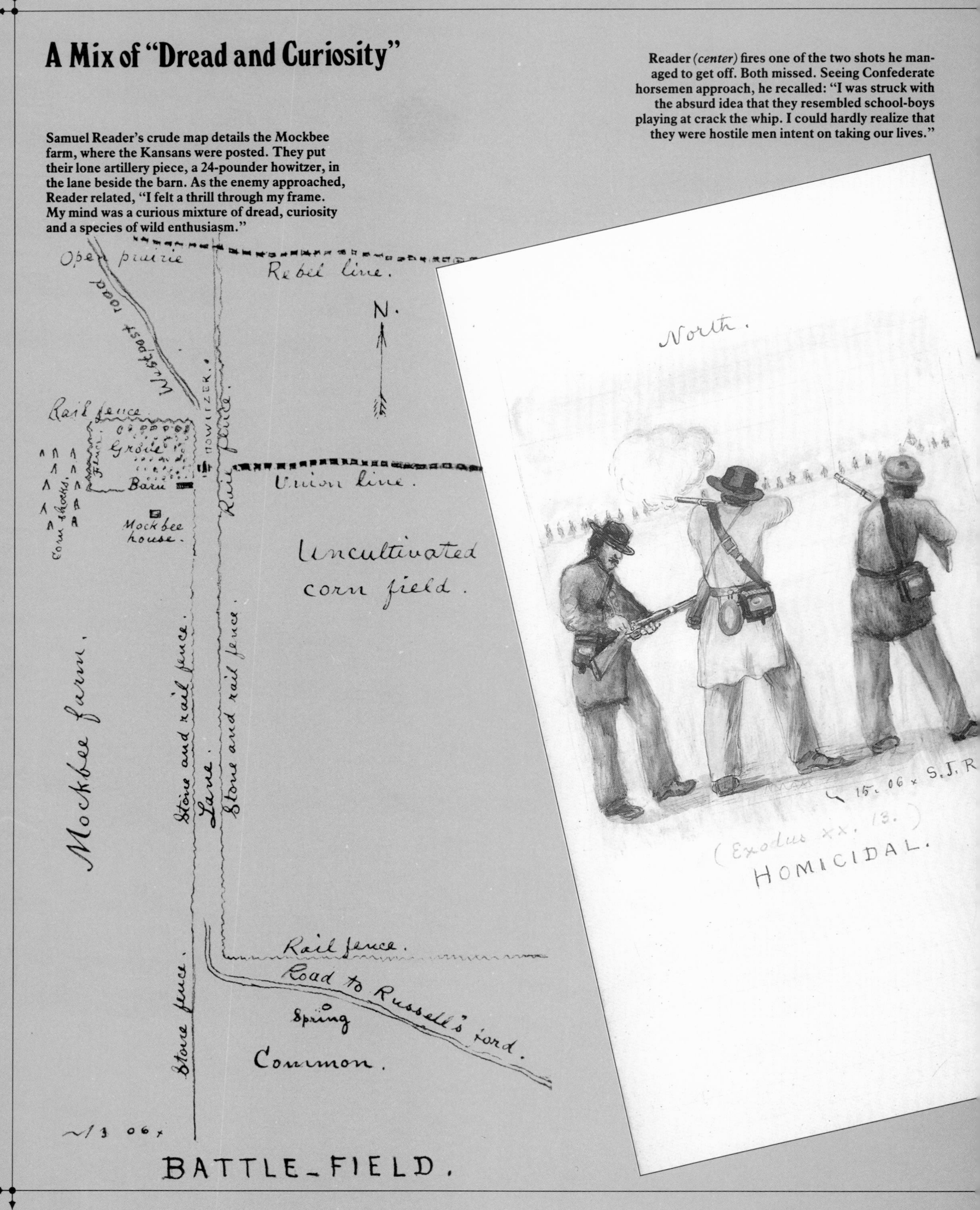

Sword in hand, Colonel George W. Veale entreats the Kansans to control their horses and maintain formation. "The air seemed alive with rifle balls," Reader wrote. "Some of them came altogether too close for comfort with a spiteful whiz-zip that made the flesh fairly creep. The lease on mortal life of more than a score could now be measured by minutes only."

13 06

Southern Battle-flag.

CUT DOWN.

"Thou knowest the storm
Of balls that swarm
In dense and hurtling flight,
When thy crossed bars
A blaze of stars,
Plunge headlong thro' the fight."

(By a dyed-in-the-wool Secesh poet.)

At right, a Confederate color-bearer falls off his horse, mortally wounded by canister from the howitzer. Soon afterward, the enemy retreated and Reader thought the fight was over. Then a bugle sounded, and "a long line of horsemen seemed to rise up in front of us. First the rebels' heads appeared; then their shoulders, and the horses, until all were fully revealed. The crisis was coming!"

Flight and Capture

Reader races for the Mockbee barn, 50 yards away. "When I reached the barn I saw instantly that the battle was lost. Everything seemed a chaotic mass of confusion and uproar. A look backward showed the advance of the rebels pouring through the gaps in the north fence. No where could I see any effort being made to meet their onset."

Outnumbered, the Kansans flee for their lives. Reader vividly described the charge that routed them: "The line broke into a trot, then a gallop, and a wild yell arose. It was the Southern war-cry — the redoubtable rebel yell, and the foe was coming down upon us like an approaching tornado. A single hasty glance and I had seen all I wanted of it."

Below, Reader surrenders to two Confederates. "A soldier's glorious death could now be mine," he wrote. "The slightest resistance — the motion of a hand towards my weapons, would bring it about, swift and sure. But I was in no mood for martyrdom. Sudden Death has an ugly look, when he sternly and unexpectedly stares one in the face."

Instead of taking shelter, Reader plays dead in the cornfield opposite the barn as Confederate riders thunder by. To get there, he confessed, "I ran as I probably never ran before. I felt a thrill of shame, but all the words in the vocabulary would not have stopped me. I was no longer a free agent. A panic had seized me. A 10 year old boy should have seen that escape was now utterly hopeless."

The Prisoners' Travail

A vengeful Confederate officer gallops toward the prisoners, screaming: "Shoot them! Kill them! They shoot our boys in cold blood. Serve them as they serve us." Reader and his comrades were saved by the timely intervention of another officer, who ordered that the prisoners not be harmed.

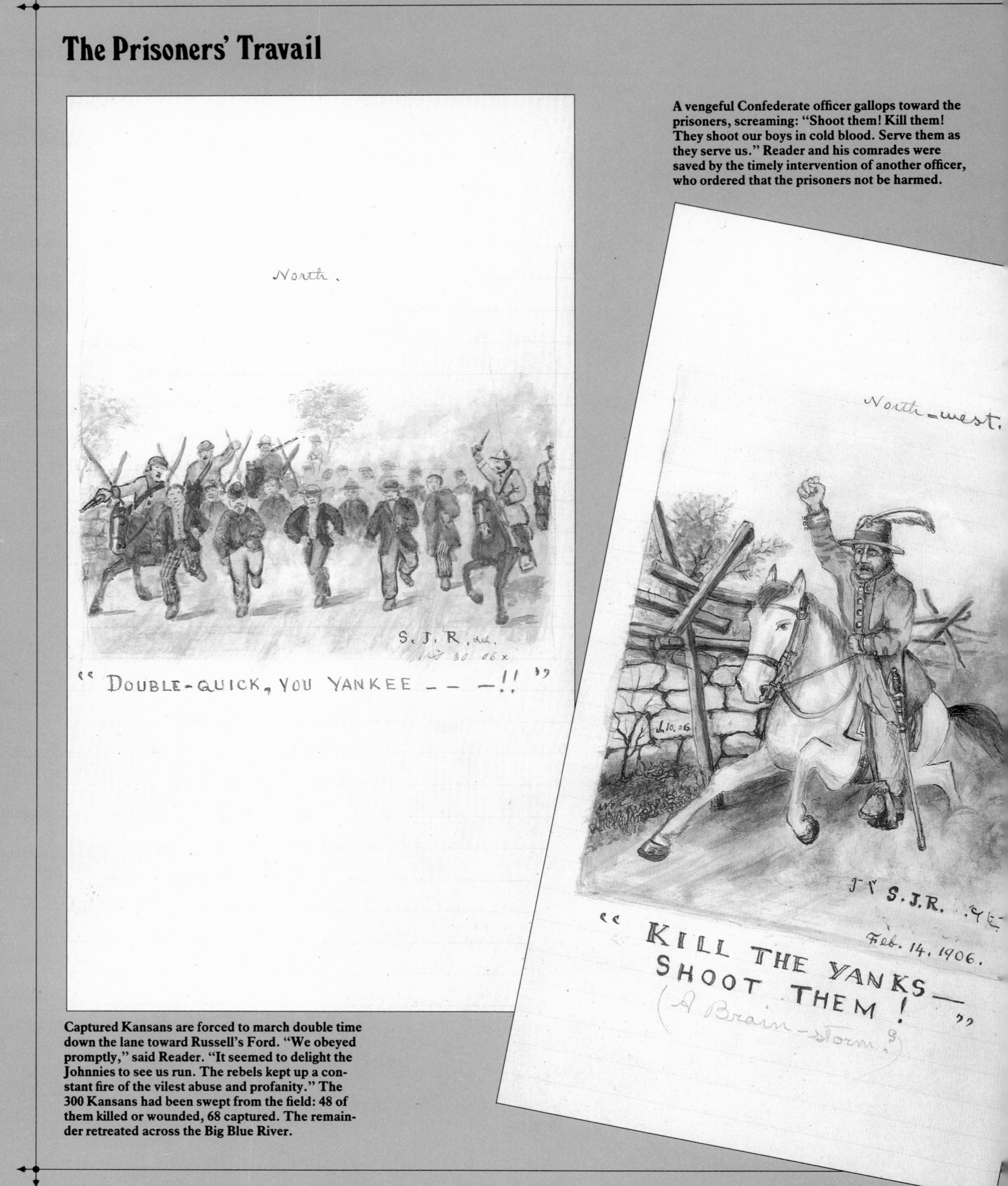

Captured Kansans are forced to march double time down the lane toward Russell's Ford. "We obeyed promptly," said Reader. "It seemed to delight the Johnnies to see us run. The rebels kept up a constant fire of the vilest abuse and profanity." The 300 Kansans had been swept from the field: 48 of them killed or wounded, 68 captured. The remainder retreated across the Big Blue River.

The exhausted Kansans drop in their tracks for a few minutes' rest at the feet of their captors. In three days of forced marching along the Kansas-Missouri border, the prisoners tramped more than 70 miles. "All were subjected to such tortures of hunger and thirst, fatigue and exposure as few mortals are called upon to suffer," Reader wrote. "My back and limbs ached as if severely beaten."

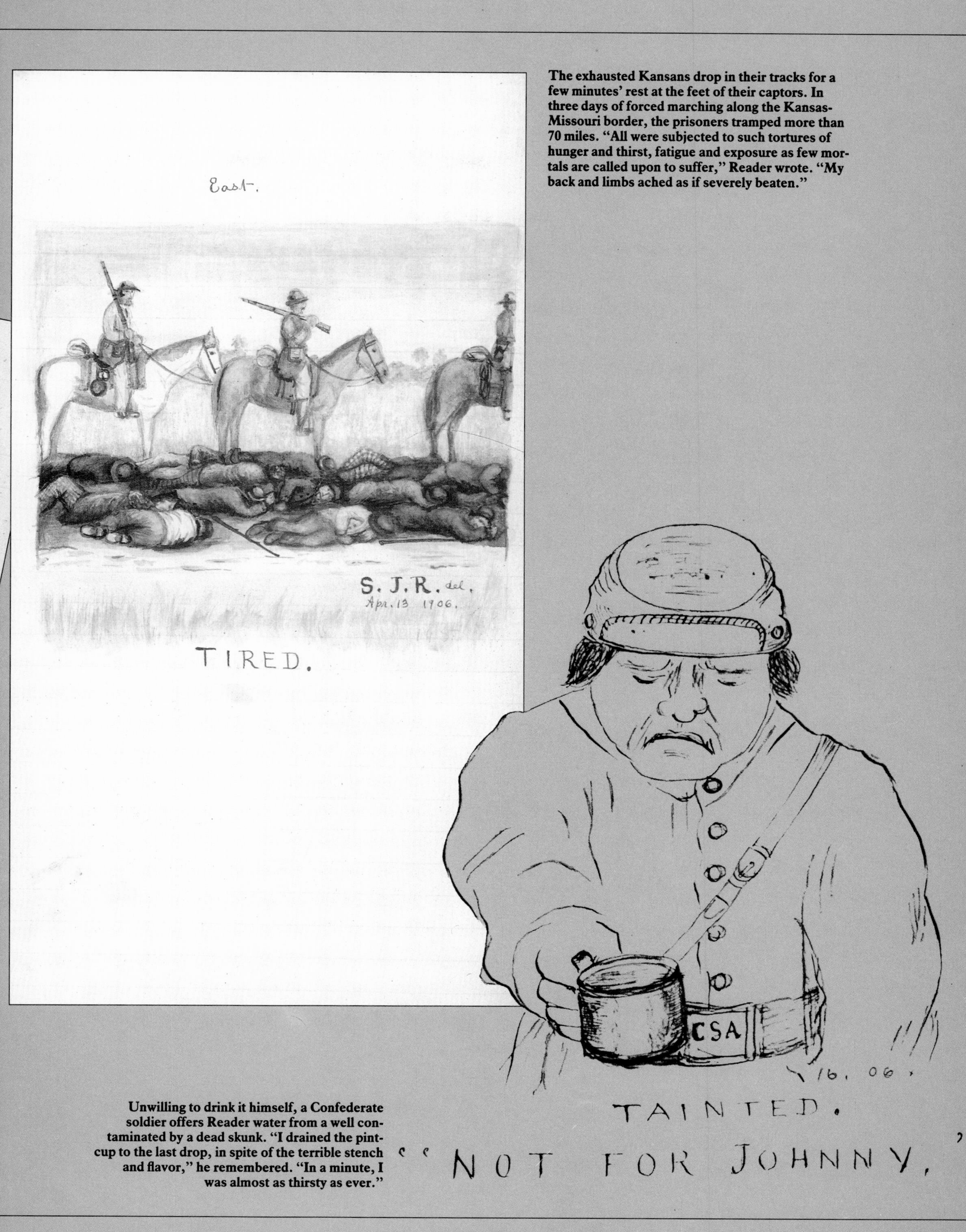

Unwilling to drink it himself, a Confederate soldier offers Reader water from a well contaminated by a dead skunk. "I drained the pint-cup to the last drop, in spite of the terrible stench and flavor," he remembered. "In a minute, I was almost as thirsty as ever."

A Fortuitous Escape

Having dismounted on the pretext of getting water from a creek, Reader cautiously approaches an enemy campfire. "Had they been grizzly bears they would hardly have inspired me with greater terror," he wrote. When the Confederates paid him no heed, he hurried off into the darkness.

Wearing a butternut coat obtained from a guard in exchange for his vest and handkerchief, Reader rides an unbridled horse lent him by a fellow prisoner so he might rest his blistered feet. In the darkness, the horse crowded in among those of the guards, who mistook Reader for one of their own. Reader felt a rush of elation: "The gates of Paradise stood ajar. I would risk escape."

fter a night spent following the North star and a ay wandering the prairie, Reader meets a pro- 'nion farmer near the Marmiton River in Kansas. t first the farmer thought he was a Confederate. ater he was treated to a dinner of biscuits, fresh ork and sweet potatoes — Reader called it "an Epi- urean feast." As a fugitive, he had survived on rain ater, hickory nuts, elm bark and wild grapes.

Reader finally turns himself over to Sergeant Pickerell of the 15th Kansas Cavalry in Barnsville, Kansas, on October 27, 1864. After examining Reader's diary, the sergeant pronounced him free to go. "I started the next morning, on foot," Reader said, "and reached Topeka at noon, October 30. I crossed the Kansas River and reached home at about 3 p.m."

ACKNOWLEDGMENTS

The editors wish to thank the following individuals and institutions for their valuable assistance in the preparation of this volume:

Arizona: Tucson — Margaret Bret Harte, Arizona Historical Society.

California: Sacramento — Col. William G. Hamilton, Historical Officer, State of California; Brigadier General Donald E. Mattson, Center for Military History, California State Military Reserve. San Francisco — Charles S. Hawkins, Fort Point National Historic Site.

Colorado: Denver — Katie Davis, David Guerrero, Mercedes Penarowski, Colorado Historical Society.

Kansas: Topeka — Patricia Michaelis, Nancy Sherbert, Kansas State Historical Society.

Minnesota: St. Paul — Tracey Baker, Tom O'Sullivan, Minnesota Historical Society; Cass Welch, Minnesota State Capitol.

Missouri: Columbia — Fae Sotham, The State Historical Society of Missouri. Jefferson City — Martin Shay, Missouri State Museum.

Nebraska: Omaha — David C. Hunt, Joslyn Art Museum.

New Mexico: Albuquerque — Don E. Alberts. Las Cruces — Austin Hoover, Library, New Mexico State University. Santa Fe — William Charles Bennett Jr., Museum of New Mexico. Taos — Lorraine D. Dyson, Kit Carson Memorial Foundation. Watrous — Carol Kruse, Fort Union National Monument.

Ohio: Columbus — Larry Strayer.

Oklahoma: Norman — John R. Lovett, Western History Collections, The University of Oklahoma. Oklahoma City — Mark Lea Cantrell, Oklahoma Historical Society Museum; Mary Jo Watson, Center of the American Indian. Tulsa — Mark Haynes, Daniel M. McPike, Anne Morand, The Thomas Gilcrease Institute of American History and Art.

Pennsylvania: Carlisle Barracks — Randy Hackenburg, Michael Winey, United States Army Military History Institute.

Texas: Austin — John Anderson, Cynthia Beeman, Archives Division, Texas State Library. Cleburne — Mildred Padon, Layland Museum.

Virginia: Richmond — David C. Hahn, Museum of th Confederacy.

Washington, D.C.: Kathleen Baxter, The National Anthropological Archives, National Museum of Natural History Smithsonian Institution; Diane Della-Loggia, Felicia Picker ing, Department of Anthropology, National Museum of Nat ural History, Smithsonian Institution; Deborah Edge, Stil Pictures Branch, National Archives; Eveline Nave, Photodu plication Service, Library of Congress.

Wisconsin: Madison — Myrna Williamson, The State His torical Society of Wisconsin.

France: Paris — Lionel Dumarche, Jean-Marcel Humbert Michèle Pierron, Col. Paul Willing, Musée de l'Armée; Juar Carmigniani, Giraudon.

Italy: Trieste — Rossella Fabiani, Soprintendenz B.A.A.A.A.S.

The index for this book was prepared by Roy Nanovic.

BIBLIOGRAPHY

Books

Abel, Annie Heloise, *The American Indian as Participant in the Civil War.* Cleveland: Arthur H. Clark Co., 1919.

Andrist, Ralph K., *The Long Death: The Last Days of the Plains Indian.* New York: Collier Books, 1969.

Bailey, L. R., *The Long Walk.* Los Angeles: Westernlore Press, 1964.

Bancroft, Hubert Howe, *History of Arizona and New Mexico 1530-1888.* Albuquerque: Horn & Wallace, 1962.

Berthrong, Donald J., *The Southern Cheyennes.* Norman: University of Oklahoma Press, 1963.

The Board of Commissioners, *Minnesota in the Civil and Indian Wars 1861-1865.* St. Paul: The Pioneer Press Co., 1890.

Brown, Dee, *The Galvanized Yankees.* New York: Curtis Books, 1963.

Bryant, Charles S., and Abel B. Murch, *A History of the Great Massacre by the Sioux Indians in Minnesota.* Cincinnati: Rickey & Carroll, 1864.

Carley, Kenneth, *The Sioux Uprising of 1862.* St. Paul: Minnesota Historical Society, 1976.

Castel, Albert:

A Frontier State at War: Kansas, 1861-1865. Ithaca, N.Y.: Cornell University Press, 1958.

General Sterling Price and the Civil War in the West. Baton Rouge: Louisiana State University Press, 1968.

Coel, Margaret, *Chief Left Hand.* Norman: University of Oklahoma Press, 1981.

Colton, Ray C., *The Civil War in the Western Territories.* Norman: University of Oklahoma Press, 1959.

Cunningham, Frank, *General Stand Watie's Confederate Indians.* San Antonio: The Naylor Co., 1959.

Drips, J. H., *Three Years among the Indians in Dakota.* New York: Sol Lewis, 1974 (reprint of 1894 edition).

Duncan, Robert Lipscomb, *Reluctant General: The Life and Times of Albert Pike.* New York: E. P. Dutton & Co., 1961.

Estergreen, M. Morgan, *Kit Carson: A Portrait in Courage.* Norman: University of Oklahoma Press, 1962.

Fehrenbach, T. R., *Comanches: The Destruction of a People.* New York: Alfred A. Knopf, 1979.

Ferris, Robert G., ed., *Soldier and Brave.* Vol. 12 of *The National Survey of Historic Sites and Buildings.* Washington, D.C.: National Park Service, 1971.

Fischer, LeRoy H., ed.:

Civil War Battles in the West. Manhattan, Kans.: Sunflower University Press, 1981.

The Civil War Era in Indian Territory. Los Angeles: Lorrin L. Morrison, 1974.

The Western Territories in the Civil War. Manhattan, Kans.: Sunflower University Press, 1977.

Folwell, William Watts, *A History of Minnesota.* Vol. 2. St. Paul: Minnesota Historical Society, 1924.

Grinnell, George Bird, *The Fighting Cheyennes.* Norman: University of Oklahoma Press, 1956.

Hall, Martin H., *Sibley's New Mexico Campaign.* Austin: University of Texas Press, 1960.

Hall, Martin H., and Sam Long, *The Confederate Army of New Mexico.* Austin, Tex.: Presidial Press, 1978.

Hanna, Alfred Jackson, and Kathryn Abbey Hanna, *Napoleon III and Mexico.* Chapel Hill: The University of North Carolina Press, 1971.

Hollister, Ovando J., *Boldly They Rode.* Lakewood, Colo.: The Golden Press, 1949.

Hunt, Aurora, *The Army of the Pacific.* Glendale, Calif.: The Arthur H. Clark Co., 1951.

Hyde, George E., *Life of George Bent.* Ed. by Savoie Lottinville. Norman: University of Oklahoma Press, 1968.

Johnson, Ludwell H., *Red River Campaign.* Baltimore: The Johns Hopkins Press, 1958.

Johnson, Robert Underwood, and Clarence Clough Buel, eds., *Battles and Leaders of the Civil War.* Vols 1-4. New York: Thomas Yoseloff, 1956 (reprint of 1887 edition).

Kerby, Robert Lee:

The Confederate Invasion of New Mexico and Arizona 1861-1862. Los Angeles: Westernlore Press, 1958.

Kirby Smith's Confederacy. New York: Columbia University Press, 1972.

Lamar, Howard Roberts, *The Far Southwest 1846-1912.* New York: W. W. Norton & Co., 1970.

Long, E. B., *The Saints and the Union: Utah Territory during the Civil War.* Urbana: University of Illinois Press, 1981.

McGuire, James Patrick, *Iwonski in Texas: Painter and Citizen.* San Antonio: San Antonio Museum Association, 1976.

Madsen, Brigham D., *The Shoshoni Frontier and the Bear River Massacre.* Salt Lake City: University of Utah Press, 1985.

Mangan, Terry W., *Colorado on Glass.* Silverton, Colo.: Sundance Publications, 1980.

Meyer, Roy W., *History of the Santee Sioux.* Lincoln: University of Nebraska Press, 1967.

Nichols, David A., *Lincoln and the Indians.* Columbia: University of Missouri Press, 1978.

Oehler, C. M., *The Great Sioux Uprising.* New York: Oxford University Press, 1959.

O'Flaherty, Daniel, *General Jo Shelby.* Chapel Hill: The University of North Carolina Press, 1954.

Orton, Richard H., comp., *Records of California Men in the War of the Rebellion, 1861 to 1867.* Detroit: Gale Research Co., 1979 (reprint of 1890 edition).

Parkman, Francis, Jr., *The California and Oregon Trail.* New York: George P. Putnam, 1849.

Peticolas, A. B., *Rebels on the Rio Grande: The Civil War Journal of A. B. Peticolas.* Ed. by Don E. Alberts. Albuquerque: University of New Mexico Press, 1984.

Petty, Elijah P., *Journey to Pleasant Hill: The Civil War Letters of Captain Elijah P. Petty.* Ed. by Norman D. Brown. San Antonio: University of Texas, 1982.

Rogers, Fred B., *Soldiers of the Overland.* San Francisco: The Grabhorn Press, 1938.

Smith, Gene, *Maximilian and Carlota.* New York: William Morrow & Co., 1973.

Spring, Agnes Wright, *Caspar Collins: The Life and Exploits of an Indian Fighter of the Sixties.* Lincoln: University of Nebraska Press, 1927.

Stanley, F., *The Apaches of New Mexico 1540-1940.* Pampa Tex.: Pampa Print Shop, 1962.

Sully, Langdon, *No Tears for the General: The Life of Alfred Sully, 1821-1879.* Palo Alto, Calif.: American West Publishing Co., 1974.

Taylor, Richard, *Destruction and Reconstruction* (Collector's Library of the Civil War series). Alexandria, Va.: Time Life Books, 1983 (reprint of 1879 edition).

Thompson, Gerald, *The Army and the Navajo.* Tucson: The University of Arizona Press, 1976.

Thoreau, Henry David, *The Portable Thoreau.* Ed. by Carl Bode. New York: Viking Press, 1963.

Thrapp, Dan L., *Victorio and the Mimbres Apaches.* Norman University of Oklahoma Press, 1974.

Trafzer, Clifford E., *The Kit Carson Campaign.* Norman: University of Oklahoma Press, 1982.

United States War Department, *The War of the Rebellion*

Series 1:
Vol. 41, Part 1. Washington, D.C.: GPO, 1893.
Additions and Corrections to Vols. 4, 8, 9, 13, 22, 34, 50. Washington, D.C.: GPO, 1902.
Utley, Robert M.:
Frontiersmen in Blue. New York: Macmillan Publishing Co., 1967.
The Indian Frontier of the American West 1846-1890. Albuquerque: University of New Mexico Press, 1984.
Ware, Eugene F., *The Indian War of 1864.* Lincoln: University of Nebraska Press, 1960.
Watson, William, *Life in the Confederate Army.* New York: Scribner and Welford, 1983 (reprint of 1888 edition).
Webb, Walter Prescott, *The Texas Rangers.* Austin: University of Texas Press, 1974.
Wheeler, Keith, and the Editors of Time-Life Books, *The Scouts* (The Old West series). Alexandria, Va.: Time-Life Books, 1978.
Whitford, William Clarke, *Colorado Volunteers in the Civil War: The New Mexico Campaign in 1862.* Glorieta, N. Mex.: The Rio Grande Press, 1971.
Wight, Levi Lamoni, *The Reminiscences and Civil War Letters of Levi Lamoni Wight.* Ed. by Davis Bitton. Salt Lake City: University of Utah Press, 1970.
Williams, Kenneth P., *Lincoln Finds a General,* Vols. 3-5. New York: The Macmillan Co., 1952, 1956, 1959.
Willing, Paul, *L'Expédition du Mexique (1861-1867) et la Guerre Franco-Allemande (1870-1871).* Arcueil, France: Société des Amis du Musée de l'Armée, 1984.
Winters, John D., *The Civil War in Louisiana.* Baton Rouge: Louisiana State University Press, 1979.
Worcester, Donald E., *The Apaches.* Norman: University of Oklahoma Press, 1979.

Other Sources
Bass, Henry, "Civil War in Indian Territory." *American Scene,* Vol. 4, No. 4, 1962.
Bean, Geraldine, "General Alfred Sully and the Northwest Indian Expedition." *North Dakota History,* summer 1966.
Blunt, James G., "General Blunt's Account of His Civil War Experiences." *The Kansas Historical Quarterly,* May 1932.
Carley, Kenneth, "The Sioux Campaign of 1862:Sibley's Letters to His Wife." *Minnesota History,*September 1962.
Carley, Kenneth, ed., "As Red Men Viewed It: Three Indian Accounts of the Uprising." *Minnesota History,* September 1962.
Chandler, Robert J., "The Velvet Glove: The Army during the Secession Crisis in California, 1860-1861."*Journal of the West,* October 1981.
Dietz, Charlton, "Henry Behnke: New Ulm's Paul Revere." *Minnesota History,* December 1976.
Fridley, Russell W., "Charles E. Flandrau: Attorney at War." *Minnesota History,* September 1962.
Hansen, Sandra, "Chivalry and Shovelry." *Civil War Times Illustrated,* December 1984.
Jacobson, Clair, "A History of the Yanktonai and Hunkpatina Sioux." *North Dakota History: Journal of the Northern Plains,* winter 1980.
Journal of the West, The Western States in the Civil War issue, January 1975.
Kibby, Leo P., "Patrick Edward Connor, First Gentile of Utah." *Journal of the West,* October 1963.
Kingsbury, David L., "Sully's Expedition against the Sioux in 1864." *Collections of the Minnesota Historical Society.* Vol. 8, 1898.
Langsdorf, Edgar, "Price's Raid and the Battle of Mine Creek." *The Kansas Historical Quarterly,* autumn 1964.
Larson, Gustive O., "Utah and the Civil War." *Utah Historical Quarterly,* winter 1965.
Lecompte, Janet, "Sand Creek." *The Colorado Magazine,* fall 1964.
Missouri Historical Society Bulletin, January and July 1961.
Pattee, John, "Dakota Campaigns." *South Dakota Historical Collections.* Vol. 5, 1910.
Rampp, Lary C., "Confederate Indian Sinking of the 'J. R. Williams.' " *Journal of the West,* January 1972.
Reader, Samuel J., *Extracts from an Old Diary, 1864, and Personal Recollections of the Battle of Big Blue Fought October 22d, 1864.* Unpublished memoirs.
Report of the Commissioner of Indian Affairs for the Year 1865. Washington, D.C., 1865.
"Taoyateduta Is Not a Coward." *Minnesota History,* September 1962.
Thomas, Lately, "The Operator and the Emperors." *American Heritage,* April 1964.
Williams, Walter, "The Other Civil War: Total War against the Navajo." *Civil War Times Illustrated,* March 1983.

PICTURE CREDITS

The sources for the illustrations in this book are shown below. Credits from left to right are separated by semicolons, from top to bottom by dashes.

Cover: From *Battles of the Civil War, 1861-1865: The Complete Kurz & Allison Prints,* published by Oxmoor House, Birmingham, Ala., 1976. 2, 3: Map by Peter McGinn. 8, 9: Painting by William T. Ranney, courtesy Martin Kodner, Gallery of the Masters, St. Louis, photo courtesy The National Cowboy Hall of Fame and Western Heritage Center, Oklahoma City. 10, 11: Painting by Albert Bierstadt, The Butler Institute of American Art, Youngstown, Ohio — courtesy AT&T Bell Laboratories; Minnesota Historical Society. 12, 13: Painting by William T. Ranney, Enron Art Foundation, Joslyn Art Museum, Omaha, photographed by Donn Doll; photo by Upton, courtesy Minnesota Historical Society — courtesy Colorado Historical Society. 14, 15: Painting by Felix Mathews, Chicago Historical Society No. 1920.150; painting by John Mix Stanley, Yale University Art Gallery, gift of Paul Mellon. 17: Courtesy Colorado Historical Society, photographed by David Guerrero. 18: Archives Division, Texas State Library, Austin, copied by Bill Malone. 19: Valentine Museum, Richmond — Library of Congress. 21: Courtesy James Patrick McGuire, San Antonio; Library of Congress — courtesy Frank & Marie-T. Wood Print Collections, Alexandria, Va. 22: Painting by Carl G. von Iwonski, courtesy San Antonio Museum Association. 24: From *Colorado Volunteers in the Civil War,* by William Clark Whitford, published by The State Historical and Natural History Society, Denver, 1906; Library of Congress. 25: Library of Congress. 26, 27: Library of Congress (2) — courtesy Gifford White, copied by Bill Malone. 29: Rio Grande Historical Collections, New Mexico State University Library — painting by C. M. Russell, The Thomas Gilcrease Institute, Tulsa. 30: Courtesy Colorado Historical Society. 31: Courtesy William J. Schultz. 33: Map by William L. Hezlep. 34: Courtesy Colorado Historical Society, photographed by David Guerrero. 36: A. B. Peticolas from *Rebels on the Rio Grande: The Civil War Journal of A. B. Peticolas,* edited by Don E. Alberts, published by University of New Mexico Press, Albuquerque, 1984. 37: A. B. Peticolas, Arizona Historical Society. 38: Painting by Hippolyte Flandrin, courtesy Musée du Château de Versailles, photo Bulloz, Paris; National History Museum, Mexico City, photo Giraudon, Paris. 39: Gemini Smith, Inc. 40, 41: Painting by Jean Adolphe Beaucé, courtesy Musée du Château de Versailles, photo Bulloz, Paris — painting by F. La Rivière, courtesy Musée du Château de Versailles, photo Lauros-Giraudon, Paris; courtesy Musée de l'Armée, Paris; painting by Edouard Detaille, courtesy Musée de l'Armée, Paris, photographed by Dmitri Kessel; courtesy Musée de l'Armée, Paris. 42, 43: Painting by Jean Adolphe Beaucé, Musée du Château de Versailles, photo Bulloz, Paris; Patrick Lorette-Giraudon, Paris — painting by Cesare Dell 'Acqua, Museo Storico del Castello di Miramare, photographed by B. and M. Fachin, Trieste. 44, 45: Archives Tallandier, Paris; painting by Jean Adolphe Beaucé, courtesy Musée de l'Armée, Paris; Patrick Lorette-Giraudon, Paris. 47: Courtesy Chris Nelson, photographed by Michael Latil. 48, 49: Library of Congress — Special Collections Department, Robert W. Woodruff Library, Emory University; courtesy Frank & Marie-T. Wood Print Collections, Alexandria, Va. — drawing by Frank Schell, Print Collection, The New York Public Library, Astor, Lenox and Tilden Foundations. 50: Courtesy Chris Nelson. 52: National Archives Neg. No. 111-B-2780. 53: Drawing by C.E.H. Bonwill, Prints and Picture Department, Free Library of Philadelphia, copied by Arthur Soll. 55: Alabama Department of Archives and History, copied by John Scott; courtesy Atlanta Historical Society. 57: Massachusetts Commandery of the Military Order of the Loyal Legion of the United States and the U.S. Army Military History Institute (MASS-MOLLUS/USAMHI), copied by A. Pierce Bounds; courtesy Frank & Marie-T. Wood Print Collections, Alexandria, Va. 58, 59: Courtesy Frank & Marie-T. Wood Print Collections, Alexandria, Va., except map by William L. Hezlep. 60: L. M. Strayer Collection. 62: Courtesy Frank & Marie-T. Wood Print Collections, Alexandria, Va. 63: Maps by Walter W. Roberts. 64: MASS-MOLLUS/USAMHI, copied by A. Pierce Bounds. 66, 67: Courtesy Paul DeHaan. 68, 69: Dam diagrams courtesy Frank & Marie-T. Wood Print Collections, Alexandria, Va.; MASS-MOLLUS/USAMHI, copied by A. Pierce Bounds, inset Michael Waskul Collection, courtesy L. M. Strayer. 70, 71: Painting by James Madison Alden, Museum of Fine Arts, Boston, M. and M. Karolik Collection of American Water Colors and Drawings, 1800-1875. 73: Smithsonian Institution, National Anthropological Archives Neg. No. 3505B. 75: Courtesy Frank & Marie-T. Wood Print Collections, Alexandria, Va. 76: Map by Peter McGinn. 78: Courtesy Chippewa County Historical Society, Montevideo, Minn. 79: Minnesota Historical Society. 80: Minnesota State Archives, Minnesota Historical Society; photo by Whitney, courtesy Minnesota Historical Society. 82: Painting by Anton Gág, Brown County Historical Society Museum, New Ulm, Minn., photographed by Gary Mortensen. 83: Library of Congress. 84: Painting by James McGrew, Minnesota Historical Society. 85: Photo by Whitney, courtesy Minnesota Historical Society — Minnesota Historical Society. 86: Painting by Alexander Schwendinger, Brown County Historical Society Museum, New Ulm, Minn., photographed by Gary Mortensen. 88, 89: Panorama scenes by Anton Gág,

Christian Heller, Alexander Schwendinger, courtesy Minnesota Historical Society. 90: Photo by Whitney, courtesy Minnesota Historical Society. 91: Minnesota Historical Society. 92, 93: Photo by Upton, courtesy Minnesota Historical Society — photo by Whitney, courtesy Minnesota Historical Society. 94: Edward Duffield Neill and Family papers, Minnesota Historical Society. 95: Panorama scene by John Stevens, The Thomas Gilcrease Institute, Tulsa. 96, 97: Insets Department of Anthropology, Smithsonian Institution Catalogue Nos. 76831(2); 76827; 76835; 76826, photographed by Vic Krantz — painting by Alfred Sully, The Thomas Gilcrease Institute, Tulsa. 98: Painting by Carl L. Boeckmann, Minnesota State Capitol, St. Paul, photographed by Gary Mortensen. 99: Courtesy Minnesota Historical Society. 100-105: Panorama scenes by John Stevens, The Thomas Gilcrease Institute, Tulsa. 107: Courtesy William J. Schultz. 109: The Society of California Pioneers, San Francisco — National Park Service (NPS), Fort Point National Historic Site. 110: California State Capitol Museum, photographed by Robert DiFranco. 111: American Heritage Center, University of Wyoming, Laramie — drawing by Caspar Wever Collins, American Heritage Center, University of Wyoming, Laramie. 113: Utah State Historical Society. 114: National Archives Neg. No. 111-SC-87289. 116: Courtesy The Bancroft Library, University of California, Berkeley 117: Courtesy Museum of New Mexico Neg. No. 22938. 119: Veterans Administration, Department of Memorial Affairs, San Francisco National Cemetery, photographed by Michael McKinley. 120: Library of Congress; Smithsonian Institution, National Anthropological Archives Neg. No. 2390. 121: National Archives Neg. No. 111-SC-87973. 122, 123: Painting by William Cary, courtesy Amon Carter Museum, Fort Worth, Tex. 124: Smithsonian Institution, National Anthropological Archives Neg. Nos. 43022; 148A2. 125-129: Courtesy Colorado Historical Society. 130, 131: Painting by Robert Lindneux, Colorado Historical Society, photographed by David Guerrero. 132: NPS, Fort Laramie National Historic Site — courtesy William J. Schultz; courtesy Roger Davis. 133: Kansas State Historical Society — courtesy Dale S. Snair; courtesy Roger Davis. 134: Library of Congress; from *Arizona,* Vol. 1, by James H. McClintock, published by The S. J. Clarke Publishing Co., Chicago, 1916 — Missouri Historical Society #307, from *They Who Fought Here,* by Bell Irvin Wiley, published by The Macmillan Company, New York, 1959. 135: Courtesy Ellis County Museum — Arkansas History Commission. 137: State Historical Society of Wisconsin. 138: Courtesy Thomas P. Sweeney. 139: The Thomas Gilcrease Institute, Tulsa; Smithsonian Institution, National Anthropological Archives Neg. Nos. 45111-F; 42913 — Library of Congress; courtesy Thom as P. Sweeney; Smithsonian Institution, National Anthrop logical Archives Neg. No. 52.917. 140: Courtesy William J Schultz. 142: Courtesy Frank & Marie-T. Wood Print Colle tions, Alexandria, Va. 143: Maps by Walter W. Roberts. 14 Painting by Hunt P. Wilson, Museum of the Confederacy Richmond, photographed by Katherine Wetzel. 145: Court sy Bill Turner, copied by Michael Latil. 147: Kansas Stat Historical Society. 148: Smithsonian Institution, Nation Anthropological Archives Neg. No. 993. 149: Courtes Thomas P. Sweeney, photographed by Ralph Duke. 15 Painting by Stanley M. Arthurs, Minnesota State Capitol, S Paul, photographed by Gary Mortensen. 154: Courtesy Fran & Marie-T. Wood Print Collections, Alexandria, Va. 15 Layland Museum, Cleburne, Tex., photographed by Davi Buffington. 156: Courtesy Steve Mullinax. 157: Louisian Historical Association Collection, Tulane University Library 158, 159: Library of Congress — The State Historical Societ of Missouri — Museum of the Confederacy, Richmond, cop ied by Katherine Wetzel; painting by Benjamin Mileham Kansas State Historical Society. 161: Mural by N. C. Wyeth Missouri State Capitol, Jefferson City, Mo., photographed b Jack A. Savage. 162-171: Drawings, watercolors by Samuel J Reader, Kansas State Historical Society.

INDEX

Numerals in italics indicate an illustration of the subject mentioned.